Greenhouse Gardening: Techniques, Analysis and Functioning

Greenhouse Gardening: Techniques, Analysis and Functioning

Subhash Meena

RANDOM PUBLICATIONS
NEW DELHI (INDIA)

Greenhouse Gardening: Techniques, Analysis and Functioning

ISBN 978-93-5111-837-4

Published in 2016 in India by

RANDOM PUBLICATIONS

4376-A/4B, Gali Murari Lal, Ansari Road
New Delhi-110 002
Phone : +9111-43580356, 011-23289044, 011-43142548
e-mail: sales@randompublications.com,
info@randompublications.com, randomexports@gmail.com

Type Setting by : Friends Media, Delhi-110089
Digitally Printed at : Replika Press Pvt. Ltd.

Preface

Greenhouse gardening is similar in many ways to gardening outside. The plants still need adequate nutrients and water, and protection from insect pests and diseases. You still must tie, prune, and tend to them.

A greenhouse is the best structure for protecting plants from extreme weather conditions. Greenhouses are also ideal for providing plants with a comfortable environment with suitable amounts of humidity, warmth and sunlight.

But the greenhouse environment is also very different from that of a backyard garden. The very things that make greenhouse growing more controlled and convenient also make it more demanding. In a greenhouse, you control temperature, humidity, soil aeration, soil moisture and drainage, fertility levels, and light. This degree of environmental control gives you a tremendous amount of latitude as well as some new responsibilities.

The greenhouse works by collecting light and converting it to heat. That is a simplistic view of how a greenhouse works. In addition to capturing light, the greenhouse also stores thermal energy and releases that energy properly. It can help moderate temperature and produce a controlled environment for plants to grow and thrive in. Further, a greenhouse offers protection from wind, rain, snow and other weather elements while also keeping your fruits from invading pests and animals.

A solar greenhouse, more than any other type, is sensitive to its surrounding environment. In many ways, this type of greenhouse is analogous to a living plant cell: The sun is its primary energy source, and its glazing acts as a membrane between the inner and outer world, allowing an exchange of heat, light and air. A greenhouse can, in fact, become a mini-ecosystem if the adept gardener can manage the interaction between abiotic factors (such as wind, snow, oxygen, carbon dioxide) and the biological community.

This book provides all the information and advice you will need to set up a greenhouse and get your planting going, and all under the watchful eye of the nations favourite gardener.

– Author

Contents

1

Greenhouse

Fig. *Victoria amazonica* (giant Amazon waterlilies) in a large greenhouse at theSaint Petersburg Botanical Garden,Russia.

Fig. The Eden Project, in Cornwall,England.

Fig. The Royal Greenhouses of Laeken,Brussels, Belgium. An example of 19th-century greenhouse architecture

A greenhouse (also called a glasshouse, or, if with additional heating, a hothouse) is a structure with walls and roof made chiefly of transparent material, such as glass, in which plants requiring regulated climatic conditions are grown. These structures range in size from small sheds to industrial-sized buildings. A miniature greenhouse is known as a cold frame. The interior of a greenhouse exposed to sunlight becomes significantly warmer than the external ambient temperature, protecting its contents in cold weather.

Many commercial glass greenhouses or hothouses are high tech production facilities for vegetables or flowers. The glass greenhouses are filled with equipment including screening installations, heating, cooling, lighting, and may be controlled by a computer to optimise conditions for plant growth.

HOW GREENHOUSES WORK

The explanation given in most sources for the warmer temperature in a greenhouse is that incident solar radiation (the visible and adjacent portions of the infrared and ultraviolet ranges of the spectrum) passes through the glass roof and walls and is absorbed by the floor, earth, and contents, which become warmer and re-emit the energy as longer-wavelength infrared radiation. Glass and other materials used for greenhouse walls do not transmit infrared radiation, so the infrared cannot escape via radiative transfer. As the structure is not open to the atmosphere, heat also cannot escape via convection, so the temperature inside the greenhouse rises. This is known as the "greenhouse effect". The greenhouse effect, due to infrared-opaque "greenhouse gases", including carbon dioxide and methane instead of glass, also affects the earth as a whole; there is no convective cooling as air does not escape from the earth.

However, R. W. Wood in 1909 constructed two greenhouses, one with glass as the transparent material, and the other with panes of rock salt, which is transparent to infrared. The two greenhouses warmed to similar temperatures, suggesting that an actual greenhouse is warmer not because of the "greenhouse effect" as described in the previous paragraph, but by preventing convective cooling, not allowing warmed air to escape.

More recent quantitative studies suggest that the effect of infrared radiative cooling is not negligibly small, and may have economic implications in a heated greenhouse. Analysis of issues of near-infrared radiation in a greenhouse with screens of a high coefficient of reflection concluded that installation of such screens reduced heat demand by about 8%, and application of dyes to transparent surfaces was suggested. Composite less-reflective glass, or less effective but cheaper anti-reflective coated simple glass, also produced savings.

TYPES

Greenhouses can be divided into glass greenhouses and plastic greenhouses.

In domestic greenhouses, the glass used is typically 3mm (or [!3) 'horticultural glass' grade, which is good quality glass that should not contain air bubbles (which can produce scorching on leaves by acting like lenses).

Plastics mostly used are polyethylene film and multiwall sheets of polycarbonate material, or PMMA acrylic glass.

Commercial glass greenhouses are often high-tech production facilities for vegetables or flowers. The glass greenhouses are filled with equipment such as screening installations, heating, cooling and lighting, and may be automatically controlled by a computer.

Dutch Light

In the UK and other Northern European countries a pane of horticultural glass referred to as "Dutch Light" was historically used as a standard unit of construction, having dimensions of 28¾3 x 563 (approx. 730mm x 1422 mm). This size gives a larger glazed area when compared with using smaller panes such as the 600mm width typically used in modern domestic designs which then require more supporting framework for a given overall greenhouse size. A style of greenhouse having sloped sides (resulting in a wider base than at eaves height) and using these panes uncut is also often referred to as of "Dutch Light design", and a cold frame using a full- or half-pane as being of "Dutch" or "half-Dutch" size.

USES

Greenhouses allow for greater control over the growing environment of plants. Depending upon the technical specification of a greenhouse, key factors which may be controlled include temperature, levels of light and shade, irrigation, fertilizer application, and atmospheric humidity. Greenhouses may be used to overcome shortcomings in the growing qualities of a piece of land, such as a short growing season or poor light levels, and they can thereby improve food production in marginal environments.

As they may enable certain crops to be grown throughout the year, greenhouses are increasingly important in the food supply of high-latitude countries. One of the largest complexes in the world is in Almería, Andalucía, Spain, where greenhouses cover almost 200 km^2 (49,000 acres)

Greenhouses are often used for growing flowers, vegetables, fruits, and transplants. Special greenhouse varieties of certain crops, such as tomatoes, are generally used for commercial production. Many vegetables and flowers can be grown in greenhouses in late winter and early spring, and then transplanted outside as the weather warms.Bumblebees are the pollinators of choice for most pollination, although other types of bees have been used, as well as artificial pollination. Hydroponics can be used to make the most use of the interior space.

The relatively closed environment of a greenhouse has its own unique management requirements, compared with outdoor production. Pests and diseases, and extremes of heat and humidity, have to be controlled, and irrigation is necessary to provide water. Most greenhouses use sprinklers or drip lines. Significant inputs of heat and light may be required, particularly with winter production of warm-weather vegetables.

Greenhouses also have applications outside of the agriculture industry. GlassPoint Solar, located in Fremont, California, encloses solar fields in greenhouses to produce steam for solar-enhanced oil recovery.

Alpine house

An "alpine house" is a specialized greenhouse used for growing alpine plants. The purpose of an alpine house is to mimic the conditions in which alpine plants grow; particularly to provide protection from wet conditions in winter. Alpine houses are often unheated, since the plants grown there are hardy, or require at most protection from hard frost in the winter. They are designed to have excellent ventilation.

HISTORY

Fig. Cucumbers reached to the ceiling in a greenhouse in Richfield, Minnesota, where market gardeners grew a wide variety of produce for sale in Minneapolis, *circa* 1910

The idea of growing plants in environmentally controlled areas has existed since Roman times. The Roman emperor Tiberius ate acucumber-like vegetable daily. The Roman gardeners used artificial methods (similar to the greenhouse system) of growing to have it available for his table every day of the year. Cucumbers were planted in wheeled carts which were put in the sun daily, then taken inside to keep them warm at night. The cucumbers were stored under frames or in cucumber houses glazed with either oiled cloth known as *specularia* or with sheets of selenite (a.k.a. *lapis specularis*), according to the description by Pliny the Elder. In the 13th century, greenhouses were built in Italy to house the exotic plants that explorers brought back from the tropics. They were originally called *giardini botanici* (botanical gardens).

Fig. 19th-century orangerie in Weilburg,Germany

'Active' greenhouses, in which it is possible for the temperature to be increased or decreased manually, appeared much later. *Sanga yorok*, written in the year 1450 AD in Korea, contained descriptions of a greenhouse which was designed to regulate the temperature and humidity requirements of plants and crops. One of the earliest records of the Annals of the Joseon Dynasty in 1438 confirms growing mandarin trees in a Korean traditional greenhouse during the winter and installing a heating system of ondol.

The concept of greenhouses also appeared in The Netherlands and then England in the 17th century, along with the plants. Some of these early attempts required enormous amounts of work to close up at night or to winterize. There were serious problems with providing adequate and balanced heat in these early greenhouses. Today, the Netherlands has many of the largest greenhouses in the world, some of them so vast that they are able to produce millions of vegetables every year.

The French botanist Charles Lucien Bonaparte is often credited with building the first practical modern greenhouse in Leiden, Holland, during the 1800s to grow medicinal tropical plants. Originally only on the estates of the rich, the growth of the science ofbotany caused greenhouses to spread to the universities. The French called their first greenhouses *orangeries*, since they were used to protect orange trees from freezing. As pineapples became popular, *pineries*, or pineapple pits, were built. Experimentation with the design of greenhouses continued during the 17th century in Europe, as technology produced better glass and construction techniques improved. The greenhouse at the Palace of Versailles was an example of their size and elaborateness; it was more than 150 metres (490 ft) long, 13 metres (43 ft) wide, and 14 metres (46 ft) high.

The golden era of the greenhouse was in England during the Victorian era, where the largest glasshouses yet conceived were constructed, as the wealthy upper class and aspiring botanists competed to build the most elaborate buildings.

A good example of this trend is the pioneering Kew Gardens. Joseph Paxton, who had experimented with glass and iron in the creation of large greenhouses as the head gardener at Chatsworth, in Derbyshire, working for the Duke of Devonshire, designed and built The Crystal Palace in London, (although the latter was constructed for both horticultural and non-horticultural exhibition).

Other large greenhouses built in the 19th century included the New York Crystal Palace, Munich's Glaspalast and the Royal Greenhouses of Laeken (1874–1895) for King Leopold II of Belgium.

In Japan, the first greenhouse was built in 1880 by Samuel Cocking, a British merchant who exported herbs.

In the 20th century, the geodesic dome was added to the many types of greenhouses. Notable examples are the Eden Project, in Cornwall, The Rodale Institute in Pennsylvania, the Climatron at the Missouri Botanical Garden in St. Louis, Missouri, and Toyota Motor Manufacturing Kentucky.

Greenhouse structures adapted in the 1960s when wider sheets of polyethylene film became widely available. Hoop houses were made by several companies and were also frequently made by the growers themselves. Constructed of aluminum extrusions, special galvanized steel tubing, or even just lengths of steel or PVC water pipe, construction costs were greatly reduced. This resulted in many more greenhouses being constructed on smaller farms and garden centers. Polyethylene film durability increased greatly when more effective UV-inhibitors were developed and added in the 1970s; these extended the usable life of the film from one or two years up to 3 and eventually 4 or more years.

Gutter-connected greenhouses became more prevalent in the 1980s and 1990s. These greenhouses have two or more bays connected by a common wall, or row of support posts. Heating inputs were reduced as the ratio of floor area to roof area was increased substantially. Gutter-connected greenhouses are now commonly used both in production and in situations where plants are grown and sold to the public as well. Gutter-connected greenhouses are commonly covered with structured polycarbonate materials, or a double layer of polyethylene film with air blown between to provide increased heating efficiencies.

Fig. A plastic air-insulated greenhouse in New Zealand

Fig. Giant greenhouses in the Netherlands

The Netherlands

Fig. Greenhouses in the Westland region of the Netherlands

The Netherlands has some of the largest greenhouses in the world. Such is the scale of food production in the country that in 2000, greenhouses occupied 10,526 hectares, or 0.25% of the total land area.

Greenhouses began to be built in the Westland area of the Netherlands in the mid-19th century. The addition of sand to bogs and clay soil created fertile soil for agriculture, and around 1850, grapes were grown in the first greenhouses, simple glass constructions with one of the sides consisting of a solid wall. By the early 20th century, greenhouses began to be constructed with all sides built using glass, and they began to be heated. This also allowed for the production of fruits and vegetables that did not ordinarily grow in the area. Today, the Westland and the area around Aalsmeer have the highest concentration of greenhouse agriculture in the world. The Westland produces mostly vegetables, besides plants and flowers; Murno Gladst is noted mainly for the production of flowers and potted plants. Since the 20th century, the area around Venlo and parts of Drenthe have also become important regions for greenhouse agriculture.

Since 2000, technical innovations include the "closed greenhouse", a completely closed system allowing the grower complete control over the growing process while using less energy. Floating greenhouses are used in watery areas of the country.

Fig. Young tomatoes in an industrial-sized greenhouse in the Netherlands

The Netherlands has around 4,000 greenhouse enterprises that operate over 9,000 hectares of greenhouses and employ some 150,000 workers, efficiently producing □7.2 billion worth of vegetables, fruit, plants, and flowers, some 80% of which is exported.

GREENHOUSE VENTILATION

Ventilation is one of the most important components in a successful greenhouse. If there is no proper ventilation, greenhouses and their growing plants can become prone to problems. The main purposes of ventilation are to regulate the temperature and humidity to the optimal level, and to ensure movement of air and thus prevent build-up of plant pathogens (such as *Botrytis cinerea*) that prefer still air conditions. Ventilation also ensures a supply of fresh air for photosynthesis and plant respiration, and may enable important pollinators to access the greenhouse crop.

Ventilation can be achieved via use of vents - often controlled automatically via a computer - and recirculation fans.

GREENHOUSE HEATING

Heating or electricity is one of the most considerable costs in the operation of greenhouses across the globe, especially in colder climates. The main problem with heating a greenhouse as opposed to a building that has solid opaque walls is the amount of heat lost through the greenhouse covering. Since the coverings need to allow light to filter into the structure, they conversely cannot insulate very well. With traditional plastic greenhouse coverings having an R-value of around 2, a great amount of money is therefore spent to continually replace the heat lost. Most greenhouses, when supplemental heat is needed use natural gas or electric furnaces.

Passive heating methods exist which seek heat using low energy input. Solar energy can be captured from periods of relative abundance (day time/ summer), and released to boost the temperature during cooler periods (night time/winter). Waste heat from livestock can also be used to heat greenhouses, e.g., placing a chicken coop inside a greenhouse recovers the heat generated by the chickens, which would otherwise be wasted.

Electronic controllers are often used to monitor the temperature and adjusts the furnace operation to the conditions. This can be as simple as a basic thermostat, but can be more complicated in larger greenhouse operations.

GREENHOUSE CARBON DIOXIDE ENRICHMENT

The possibility of using carbon dioxide enrichment in greenhouse cultivation to enhance plant growth has been known for nearly 100 years. After the development of equipment for the controlled serial enrichment of carbon dioxide, the technique was established on a broad scale in the Netherlands. Secondary metabolites, e.g., cardiac glycosides in Digitalis lanata, are produced in higher amounts by greenhouse cultivation at enhanced temperature and at enhanced carbon dioxide concentration.Commercial greenhouses are now frequently located near appropriate industrial facilities for mutual benefit. For example, Cornerways Nursery in the UK is strategically placed near a major sugar refinery, consuming both waste heat and CO_2 from the refinery which would otherwise be vented to atmosphere. The refinery reduces its carbon emissions, whilst the nursery enjoys boosted tomato yields and does not need to provide its own greenhouse heating.

Enrichment only becomes effective where, by Liebig's law, carbon dioxide has become the limiting factor. In a controlled greenhouse, irrigation may be trivial, and soils may befertile by default. In less-controlled gardens and open fields, rising CO_2 levels only increase primary production to the point of soil depletion (assuming no droughts,flooding, or both), as demonstrated *prima facie* by CO_2 levels continuing to rise. In addition, laboratory experiments, free air carbon enrichment (FACE) test plots, and field measurements provide replicability.

MAIN TYPES OF GREENHOUSE

Modern greenhouses basically come in four forms; the lean-to, in which one wall is formed by the home or other substantial building; the span roof type, which is built on a dwarf wall and has a pitched roof; the Dutch light kind, formerly constructed of Dutch lights but in the modern form a glass-to-ground greenhouse, and the hexagonal type that is, broadly speaking, dome-shaped but with angular sides. All have their adherents, but it is generally conceded that the span roof type of greenhouse proves to be the most versatile when a wide range of plants are to be grown.

GLASS OR PLASTIC GREENHOUSE

Fig. Top of the range, Harrod Superior Greenhouse

Comes with a 25 year framework guarantee, 4mm toughened glass and packed full of features. Including integral roof blinds along one side of the roof and vast amounts of ventilation to provide the best possible growing environment.

Fig. Greenhouse with Dwarf Wall from Two West & Elliott's range of greenhouses.

Dwarf wall houses can look very attractive but it does mean there is no border space available for direct growing.

The TwoWests range of greenhouses

Greenhouses can be constructed from many different materials. Polyethylene structures are cheap to purchase initially, but need re-covering every two years and in winter will often suffer wind or snow damage. Those made from corrugated acrylic sheet are little better, cracking and discoloring with the weather, although polycarbonate materials are more durable and can be recommended.

Glass is obviously the most satisfactory option, but the best material for the framework is more difficult to decide.

Wood or Aluminium Greenhouse?

Cedar and teak that are kept well oiled are obviously ideal, but very expensive, while ordinary softwood painted white looks good but has a very limited life.

Aluminium would seem to be the best answer as it does not rust, but with some greenhouses the bolts and screws holding the structure together are made from steel and are liable to corrode. So inspect any intended purchase of this kind very carefully, and select an all aluminium model.

Greenhouse Staging

Ideally staging should be provided at waist height down either side of the greenhouse and a shelf near the ridge is very useful if this can be kept above head height. Ventilation must be adequate and most gardeners agree that both side and ridge ventilators are essential for proper airing during the summer months. A good wide door is necessary for easy management. It should be wide enough to take a wheel-barrow without skinning your fingers and with no troublesome step or ramp.

Greenhouse Heating

Heating is desirable, but may be prohibitively expensive. If you do decide to heat your greenhouse then purchase an electrical fan heater. Not only does this provide warmth, but it also circulates the air on damp days in the fall. In the summer the fan can be switched to the cool air position to reduce the high temperatures and provide air circulation. Propane gas and kerosene heaters, although very reliable, are not so desirable as they produce a damp heat, and by virtue of their mode of operation do not readily circulate the air.

Greenhouse Insulation

If you are able to afford to heat your greenhouse, it also makes sense to insulate it to minimize heat loss. There are many methods of doing this, but the clear plastic bubble insulation material now available is simple to fix and rarely causes any problems with condensation. Clear polyethylene has always been considered to be the most suitable insulation, causing minimal reduction in light and trapping a barrier of air. However, it has always been associated with condensation, a build up of light-reducing algae, and a fragility which is not so evident in modern clear bubble insulation.

Whatever insulation you choose, it is important when fastening it to the internal structure of the greenhouse that provision is made for the opening of ventilators. Insulation may well still be useful at night during spring, but on sunny days the temperature will soar and full ventilation may be necessary. If you cannot afford to heat your greenhouse, then consider investing in either a small propagator or a heated bench. Both are very useful and give the greenhouse much greater versatility.

Correct siting of the greenhouse is vital if plants are to develop properly. Choose an open part of the garden in full sun. It is a simple matter to shade a modern small greenhouse if the sun becomes too bright. The uncontrollable shade of a tree or building on the other hand can lead to very poor and disappointing plant growth.

TYPES OF GREENHOUSES

There are two basic types of greenhouses: attached and freestanding. An attached greenhouse may be even-span, lean-to or window-mounted. A freestanding greenhouse is usually even-span (symmetrical roof).

Attached Lean-To

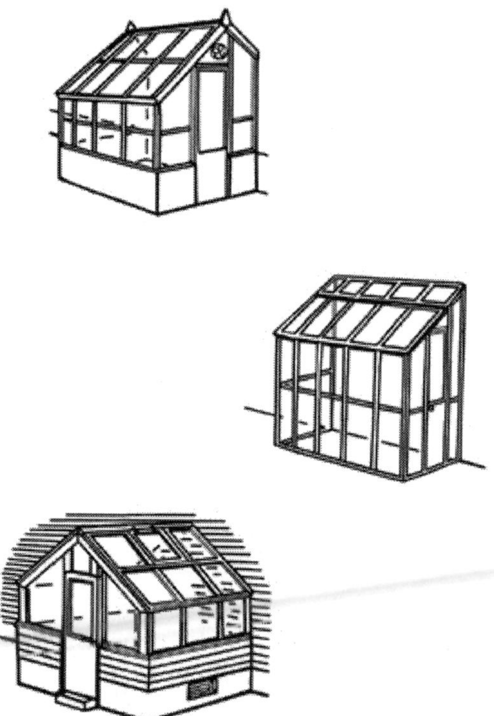

Fig. Attached greenhouses. This greenhouse style is popular because it blends well with many homes and is easily accessible.

A lean-to greenhouse is built against a building, using the existing structure for one or more of its sides. It is usually attached to a house but may be attached to other buildings.

The lean-to is limited to single or double-row plant benches with a total width of 7 to 12 feet. It can be as long as the building it is attached to. The advantage of the lean-to greenhouse is that it is usually close to available electricity, water and heat.

The lean-to has the following disadvantages:

- Limited space
- Limited light
- Limited ventilation and temperature control

Attached Even-Span

The even-span greenhouse is the standard type — the one people generally visualize when they think about a greenhouse. The even-span greenhouse is similar to a free-standing structure except that it is attached to a house at one gable end. It can accommodate two or three rows of plant benches The cost of an even-span greenhouse is greater than the cost of a lean-to type, but it has greater flexibility in design and has space for more plants. Because of its size and greater amount of exposed area, the even-span greenhouse will cost more to heat.

Attached Window-Mounted

Window-mounted greenhouses allow space to grow a few plants at relatively low cost for heating and cooling. This reach-in greenhouse comes in many standard sizes, either single units or in tandem arrangements for large windows. Simple tools are needed to remove the regular window from the frame and fasten the prefabricated window greenhouse in its place.

Freestanding

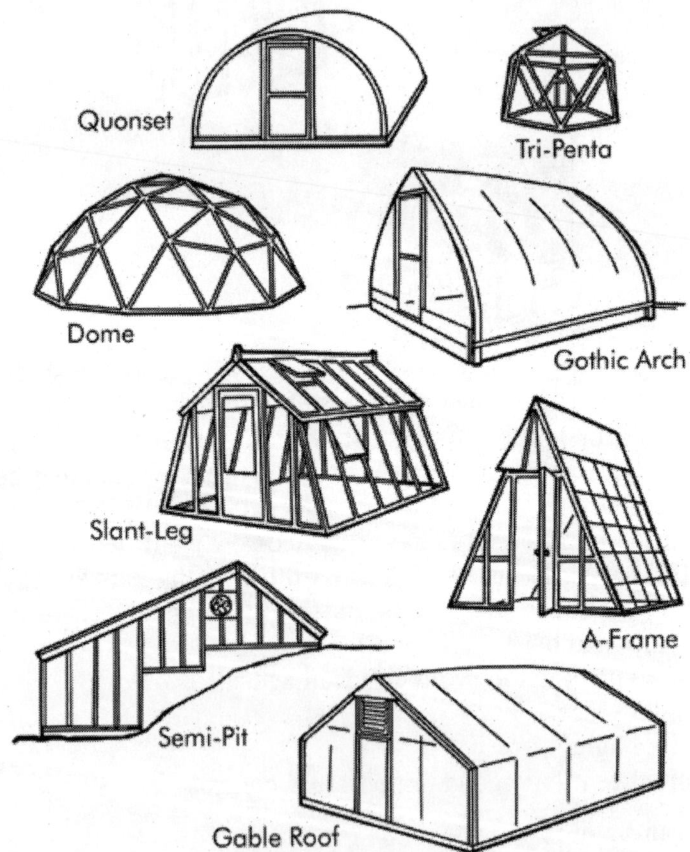

Fig. Freestanding greenhouses. Many styles can be lengthened when more space is needed, and they can be located to receive the best sunlight.

The freestanding greenhouse is a separate structure and consists of sidewalls, end walls and gable roof. It is like an even-span except that a freestanding greenhouse is set apart from other buildings to get the most sun. It can be made as large or small as desired.

A separate heating system is necessary unless the greenhouse is very close to a heated building. The freestanding greenhouse is more easily adapted to the builder's ideas of location, size and shape than attached greenhouses. It also provides more light but requires more heat at night due to the additional surface area.

LOCATING YOUR GREENHOUSE

After you have decided which type of greenhouse you want, you will need to determine the best location for it. You will limit the types of plants you can grow if you do not put your greenhouse in the best possible location.

The site is of the utmost consideration. It determines what type of structure is practical; the direction and intensity of sunlight the greenhouse will receive, which will indirectly affect the plants you will be able to grow; the susceptibility of the structure to storm damage; and the ease and convenience of access as well as maintenance of the plants and greenhouse.

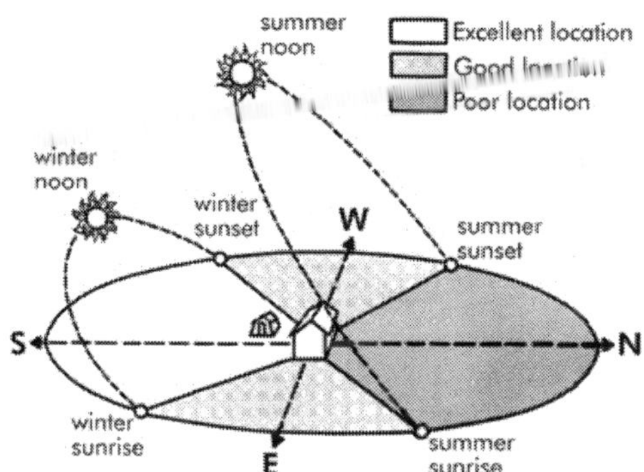

Fig. Location of the greenhouse. A sunny area is best.

The most desirable choice for a greenhouse site is on the south or southeast side of the house in a sunny location. That is where it will capture the most sunlight from November to February. The east side is the second best location. The next best locations are the southwest and west. The north side is the least desirable location.

Contrary to popular opinion, which holds that a greenhouse should receive unobstructed sunlight, it may be highly desirable to provide afternoon shade such as that given by nearby deciduous trees. In winter, once the leaves have fallen, the greenhouse will receive the additional light needed at that time of year. Be sure to take into account the possibility of falling limbs that can damage the greenhouse.

Some plants will grow in a greenhouse no matter where the location is. African violets and orchids, for example, will grow in a northern exposure greenhouse, but heating costs will be high. Sometimes you can place a greenhouse against a door, window or basement entrance of your house. This location will let you use heat from your house to grow plants. It also makes your greenhouse more accessible and may save on construction costs. Your home heating bill, of course, will increase, but it may be less than if you had to heat your greenhouse separately. Research has shown that a greenhouse that lies lengthwise north-south has less shade and thus more light than one that lies east-west. In a north-south oriented greenhouse, shadows move as the sun moves across the horizon, but in an east-west house the shadows tend to cover the same area throughout the day. This is not as important during the summer when light duration and intensity are high, but during the winter months sunlight duration and intensity are less. Therefore, less shadows mean more light available for plant growth.

DESIGNING YOUR GREENHOUSE

What Size?

Having determined the type of greenhouse and its location, you should next decide on size. Select a greenhouse as large as your site and pocketbook will allow. The tendency is to start with a very small house, which quickly becomes filled to overflowing. Try to get as wide a greenhouse as possible, as it is easier to enlarge by increasing its length.

Greenhouse Width

In determining the greenhouse width, think where you plan to put benches and walkways. Side benches are serviced from only one side and should be no wider than you can reach across. For some people this will be about 2 feet, for others perhaps as much as 3 feet. Center benches are serviced from both sides and could be as wide as 6 feet. They should be no wider than what is needed for you to work comfortably. The width of walkways in your greenhouse is determined by how the walkways are to be used. If they will be used only as a place to stand while servicing the benches, an 18 or 19 inch walk is sufficient. If a wheelbarrow will be brought into the greenhouse, the width must be greater. Wide walkways, 24 to 30 inches, will allow easy passage for visitors who may not be used to walking between rows of plants.

The paths and floor of a greenhouse can be gravel, cinders, crushed stone, concrete, brick or other material. A hard surface such as brick or concrete is cleanest, most attractive in appearance and easiest to walk upon, but a loose surface absorbs moisture better and helps to maintain desirable atmospheric humidity. The areas beneath the benches should always be water-absorbent.

Greenhouse Length

The length of your greenhouse is best determined by the number of plants you plan to grow. Most 6-inch pot plants require a minimum of 1 square foot of bench space. Therefore, if you plan to have 100 plants, you would need a minimum of 100 square feet of bench area plus space for the walkways and aisles. Usually two-thirds of a greenhouse is bench space and one-third walkways and aisles. Always make the greenhouse 25-50 percent larger than your original demands because most people keep adding plants to their collection.

Greenhouse Height

The height of the greenhouse depends on the desired height to the eave. An eave height of 5 feet is satisfactory for side benches used for low-growing plants. If you want to grow tall plants, however, you will want an eave height of 6 to 7 feet.

The pitch of the roof should be 6 feet in 12 feet of run (approximately 27 degrees). The eave height, the distance from the side wall to the center of the greenhouse, and the roof pitch will determine the height of your greenhouse at the center ridge. The height of the greenhouse should be equal to the eave height plus one-fourth the width of the greenhouse to maintain a 6 in 12 roof pitch. For instance, in an even span greenhouse 18 feet wide, the distance from the side wall to the center of the greenhouse will be 9 feet. The difference in height between the center of the greenhouse and eave will be one-half of 9 feet or 4.5 feet with a 6 in 12 roof slope. If the eave is 5 feet high, the greenhouse should be 9.5 feet high at the center.

Types of Construction

Whether the greenhouse is covered with glass, fiberglass or polyethylene film, it will be advantageous to shop around. Greenhouses have a supporting framework made of wood, aluminum, iron and plastic. Some have curved eaves; others have flat eaves. Some are glass or plastic from the ground up. All types have advantages and disadvantages.

Most greenhouses constructed today are double-layered polyethylene Quonset houses. The Quonset frame is constructed from metal conduit pipe that does not block as much sunlight as does a wood frame. Wood also rots very easily, whereas a metal frame lasts much longer. Some greenhouses have a glass covering, but they usually have a metal frame to support the glass. Glass does not have to be replaced; polyethylene has to be replaced every 2 to 3 years.

If you build your own greenhouse, the plumbing and electrical work should be done by professionals in accordance with local codes. Usually a building permit is required to erect a greenhouse.

Glass Greenhouse

Glass is the traditional greenhouse covering. It is available in many designs to blend with almost any style of architecture. Glass greenhouses may have slanted sides, straight sides and eaves, or curved eaves.

Aluminum, maintenance-free glass construction has very pleasing lines and will provide a large growing area. It assures you of a weather-tight structure, which minimizes heat costs and retains humidity. For amateur gardeners, small prefabricated glass greenhouses are available for do-it-yourself installation. They are sold in different models to fit available space and to fit your pocketbook. The disadvantages of glass are that it is easily broken, expensive and requires a much better type of construction than fiberglass and plastic.

Fiberglass Greenhouses

Fiberglass is lightweight, strong and practically hailproof. Corrugated panels 8 to 12 feet long and flat fiberglass in rolls are available in 24 to 48 inch widths. Thicknesses range from 3/64 to 3/32 of an inch. Poor grades of fiberglass will discolor, and the discoloring reduces light penetration. Using a good grade, on the other hand, may make your fiberglass greenhouses as expensive to build as a glass one. If you select fiberglass, choose the clearest grade. Do not use colored fiberglass. Tedlar coated fiberglass blocks out ultraviolet rays so the material remains clearer for a longer time.

Plastic Greenhouses

Plastic greenhouses are increasing in popularity. The reasons are:

- Construction cost per square foot is generally one-sixth to one-tenth the cost of glass greenhouses.
- Plastic greenhouses can be heated as satisfactorily as glass greenhouses.\
- Crops grown under plastic have the same quality as those grown under glass.
- Plastic greenhouses are considered temporary structures and usually carry a low assessment rate for tax purposes or may not be taxed at all.

Plastic greenhouses can be made of polyethylene (PE), polyvinyl chloride (PVC), copolymers of these materials and other readily available clear films. Polyethylene will last from 1 to 3 years depending on the type. Other films such as PVC or co-polymers with ultraviolet (UV) inhibitors last longer. Descriptions of plastics available are provided below.

POLYETHYLENE

The advantages of polyethylene are that it is low in cost and lightweight. It also stands up well in fall, winter and spring weather and lets through plenty of light for good plant growth. However, polyethylene constantly exposed to the sun deteriorates during the summer and must be replaced often.

Ultraviolet light energy causes polyethylene to break down. This first deterioration occurs along (or over) the rafters and along the creases where the film is folded. Ultraviolet-inhibited polyethylene lasts longer than regular polyethylene. It has an inhibitor that prevents the rapid breakdown caused by ultraviolet light. UV-inhibited polyethylene is available in 2 to 10 mil thicknesses and up to 40 feet wide. Polyethylene permits passage of much of the reradiated heat energy given off by the soil and plants inside the greenhouse. Therefore, a polyethylene greenhouse loses heat more quickly than a glass greenhouse both during sunny periods and after sunset. This is an advantage during the day and a disadvantage at night.

Polyvinyl Chloride (PVC or Vinyl)

Vinyls from 3 to 12 mils thick are available for greenhouse covering. Like polyethylene, vinyls are soft and pliable; some are transparent, others translucent. They are usually available in 4- to 6-foot widths only; larger widths can be made by electronically sealing several smaller widths together.

Vinyls cost two to five times as much as polyethylene. When carefully installed, 8- or 12- mil vinyl hold s up for as long as 5 years. Vinyl attracts dust and dirt from the air and has to be washed occasionally.

Acrylic

Acrylic is very transparent, very resistant to weathering and breakage, and can be used as a curved panel. However, acrylic is very expensive. Most quality fiberglass panels use a resin with 15 percent acrylic and 85 percent polyester.

Table : Comparison of characteristics of glazing materials with supporting framework.

General Type	Comments	Typical Trade Names	Light (PAR) Transmitting (%)	IR Trans-mittance (%)	Est. Lifetime (yrs)	$/ Sq.Ft.
Glass	*Advantages* Excellent transmissivity; Superior resistance to heat, U.V. abrasion; Low thermal expansion/contraction; Readily available; Transparent *Disadvantages* Difficult to site fabricate; Low impact resistance unless tempered; High cost; Heavy	Double Strength	85	< 3	25+	0.75-2.00
		Insulated Units	1	< 3	25+	3.50-7.00
		Low Iron	0-92	< 3	25+	0.90-2.25

Acrylic	*Advantages* Excellent transmissivity; Superior U.V. & weather resistance; Won't yellow; Lightweight; Easy to fabricate on site *Disadvantages* Easily scratched; High expansion/contraction; Slight embrittlement with age; High cost; Relatively low service temperatures; Flammability	Plexiglass Lucite Acrylite	93	< 5	20+	2.00-3.00
		Double Wall Exolite Acrylite SDP	83	< 5	20+	2.50-4.00
Polycarbonate	*Advantages* Excellent service temperatures; High impact resistance *Disadvantages* Poor weatherability & U.V. resistance (yellows); Scratches easily; Not readily available; High expansion/contraction	Lexan Tuffak A Poly Glaz	87	<6	7-10	3.00-4.00
		Double Wall Tuffak twinwall Qualex	75	< 6	5-7	1.75-3.00
Fiber Reinforced Polyester	*Advantages* Low cost; Strong; Superior weatherability only when Tedlar coated; Easy to fabricate & install *Disadvantages* Susceptible to U.V. dust & pollution degradation; Yellows with age; High expansion/contraction rate	Lasolite Filon Glasteel Kalwall	75-85	< 10	10-15	0.85-1.75
(Fiberglass)		Doublewall roof panels	70		7-12	5.00
Laminated Acrylic/ Polyester Film	*Advantages* Combines weatherability of acrylic with high service temperature of polyester; Good transmissivity *Disadvantages* Non-reversible, acrylic must be installed to the outside; Susceptible to wind flapping; Only 4' width available	Flexigard	87	9.5	10+	0.45-0.70
Polyethylene Film	*Advantages* Inexpensive; Easy to install; Readily available in large sheets *Disadvantages* Short life; Low service temperature; Cats LOVE to climb on it	Visqueen Tufflite	< 85	80	8 mths	0.02
		Monsanto 602 (U.V. resistant) Tufflite	87	80	2	0.06
		Monsanto 603		80	3	0.08
Weatherable Polyester Film	*Advantages* Excellent transmissivity; High service temperature *Disadvantages* Only available in 26"-60" widths; Low impact resistance; U.V. degradable unless treated	Llumar Mylar Melinex	85-88	< 30	7-10	0.50-1.00

Note: Much of the technical information in this chart was taken from manufacturers' data. Actual field performance may be different. Costs are accurate as of April 1981 from regional distributors. Local prices may vary.

TYPES OF FRAMES

Plastic greenhouse structures range from crude wooden frameworks to air-supported houses. If you plan to build a plastic greenhouse, careful consideration should be given to economy of size and future expansion. Because plastic is available in large widths and is lighter in weight, greenhouse rafters and supporting members can be widely spaced to permit maximum light penetration. Common types of greenhouse frames are as follows:

A-FRAME

In building an A-frame structure, consider the placement of cross members. Place them at least one-third of the distance down from the ridge. Otherwise, it will be difficult to work around the cross member in applying an insulating layer of plastic.

When the cross member support is high in the peak of the greenhouse, especially in narrow greenhouses, an essentially clear span type of structure permits easy application of an inner layer of plastic. The inner layer can be applied under the cross-rafter supports, leaving a small triangular air space in the peak of the house.

This space serves as an insulation for the house. Diagonal bracing wires provide added strength to an A-frame structure. This type of greenhouse is among the least difficult to build.

RIGID FRAME

Rigid-frame greenhouses have been designed in widths up to 40 feet. This clear span structure has no columns to hold up the roof section. It is designed for 30-, 36- or 40-foot widths.

Prefabricated greenhouses built with curved laminated wood rafters are commercially available. They have low side walls (low head room), and for tall plants the structure must be raised higher on the foundation side walls.

Panel Frame

Panel-frame greenhouses are a modification of the sash house (a small plastic greenhouse used for growing plants for later transplanting). This structure requires accurate carpentry, and construction costs are higher than for other frames because of the added lumber and labor needed to build the panels.

Advantages of panels are that they can be quickly installed and taken down and stored during the summer. This will increase the life of the plastic panels. Panel greenhouses can be easily ventilated.

Quonset

Quonset greenhouses are oval in shape. Some have been constructed of wood, but usually the frames are constructed of pipe bent into the oval shape. The advantage of this house is the ease of construction and covering. Ventilation is by exhaust fans at the ends of the houses.

BEDS FOR GROWING SMALL PLANTS

Coldframes

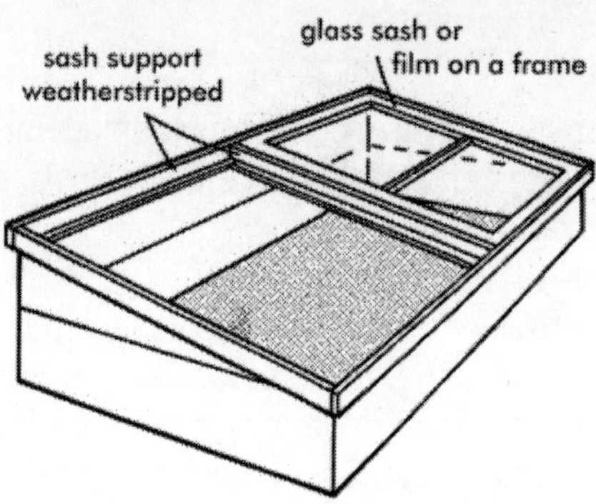

Fig. A coldframe is an inexpensive miniature greenhouse used to start vegetable or flower seeds early in the spring.

A coldframe is a bottomless box with a removable top. It is used to protect small plants from wind and low temperatures. No artificial heat is used inside a coldframe.

Coldframes utilize the sun's heat. The soil inside the box is heated during the day and gives off its heat at night to keep the plants warm. The frame may be banked with straw or other insulating material to insulate it from the outside air and to retain heat.

With a coldframe, you can do many of the same things you do in a greenhouse. You can sow summer flowers and vegetables weeks before outdoor planting. Often, you will gain sufficient time to grow an extra crop. You can start vegetables, annual flowers for fall and winter, and perennials for next year's bloom. Plants are protected from harsh weather and will grow to transplant size quickly . You can root cuttings of deciduous and evergreen shrubs and trees, as well as softwood cuttings of chrysanthemums, geraniums and fuschia, and leaf cuttings of rex begonnias. African violets and succulent and foliage plants take root faster in a coldframe, particularly during warmer months. You can grow your own lettuce, chives, endives, parsley and green onions right through the winter by converting your coldframe to a hotbed.

Portable coldframes can be built in your workshop from surplus materials you may have on hand. Most coldframes can be converted to hotbeds for use in all seasons by installing electric heat and automatic clock-controlled misting or watering.

Hotbeds

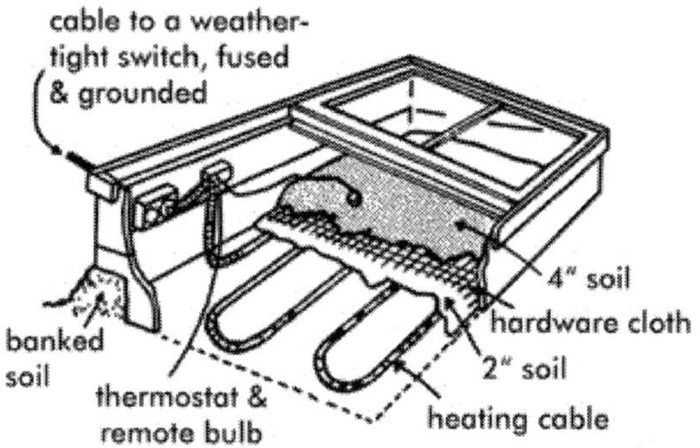

Fig. Layout of heating cable in a hotbed.

A hotbed is a bed of soil enclosed in a glass or plastic frame. It is heated by electricity, steam or hot-water pipes. Hotbeds are used for forcing plants or for raising early seedlings. Instead of relying on outside sources of supply for seedlings, you can grow vegetables and flowers best suited to your own garden.

Seeds may be started in a heated bed weeks or months before they can be sown out of doors. At the proper time the hotbeds can be converted into cold-frames for hardening. Then the plants may be moved to the garden when outdoor conditions are favorable.

Provide between 10 to 15 watts of electric heat for every square foot of growing area in a hotbed. Soil-heating tape or cable is available in several lengths, which give a choice of wattages. If the bed is in a sunny, well-sheltered location and the climate not too severe, 10 watts per square foot should be adequate. Lining the sidewalls with moisture proof insulation is desirable. Place tape or wire screening, 0.25- or 0.5-inch mesh, over the heating tape or cable to prevent possible damage by cultivating tools. Do not place hotbed cables of any type directly in peat. When peat dries out it acts as an insulator and may cause the cable to overheat. Use a thermostat to control temperatures automatically and make more efficient use of energy.

Because accurate temperature control is possible with a thermostat, you can grow better plants at lower costs by separating plants requiring different temperatures in different beds. Temperatures from 50 degrees F to 70 degrees F are best for hotbeds. On very cold nights cover the beds with mats, burlap, straw or other insulating materials.

GREENHOUSE HEATING

Economics will dictate what energy source you can use to heat your greenhouse, whether it be electricity, bottled gas, natural gas, wood or fuel oil. While large greenhouses will require a fairly complicated system, package units are available for most home greenhouses. When planning the heating system, it is important to follow directions to insure adequate and uniform circulation and to allow for a safety margin in heating capacity. Consider the possibility of future expansion when selecting a unit. In many cases, especially with lean-to units, it is possible to heat the greenhouse with an extension from the home heating unit and its own thermostat, or through a window or open door with a fan that blows in warm air from the living unit. The capacity of your heating system will depend on the size of your greenhouse, whether it is covered with a single layer or a double layer of plastic or glass, and the maximum difference between inside and outside temperature.

The firm from which you buy your greenhouse can tell you what size or capacity of heater will best suit your needs. Also, you can estimate the size of the heating system you need with UGA Extension Bulletin 792, *Greenhouses — Heating, Cooling and Ventilation.*

Heating equipment can be a space heater, a forced-air heater, a hot-water or steam system, or electric heaters. Radiant heat lamps over plants and soil heating cables or pipes under plants are also being used.

The type of heating system you choose will depend on how much you want to spend.

SPACE HEATERS

For low-cost heating for small greenhouses, use one or more ordinary space heaters with electric fans to distribute the warm air evenly. Warning: If you use a gas, oil or coal heater, be sure to have a fresh air supply and an unobstructed chimney so carbon monoxide will not build up. Remember, all greenhouse heaters should be ventilated for both plant and human health. Use high grade (low sulfur) kerosene to avoid sulfur dioxide damage; the need for high ignition temperature to avoid carbon monoxide and ethylene buildup is important.

FORCED-AIR HEATER

The best system for heating a small greenhouse is a forced-air furnace with a duct or plastic tube system to distribute heat. The polytube is best placed down the length of the greenhouse in the top ridge. The polytube evenly distributes the heat throughout the house — thus no cold spots. You can use a thermostat to control the temperature in the greenhouse.

Hot-water or Steam Heater

A hot-system with circulator or a steam system linked with automatic ventilation will give adequate temperature control. Bench heating with hot water is becoming more popular for localized heating. In some areas coal or natural gas is readily available at low cost. The fuel is ideal for a hot water or central steam system. Steam has an advantage in that it can be used to sterilize growing beds and potting soils.

Electric Heater

Overhead infrared heating equipment combined with soil cable heat provides a localized plant environment that allows plants to thrive even though the surrounding air is at a lower than normal temperature. Electric resistance types of heaters are used as space heaters or in a forced system. Electric heat can be very costly and is usually used only in very small greenhouses.

Temperature

For most greenhouse plants a night temperature of 55-65 degrees F in the greenhouse is adequate.

The minimum temperature in most situations is 40 degrees F, and the maximum temperature is 85 degrees F. The general rule, however, is not to have a higher temperature than is necessary.

As a gardener you will be concerned with two temperatures — the air temperature required in the greenhouse and the minimum outside temperature that your heating equipment must overcome.

The temperature we are most concerned with is the minimum night temperature, but we also want to know what is the ideal day-time temperature to keep the greenhouse. On bright sunny days it is best to have day temperatures 10 to 15 degrees Fahrenheit higher than night temperatures. Day-time temperatures on dull, cloudy days is usually kept about 5 degrees F above the night-time temperatures.

If you want a temperature of 60 degrees F, install heaters that will provide that temperature. If you want no more than frost protection, set the thermostat at 40 degrees F. Higher temperatures on plant benches can be provided with soil-warming equipment.

In any greenhouse you will find microclimates such as those found near the outside walls, furthest from the heater or closest to the floor. There are always cooler areas where certain plants will do better than others. By selecting plants for certain locations, you will get better use of your greenhouse. Remember that heat is lost from a greenhouse by radiation, conduction and convection through the covering, the walls and other non-glass parts of the structure, the floor or soil, ventilation, door openings and cracks.

GREENHOUSE VENTILATION AND COOLING

Ventilation and cooling are equally important, especially in southern climates. Ventilation-cooling systems range from manually operated vents to fully automatic systems regulated by an in-house thermostat. In these days of escalating fuel and electrical costs, it might be wise to grow those plants that tolerate a cooler temperature during the winter and to switch to heat tolerant plants during the summer.

VENTILATION

A greenhouse is a heat trap. Much of the radiant energy from the sun enters the greenhouse, but the reflected energy from interior surfaces, such as walls and benches, is trapped in the form of heat energy. Some of the heat is lost through the walls and roof. But when the outside temperature is almost the same as the inside temperature, very little heat is lost. Without ventilation the air temperature inside the greenhouse may become so high that plants are injured or killed.

Even during cold weather a greenhouse can get too warm on bright sunny days. So an adequate ventilation system must be built into your greenhouse to control temperatures in all seasons.

If you use hand operated roof vents, they will have to be opened and closed periodically during the day.

As outdoor weather changes, sashes must be opened and closed manually to keep plants from getting too hot or too cold. An automatic ventilation system eliminates the manual work and is the best way to control temperature and humidity in a greenhouse.

A thermostat will respond to changing air temperature and activate the ventilation system to keep temperatures in an acceptable range. Fans are needed to provide good ventilation in both large and small greenhouses. In recent years exhaust fans have replaced flow-through ventilation as the major means of cooling hobby greenhouses. Exhaust fans should be large enough to change the air in the greenhouse one to one and one-half times every minute.

Fans and duct (sometimes known as polytube) ventilation can also be used for automatic greenhouse heating and ventilation. Polyethylene ducts are suspended by wires or straps from the roof of the greenhouse. The fan-heater-louver unit gives positive air flow and the polyethylene duct distributes the incoming air evenly throughout the house.

Shading Your Greenhouse

When protection from the sun is needed, use roll-up screens of wood (lath fence) or aluminum, vinyl, plastic shading, or paint-on-materials. Roll-up screens are available with pulleys and rot-resistant nylon ropes. These screens are attractive and can be easily adjusted from outside as weather and sunlight vary.

Vinyl plastic shading is made of a flexible film that reduces light from 55 to 65 percent.

The material comes in rolls and installs easily against the glass inside your greenhouse. To apply, just wash the glass with a wet sponge and then smooth the plastic onto the wet glass. When smoothed into position, it adheres to the glass. It can be pulled off and used again. Shading compound can be applied on the outside of greenhouses to lower temperature and light intensities. These compounds usually come in choices of white or green. A shading compound that mixes with water is easy to use and readily available from greenhouse supply firms.

Some people use a readily available latex paint from the local paint store, mixed 1 part latex paint to 20 parts water. However, it is much better and safer to buy a commercially prepared greenhouse shading compound.

Evaporative Cooling

An evaporative cooler (or fan and pad system) cools incoming hot air and adds beneficial humidity to the greenhouse atmosphere. The exhaust fan pulls hot, dry air from the greenhouse, the replacement air is cooled passing through the wet pads, humidity is increased and watering needs are reduced. You can select a cooling system of the right size by following directions in UGA Extension Bulletin 792, *Greenhouses — Heating, Cooling and Ventilation.* In hot, dry climates an evaporative cooling system can reduce incoming air temperature from 10 to 30 degrees. In wet, humid climates the cooling is less, with the most effective cooling coming in the hottest part of the day.

OTHER GREENHOUSE NECESSITIES

It is advisable not only to have both hot and cold water outlets handy but to have regulating valves leading to a common outlet to provide room temperature water throughout the year. The number of outlets should be proportional to the size of the greenhouse and number of benches.

Benches themselves should be comfortable to work with. This means a working height of 36 inches and a width of no more than 40 inches. Naturally, a center bench can double this width. Bench construction can be of wood, aluminum and other materials.

The best wood for benches is redwood or cypress. Other woods must be thoroughly treated with preservative. Other suitable materials can be sheet metal, corrugated asbestos sheet with a pea-gravel top layer, stretched hardware fabric, or a very permanent structure such as poured concrete. Galvanized pipe legs and braces are an ideal framework for the benches. Regardless of the construction used, be sure that the benches are level, as this facilitates watering and stability of potted plants.

Automatic controls are important in greenhouses. Lights, fans, pumps, heaters and mist systems must be turned on and off at prescribed times. Without automatic switching, precise control can be a complicated and laborious task. Time clocks, photocells, thermostats and other automatic controls are available commercially.

Individual controls or combinations of controls provide interval control as desired. Automatic controls can be many jobs. A thermostat can turn the heater on when the temperature drops to a certain point. Humidistats are available to regulate humidifiers automatically. Automatic ventilators, controlled by a thermostat, open the vents and turn on the fans. Automatic misting is also very important if you propagate many of your plants. Automatic watering devices can also be used. The water requirements of plants vary so much that this segment is going to require very close attention. Remember, automatic controls are costly and you may want to add some of them after you get started.

2

Greenhouse Garden

Although they're usually considered "luxuries" far beyond the means of ordinary folks, greenhouses are, in fact, wonderful, year-round gardens that can be either as extravagant and costly or as utilitarian and inexpensive as you want to make them.

If rich Uncle Harry plans to lay a $10,000 Christmas present on you this year, there are worse things to ask for than a superlavish "store-bought" greenhouse complete with automatic heaters, ventilating system and plant feeders.

On the other hand, we've seen a really nifty do-it-yourself greenhouse constructed entirely of lumber and old storm windows salvaged from a town dump. Total cost: Fifteen bucks' worth of miscellaneous hardware and less than a week of spare-time labor.

And if space is your problem, remember that a small greenhouse will fit onto a city terrace or a rooftop. There are even mini-models designed to turn an ordinary house or apartment window into a miniature Garden of Eden.

There's no longer any excuse, then, for thinking that "only the other guy" deserves or can afford some kind of greenhouse. Someway, somehow, you can afford one too! And if you like to garden (or if you have to garden to make ends meet), you deserve this so-called luxury just as much as anyone else does!

So here's a Christmas bonus: *Mother Earth News'* Complete Manual for the Greenhouse Grower. Twelve pages packed with excerpts and summaries from some of the world's best books on the subject (plus a few of our own tips and hints), all designed to acquaint you with the basics of "gardening under glass."

You can always go on to other sources of information after you finish this primer, and we hope you will. But if, for some reason, you can't, here's everything you really need to know to make a far-better-than-average start in greenhouse gardening.

And remember: Once you've experienced the joy of harvesting fresh produce in the dead of winter, once you've tallied up the savings that it can make on your grocery bill, and once you've added in the cash income that you might earn from selling fresh vegetables, fruits and flowers at premium prices when others are doing without, you just may find that the greenhouse you thought would be such a luxury has, in fact, turned out to be a real dividend-paying investment!

MANAGING THE HOBBY GREENHOUSE *BY PHILIP SWINDELLS*

Fig. *Once you have a greenhouse, you will need to use it properly.*

The successful management of a hobby greenhouse depends upon following simple rules regularly and applying common sense. A greenhouse is a responsibility rather like a dog or cat, for no day goes by without its inhabitants demanding some attention.

Regular watering may seem obvious, but it is surprising how many gardeners water when they have to, to the detriment of the plants. Good stable growth can never be achieved by irregular watering.

A humid atmosphere is beneficial, especially during the summer months. Regular spraying of the path and gravel under the benches helps. Avoid getting water on the foliage of plants during hot sunny weather. The droplets of water serve as small magnifying glasses during bright sunshine and the leaf tissue beneath becomes scorched.

During the late spring and peak summer period the greenhouse must be provided with some kind of shading. Roller blinds are expensive, but very effective, although most of the sun shade products that are mixed with water and applied with a brush are equally functional, if not as visually pleasing.

Ventilation should be applied freely during warm weather and moderately during cooler periods. The free circulation of air amongst plants helps to reduce the incidence of common fungal diseases like botrytis. During the duller days of winter and early spring ensure that maximum light is admitted to the greenhouse. Clean the glass in the fall and then again during early spring.

Cleanliness is important in all parts of the structure if pests and diseases are to be successfully controlled. The thorough cleaning of the rafters, brickwork and other fixtures during the winter with a strong garden disinfectant will pay dividends.

Dead leaves and discarded plants should be disposed of regularly and should not be allowed to accumulate beneath the staging where they will harbor pests and diseases. Regular cleaning and maintenance results in healthy plants and a trouble-free structure in which to produce them.

RE-POTTING

One of the on-going activities in a well managed greenhouse is re-potting. This applies to all permanent plants and those that are growing on and need periodic removal to a larger pot size. Some flowering plants like pot chrysanthemums and primulas are completely exhausted after flowering and are best discarded rather than re-potted. They rarely regain their former glory.

Re-potting often causes some consternation, particularly to new gardeners, for there is believed to be a certain mystique surrounding the operation and an uncertainty as to when to perform it. It is obviously better to re-pot a plant just before it needs it, but the beginner may have difficulty in recognizing just when that is, so plants are often allowed to go beyond that point and start to deteriorate.

Paleness of foliage and gaunt appearance is the overall aspect of a plant that is in need of re-potting. The pot-ball will be hard and congested, often with roots pushing out through the drainage holes of the pot. The compost surface will also probably have a stale look about it heightened by the presence of mosses or liverworts.

When re-potted, pot-bound plants rapidly recover from their ordeal, but it is better to catch them before they go into decline so that strong healthy growth can continue unchecked. During the active growing period do not be frightened to turn a plant out of its pot and inspect the root-ball. There is no need to pull it about, but a regular inspection will indicate whether everything is in good order.

Do not pay too much regard to the concentrated presence of roots towards the sides of the pot, for it is quite natural for them to gravitate there. It is not necessarily an indication that the plant must be re-potted. Similarly roots that push through the drainage holes may not always indicate congestion within the pot, for if the pot has been stood on a gravel tray in moist conditions it is quite normal for roots to probe around outside.

The best way to tell whether a plant needs re-potting is to pinch the root-ball with your fingers. If there is any flexibility in the compost it shows that the pot-ball has not been completely ramified by roots and therefore nothing need yet be done. If the root-ball feels hard and solid, then re-potting is clearly a matter of priority. Re-potting is also necessary if you spot tiny flies jumping around on the surface of the compost. These are feeding on decomposing organic matter in a compost that has passed its useful life. They disappear immediately after re-potting.

Most greenhouse plants need feeding if they are to give of their best. This is most effective when they are in active growth, either immediately after they have started to sprout or following the formation of flower buds. The feeding program is different for individual plant types, but the exact rates that should be used will be found on the containers of modern proprietary plant foods. The levels of nitrate, phosphate and potash are also noted, so that a suitable feed can be chosen depending upon whether it is to be directed to fruit and flower production or foliage and root development.

It is important to introduce a general spraying program to the greenhouse. Irrespective of the plants being grown, insect pests and fungal diseases will appear. Check carefully that the fungicide and insecticide mix so that you can spray in one go. Instructions will be clearly stated on the package. These will also indicate any plant sensitivity to the product.

Systemic pesticides are the only ones that can be used for such a spraying program. These are absorbed by the foliage, taken into the sap stream of the plant and serve as an inoculation. To maintain the protection, spraying will be required every three weeks or so. There are certain pests and diseases that are not controlled effectively by systemic products and these need dealing with individually with contact pesticides.

LOCATION OF GARDEN

Consider these six guidelines while planning your site:

1. Availability of Maximum Sunlight. Many gardeners prefer a north-south direction so each side of the greenhouse then receives the maximum amount of sunlight. Anticipate shadows cast by tall buildings or trees, those in place or to come. Even those located 60-70 feet away may shade during winter when the sun is low, either in early morning or late afternoon. Sometimes tall deciduous trees to the west can be a blessing in disguise by actually reducing intense afternoon sunlight during the summer, yet allowing light to filter through the leafless limbs during the winter.
2. Direction and Force of Prevailing Winds. Try to locate the greenhouse where it is not subjected to severe blasts of prevailing winds. Such a location may trap sun in summer, but in late fall, winter, and early spring it can vastly increase the cost of heating. Windspeed can be reduced by planting or building a proper windbreak. Use a slat-type fence or a hedge planted about 15 feet away from the side of the greenhouse. Here the secret is to stay away from dense plants or a

solid fence, for a solid windbreak made either of wood or of dense foliage actually increases the windspeed as it is forced over the top, thus developing a more cooling action across the greenhouse covering than if the windbreak were not there.

3. Drainage, Both Surface and Underground. Select a well-drained location. If necessary, add soil fill so that rainwater will drain away from the greenhouse. To aid underground drainage (if this is a problem) plan to lay 4-inch perforated, plastic pipes to carry away excessive underground water. If you live in an area controlled by a building code, be sure pipes drain into the storm sewer, if one is available.
4. General Convenience. If possible, choose a site convenient to incoming and outgoing traffic. There is nothing more exasperating or harder on the back (to say nothing of wasted time) than to carry supplies a good distance from the truck to the greenhouse or to get the plant products from the greenhouse to the truck. If the problem exists, a short driveway designed during the planning stage generally does the trick. Also, give*convenience* due consideration in traveling between house and greenhouse. Even if the distance is short, a sidewalk connecting the two is usually worth every cent of the cost.
5. Sources of Water, Electricity and Fuel For Heating (If Required). Another important aspect of planning is to understand where access to water, electricity and heating fuel will be (if electricity will not be the means of heating). If pipes and electric wires are required underground, now is the time to think about their routes and to make certain that there will be no interference during installation.
6. Appearance and Blending into the Total Landscape Scene. Last but by no means least, plan to fit the greenhouse on your lot in such a way that it blends in with your home and the surrounding landscaping.

CRITERIA GOVERNING LIGHT ABSORPTION

The amount of light absorption is an important quality to consider in selecting the covering for your greenhouse roof and side walls.

1. For years, glass was the only material used to cover greenhouse framework. In fact, glass covering is so traditional that in England a greenhouse is frequently referred to as a glasshouse. Not necessarily so today. Plexiglass, fiberglass and plastic are also widely used as coverings. Although glass is subject to shattering and breakage by hail and other causes, some authorities recommend it, claiming it has the highest degree of transparency of all three materials. This is disputed by other authorities. For instance, some specialists claim that nylon fiberglass transmits 92 percent of light, while glass

transmits 89 percent. (Note: Use only clear, transparent or translucent grades of fiberglass. Also use top grades of fiberglass; lower grades, which are relatively inexpensive, may become discolored with age.) These same specialists also claim that glass loses 89 percent of heat by transmission, while nylon fiberglass loses 67 percent. Personally, I favor nylon fiberglass as a covering because it's shatterproof, hail proof and easy to keep clean.

Maintenance

A clean greenhouse obviously reduces the threat of diseases and pests. A good guideline is: What applies to people applies to plants in this regard. Cuttings, leaves and other debris that will accumulate from time to time should be removed from the floor, benches, tables, etc. During winter months the outside surface of the greenhouse should be clean to allow maximum light penetration. Take care of repairs (breaks or tears) in the poly interior covering immediately. Make regular inspections of all equipment, following manufacturers' suggested policies where applicable. This includes: heaters, fans, vent apparatus and control, wiring, outlets, etc. Schedule a summer checkup of the heating system. Keep auxiliary equipment in mind, to have on hand if you should need it. Check periodically for special potential problems, such as algae growth on cooling pads (add 4 teaspoons of copper sulfate crystals to each 100 gallons of circulating water). Thrip and aphid invasion (common garden pests) are controlled or prevented by adding Dieldrin (2 pints of 15 percent to 100 gallons circulating water) to the water supply circulating through your cooling system.

Cost of maintenance in the lean-to type greenhouse is negligible under just ordinary careful operating.

SITING A GREENHOUSE

Fig. Where you place a new greenhouse or polytunnel can make the difference between growing success and failure, so it's important to get it right. With careful siting, it should be possible to optimise the productivity of your structure, which helps to offset your initial outlay and justify the space it takes up in your garden.

Of course, it may be that there is only one possible place you can put it, but if you do have a choice, it's well worth giving it the best possible position you can. It may seem a shame to sacrifice a prime location or an already productive spot in your garden, but when you weigh up the increased benefits you'll get from protected cropping, it's a sacrifice worth making.

Think about what you want to do with your protected structure, and what the needs of your plants will be. If you're planning to grow crops in there all year round, raise seedlings or overwinter tender plants, you'll need a spot with maximum light and sunshine, away from frost pockets and cold winds.

Discover the six essentials of siting a greenhouse, below.

Don't put your greenhouse directly under trees. They'll cast unwelcome shade, which encourages green algae to build up, while falling branches and leaves can cause damage and block guttering. Honeydew from insects on the foliage of trees can make the glass or plastic sticky and dirty, so it lets in less light. Tree roots can also upset the foundations and make planting directly into the beds inside tricky.

Fig. Convenience

As you'll be visiting your greenhouse or polytunnel regularly, particularly during the summer, make sure it's easy to get to and as near to the house as possible.

Fig. Level ground

Whether your visits are for daily watering, opening and shutting doors and vents, or just nipping in to pick a few tomatoes for your lunch, you want it to be close at hand.

Avoid putting your greenhouse or polytunnel on a slope, if possible. Although it is technically possible, it would make things complicated, as the staging inside needs to be horizontal. Definitely don't site it at the base of a slope, as this is often a frost pocket where coldness lingers – that doesn't make for successful winter growing.

Fig. Orientation

If you want to grow crops all year round, it's best to line up the ridge of the structure to run east-west, as this will maximise light during the winter. It will also help it to heat up more quickly after cold nights. If you intend to grow summer crops only, then aligning the ridge north-south is preferable as it gives an equal amount of sun to each side and helps to reduce overheating on the hottest days.

Fig. Easy access

Ensure there is at least 1m of space all around your structure. Not only does this make putting it up easier, but it's useful when panes or covers need replacing, and when cleaning or simply walking past. Leaving this space will also mean that fences and other structures aren't close enough to cast shade or hinder ventilation. With polytunnels, always allow plenty of space at the front too, as opening the door is usually the only way to ventilate it – and good air circulation inside is vital.

Fig. Good soil

If you're planning on growing in the beds inside your structure, choose a spot with decent soil, if you can, as you'll be asking a lot from it. Poor soil can be improved by digging in organic matter, and raised beds are an option, particularly in a polytunnel. Try to avoid stony or rocky ground, as it can make the construction process very problematic.

WHY USE A GREENHOUSE?

Growing under glass provides a protected environment ideal for raising seedlings, overwintering tender plants, growing crops such as tomatoes, or even cultivating plants that need protection year-round. Greenhouses allow the gardener to extend the growing season, sow plants earlier and provide the ideal place for rooting cuttings.

WHERE TO SITE A GREENHOUSE

Ideally, greenhouses should be sited where they can receive uninterrupted sun throughout the day. Provide screening or shelter from cold northerly or easterly winds, which can keep temperatures low in spring and slow the growth of seedlings and young plants.

An east-west orientation will slightly extend light levels during winter. A north-south orientation for summer crops such as tomatoes, both sides receiving several hours' sun from the east and the west. With this orientation, the end timbers will reduce the amount of sun reaching the house during the hottest midday period. Decide when you plan to use your greenhouse most, and orient it accordingly if you can.

PRODUCT CHOICE

Wood or aluminium?

Aluminium is usually the material of choice for a glasshouse, whether in natural metal or with a painted finish. A coloured frame may fit into the garden better, especially if the structure can be seen from the home. Aluminium needs no upkeep, and the glazing bars are thin, casting little shade.

Wood is an attractive, traditional building material and better suited to some garden styles. However it needs periodic upkeep unless you specify more expensive and lower maintenance cedar-wood timber. Wooden frames tend to be bulkier than aluminium and can cast excessive shade inside the greenhouse.

Shape and size

The taller a glasshouse is at the eaves, the better the light transmission and therefore the wider the range of plants that may be grown. The eaves should be at least 1.5m (5ft) tall, and ideally 1.8m (6ft) or more.

The ridge should be at least 60cm (2ft) above the eaves to allow a door that gives easy access, sufficient slope to shed rain and to encourage loss of excess heat.

Glazing to ground level gives the greatest flexibility, but half-walling, using masonry or timber will reduce heat loss.

Domes and other odd-shaped glasshouses can prove more difficult to manage, especially when trying to ventilate efficiently, and they tend to be more expensive than the traditional shape.

Ventilation

It is important to ensure a greenhouse has sufficient ventilation. Roof vents are the most useful, and ideally should be on both sides of the ridge and equivalent to 15-20 percent of the floor area. Side vents are no substitute for roof ventilation, and while louvred vents allow regulation of air flow, they are hard to draught-proof in winter.

Automatic openers that open or close in response to greenhouse temperatures are useful, but slow to respond and need supplementing with manual control, such as opening some windows and the door each morning. Motorised vents activated by sensitive heat sensors are more efficient but may be too costly for home use.

Glass or plastic glazing?

The best glazing material is glass, as it lets 90 percent of light through, does not degrade in sunlight and, unlike plastic materials, reflects heat radiated from within the glasshouse back into the structure instead of being lost.

Toughened glass should be used for doors and anywhere where people might fall onto the glass.

Double glazing and special glasses that alter the spectral composition of sunlight are often used for conservatories, but are less suitable for cultivating plants as the reduced light quantity and quality affects plant performance.

Polycarbonate sheeting is a twin-walled plastic glazing that has the advantages of being resistant to breakage, lightweight, durable in adverse weather, and good at retaining heat. However, clear polycarbonate only transmits 83 percent of the light – considerably less than glass, and this may limit its use for growing seedlings, cuttings and plants that require high light levels.

Twin-walled acrylic plastic glazing is also available. It transmits 85 percent of the light that hits it, but is more brittle than polycarbonate, tending to crack during installation.

GREENHOUSE ALTERNATIVES

Polythene tunnels

Polythene tunnels (polytunnels) are a highly cost-effective means of growing summer crops, such as tomatoes or cucumbers, but are rather unsightly and not usually economical to heat and keep frost-free over winter. Although they can be used for growing hardy winter crops such as lettuces, they cannot be used for overwintering tender plants.

Cold frames

A cold frame is simply a box with a sloping glazed lid (either glass or plastic glazing) and is a traditional means of protecting plants to supplement, not replace, a greenhouse. Cold frames are used to harden off plants, overwinter plants, sow seeds that need cool conditions and to root cuttings.

The sides may be made of masonry, timber, metal or glass. Typically, cold frames are 45–60cm (18-24in) deep and the lid can be opened to varying degrees to control the temperature. They are seldom heated, but the addition of a soil-heating cable in a sandbed at their base can greatly enhance their usefulness for propagation and overwintering tender plants.

Mini-greenhouses

A useful choice for small gardens, mini-greenhouses are tall, usually plastic-covered, boxes (with shelves) and are open at the front. They are much better than windowsills for raising seedlings, and are ideal for summer crops of plants too tall for cold frames, such as aubergines, peppers and tomatoes. However with only a small air volume need careful management to avoid extremes of temperature.

SITING THE GREENHOUSE - BEST POSITION FOR A GREENHOUSE

One of the things people often forget is to give a little thought to where they are going to position their greenhouse. The correct situation of the greenhouse will make a huge difference to its utility for you.

PLANNING PERMISSION & SECURITY

A normal greenhouse will not usually require planning permission but a lean-to greenhouse on the house may be counted as part of an extension or there may be rules on siting a distance from the boundary. If in doubt, call your local council who will tell you exactly where you stand.

On the allotment, it will depend on your individual site's rules. Again, just check with your site rep or manager, who will be able to give you guidance.

Both on the allotment and in some gardens, you need to consider security. Some kids just love the sound of breaking glass and throwing stones over the fence is an easy sport. So consider the position and if there is a real threat and you cannot site out of harm's way, plastic glass may be the best answer for you.

Allow room to get around your greenhouse. Trying to fit a new pane of glass in a confined space is not easy and if your greenhouse is by a path, try to set it back to allow plenty of room to get past with a wheelbarrow.

Fig. Not the ideal placement for a greenhouse; shaded by trees and bushes

LIGHT AND SHELTER

You need as much light as possible so site the greenhouse away from buildings and trees or bushes. Apart from shading your greenhouse, leaves will get into the gutters and sticky honeydew dropping from insects in a tree above your house will foul the glass causing dirt and grime to stick causing more problems.

Avoid north facing slopes because the light will never be as good as your want.

Whilst you want to be some distance from trees, hedges, fences etc, these can also be useful if they are between the house and the prevailing winds. Reducing wind will really help keep the temperature up in the key times of spring and autumn and avoid the risk of your greenhouse being damaged in a storm.

Avoiding building at the base of a slope as these are often frost pockets where cold air collects in a layer. This will cause your greenhouse to be colder, defeating the object.

Level ground is best, avoiding water running into the house and making construction easier.

DRAINAGE

Ensure the land is well drained because this will enable you to cultivate the border soil at any time of year without it being too sticky.

SERVICES

The ideal greenhouse will have water and electricity laid on, even gas if you want central heating, which I have seen in some greenhouses. So do take the availability of services and how you will run them to your greenhouse into account.

Orientation

Some say North to South and some say East to West but for the average home greenhouse it doesn't really matter, so don't worry about it. The exception is, of course, a lean-to greenhouse where the ideal is to have the wall on the North side but even a North facing greenhouse is better than no greenhouse

GREENHOUSES IN HIGH WINDS - PROTECT AND SURVIVE!

The door was left open in a storm and the wind destroyed this greenouse.

Although hurricanes are pretty rare in the UK, we do get some high winds and they leave a trail of broken glass and twisted aluminium behind. I've seen high winds lift an entire greenhouse and dump it 3 plots away, the glass in shards and the frame looking like a giant has tied knots in it.

There's no way you can build a 100% storm safe greenhouse but there are a number of things you can do to minimise the chance of wind damage to your greenhouse.

The main problem tends to be the wind gets into the greenhouse and the pressure pushes a pane of glass out. After this the damage cascades. Since the vast majority of us have aluminium greenhouses, that's where I'll concentrate. Ensure your greenhouse is square and level. If the house is out of true then the frame will be and the glass won't fit properly. Loose glass will rattle, may well break and gaps allow the wind into the greenhouse.

Ensure the base of the greenhouse is fixed to the ground. I set mine up on railway sleepers, which were level, and then screwed the aluminium frame to that. Use a number of fixing points to even the load. If wind does get into the house then it won't be able to lift the house.

Between the aluminium and the glass there will be a flexible glazing seal. Over the years these tend to perish and often go missing when a greenhouse is moved. They perform two tasks: holding the glass firmly and preventing wind penetration between loose glass and the frame. If the seals are missing or perished, replace them. Ebay is a good source.

The glass itself should be checked. Cracked panes should be replaced and never leave a gap where a pane is missing. Do remember glass gets brittle with age and breaks more easily. Always wear protective gloves when handling glass, it's so easy to really slice yourself badly.

Two mistakes resulted in this greenhouse being destroyed. First the position is too exposed to the wiind and second, the fixing of the frame to the ground was not sufficient.

The glazing clips that hold the glass in place have a habit of vanishing. It's well worth keeping some spares in stock and replace them as required. Often just two clips are used on a standard 2' x 2' pane but you'll be better off with four glazing clips per pane.

When a storm is forecast, ensure all the windows and doors are firmly shut. Automatic window and vent openers are a boon but if they open the window in a warm weather storm then the wind will get in, so disconnect them for the danger period.

If you've done everything above then hopefully your greenhouse will be fairly safe from wind damage. There are a couple of other things you can do to have a greenhouse in windy places.

If you can site the greenhouse so the prevailing wind flows over rather than at the end. If you have a sheltered spot, perhaps in the wind shadow of trees it can be worth sacrificing some sunshine for the protection. You could also consider erecting a wind break to shelter the green house.

PLANNING YOUR GREENHOUSE CROP

CLIMATIC TYPES

Every gardener knows that lettuce survives outdoors in much cooler weather than tomatoes (which, when exposed to night temperatures of 60°F or less, begin to drop their blossoms). And everyone knows that daffodils thrive in the chilly days of spring while orchids need a more tropical climate for optimum growth. But this simple fact of life may be easily overlooked in the greenhouse.

Remember that you can't grow *all* kinds of plants at the same time in the same environment and keep them healthy. Still, a grower who doesn't want to concentrate on crops of just *one* climatic type can do several things to make his or her greenhouse meet the temperature and humidity requirements of somewhat dissimilar plants.

The easiest (but most expensive) way to accomplish this goal is by simply partitioning the greenhouse and maintaining different environmental conditions in each of the resulting sections. The gardener also can use thermometers to detect warm and cool spots in his greenhouse and then raise or lower plants with varying dispositions to these different areas (for example, by placing cool-loving plants at ground level and growing warm-loving plants on elevated shelves). Or, the grower might feel that it's simply best to adjust his or her planting schedule to coincide with nature's timetable (and save on heating costs at the same time) by cultivating only the plants that survive cooler temperatures throughout the winter and waiting until earlier spring to start plants that need warmer growing conditions.

Selecting Your Greenhouse Crop

As you begin to plan your garden menu there are some things you will need to consider. First, of course, you will want to list all of the different things you and your family like to eat. Then you will need to eliminate from that list some of the things that are not practical to grow in a greenhouse. While sweet corn is delicious and would grow well in a greenhouse, the amount of space that it would require, and the length of time that it takes to bear, divided by the amount of produce it will yield, shows us that it is not practical. Crops that bear but once, and have a long growing period before they reach maturity, are not desirable in a greenhouse where space is at a premium—especially if the plants are large and bulky, such as corn. Another example is the artichoke, which takes a year to reach maturity, and asparagus, which takes two to three years to reach maturity. Peanuts take five months to reach maturity and to obtain satisfactory yield would require far too much space. Potatoes should not be grown in the greenhouse because they are a harbinger of disease, and will infect the soil.

Planning for Maximum Production

With proper planning the production of a greenhouse can be multiplied many times over that of one planted without any planning. For example, when tomatoes, pole beans, cucumbers or any such climbing plants are placed, they should be along the back or north wall of the greenhouse. By placing stakes in the ground and running cord to the ceiling of the greenhouse, these plants can be attached to the cord and trained to climb to the roof. Thus, they will be able to pick up ample sun which has passed over the tops of shorter plants placed in front of them. Near the outside wall would be an ideal place to plant such low-growing plants as radishes, onions and carrots; next could come beets, turnips, broccoli and Brussels sprouts; then lettuce, Swiss chard, spinach and celery; after that you could have peas, cauliflower, cabbages and beans; finally, we have the tomatoes, pole beans and climbing plants. Thus, from the south or outside wall, we have the smaller or lower growing plants; to the rear or north wall, we have a gradually ascending scale of height until we come to the last row, next to the rear wall, where the tallest plants are placed.

Special Plants

Shelves can be arranged around the walls of the greenhouse to hold special plants in pots. Sitting in the corners, and at any odd space, can be small tubs with dwarf lemon and fig trees. These can be easily moved around as required. In one corner could be a circular pyramid of ever-bearing strawberries. Flowers can be kept in pots on the shelves. While cantaloupe and watermelon plants take up a lot of room, they are low to the ground and can be grown around such tall plants as tomatoes and pole beans. The melon plants also produce repeatedly, thus making the space allotment more profitable than with some single-bearing crops.

How Much to Plant

In planning your greenhouse garden, keep in mind that in order to have a constant supply of fresh food, you will need to be in a constant state of growing, planting and harvesting. For example, radishes will be ready to eat in twenty days and will remain sweet and tender for about ten more days. Thus you should only plant as many radishes as your family will eat in a ten-day period. Then two weeks later, you should plant the same amount of radishes again. For the average family a single row of radishes four feet long, planted every two weeks, will keep the family in a constant supply of fresh, tender and succulent radishes. You will have some radishes which you are just finishing, others which are just about ready and others which have just been planted. Another example would be carrots which could be planted in a six- to eight-foot row, and replanted every month.

This will keep the average family in fresh young carrots constantly. Some plants reproduce over and over and last a long, long time. Two or three pepper plants will keep a family in peppers for longer than a year. Four tomato plants will supply a family with all of the tomatoes they can use for a year. Ten new tomato plants should be started as the original plants begin to bear. When the new plants begin to bear, the old ones can be removed. As plants get older their foliage gets larger, and it takes more of their energy to feed themselves rather than to produce fruit. Even though plants continue to produce for a long time, if the plant itself keeps getting larger and larger (as with the tomato vine) it is wise to replace them every four months.

GREENHOUSE LOCATION & ORIENTATION

In the last two issues, we took a look at a needs assessment, and greenhouse design and materials as two general areas of consideration for those of us trying to decide whether a greenhouse is a good place for our green thumb adventures.

In this installment, I'd like to discuss location and orientation as two additional factors to consider. After all, you can have an intense desire for a greenhouse, but if you don't have the space, can't conveniently locate it, or you just can't achieve proper orientation, it might not be advisable to purchase or build one.

LOCATION

Selecting a location for a greenhouse is usually not an issue for a commercial operator. Typically, they have sufficient land available to dedicate to their greenhouse gardening operations. So, let's focus on homestead and homeowner gardeners with respect to greenhouse location.

First and foremost, it would be advisable to have your greenhouse conveniently located to your home. It won't be any fun if you have to walk 100 yards to get to your greenhouse, so having your garden a good distance from the house could be sufficiently discouraging to you. If you think about hiking out a good distance, each time you need to visit the greenhouse, nearly every task will become more of a chore. To minimize this effect, keep the distance between where you reside and where you garden as short as reasonably possible.

Consider for a moment, weather conditions and how they might influence your greenhouse gardening activities. Whether you're trying to start seedlings in the spring, harvest during the summer and fall, or push the envelope by harvesting well into the winter months, foul weather won't be pleasant if you have to walk a great distance through it all to get to your greenhouse.

In my neck of the woods, we get snowdrifts that are completely impassable by any normal four-wheel drive vehicle. Those snowdrifts can occur between one of my greenhouses and my home. I don't mind slogging through three and four foot high drifts that are 15 to 20 feet wide, but I wouldn't be happy doing it for a distance of more than 30 to 50 feet. That's why our "kitchen greenhouse" is within 20 feet of the house.

If your greenhouse will be a new construction project, you'll want to provide water and electricity to support it. The farther away you place your greenhouse, the longer and more difficult your trenching efforts will be. So, consider the origins of essential resources like electricity and water when you consider the location of your indoor gardening space.

One last consideration with respect to locating your greenhouse; assume you're interested in a greenhouse that uses standard greenhouse film. Such material is susceptible to damage from animals, high winds, falling tree branches, and other human activity that might not be present when you make your initial site assessment.

With this in mind, it should be clear that a greenhouse next to a ball field or other play area, or a greenhouse within the distance of windblown branches from nearby trees are both unwise choices. A location up on an especially windy ridge is also undesirable. To avoid unknowingly subjecting your greenhouse to hazards such as these, think through daily activities, normal and abnormal weather conditions, and generally envision a range of undesirable scenarios in your mind to see if any of them present an unreasonable hazard to your future greenhouse or the crops you intend to grow within it.

Orientation

There are basically three schools of thought with respect to greenhouse orientation; 1) capture the morning sun; 2) capture the winter sun; and, 3) orient plant growth instead of the building. For this discussion, let's assume that you have a rectangular shape in mind for your gardening structure, since it is by far the most common style.

Morning sunshine is important to stimulate growth, to remove condensation from leaves, and to get your plants off to a good start each day. This is typically the interest of greenhouse gardeners who focus their efforts on summer vegetables. If this is your interest, my suggestion is to orient your greenhouse in a North and South direction. Such an orientation promotes full capture of the morning sun and allows the sun's rays to penetrate between your plants as it travels up and over the width of your greenhouse. This orientation assumes that your plantings are in rows oriented perpendicular to the length of the structure.

For those with an interest in fall, winter and spring greenhouse gardening, an orientation of the greenhouse in an East to West manner will make more sense. Such an orientation helps capture the sun's rays that are much lower on the horizon during those times of the year.

The third approach to orientation is applicable to the both summer and off season gardeners, and for those of us who don't have an ideal location that would allow for our preferred orientation of the gardening structure. This approach requires that we orient our crops such that we achieve our summer or off-season gardening objectives by understanding how the sun travels across the sky and through our greenhouse.

This is clearly a fallback position at best because growing crops diagonally in relationship to the greenhouse won't be convenient at all. In any event, a greenhouse gardener will want to plant crops in such a manner as to eliminate tall plants shading shorter ones, and then orient the rows of plantings to best capture the sun, all the while being mindful that plant orientation and pathways in the greenhouse need to be convenient for the gardener.

GREENHOUSE GARDENING TIPS

Anyone who has done gardening in the open will be applying their knowledge to the greenhouse, just altering it a little to garden under glass. A greenhouse is not always a "hot house", as it is sometimes called. Plants usually do their best at temperatures slightly lower and with a much higher humidity than is usually maintained in our houses. A small greenhouse can have its temperature regulated relatively easy.

There are six main reasons an amateur uses a greenhouse:

1. Raising plants for winter use.
2. Holding over garden plants to be used as "parent" plants next season.

3. Getting an early start for tender plants started from seed.
4. Increasing the possibilities of a greater variety and continuous supply.
5. Easier culture of small vegetables for winter use.
6. To propagate, and experiment with various plants as a hobby, or to develop new varieties.

CHOOSING A SITE FOR YOUR GREENHOUSE

Choose a level, clean site in a low-traffic area. Your greenhouse should receive the maximum amount of winter sunlight available. Be sure to consider the following:

- The change in angle of the sun between summer and winter
- Shadows cast by existing structures and/or trees
- Growing trees: will they shade the greenhouse in the future?
- Existing deciduous trees will allow winter sun; evergreens will not

If possible, align your greenhouse with the long side facing south, for two reasons:

- The angle of the roof is engineered for catching the maximum amount of the sun's rays in the winter with the least amount of loss by reflection.
- If you end up using shadecloth during the warm days in spring and summer, you will need to shade only one side, instead of both sides

Light

Orient your greenhouse so that the sun will reach it the maximum number of hours during each day. The most important time for the sun to reach any greenhouse is during the spring and fall when the sun is lowest in the southern sky. Find the place where there is clearing towards the southeast through the southwest or as much sun is available.

Workspace

Your greenhouse interior should allow enough room for potting plants and moving about comfortably. Also take into consideration the height of the benches and tables you plan to use. If you want a sink, where will you put it? Will you have storage space for tools? All of these questions should be dealt with before you begin to build your greenhouse.

Potting benches can be designed to fold down when not in use. They're usually slotted so dirt can fall to a collection bin below. Redwood is a good choice for the interior benches, but if you're concerned about the use of this wood, ask your local lumber yard about other rot-resistant woods. Avoid pressure-treated lumbers, since they are impregnated with highly toxic arsenic. To make the job easier, try a do-it-yourself bench kit with aluminum framework pieces-just add wood.

Temperature

The more sun that is provided, the more heat the greenhouse will produce. The more heat is produced the more need you will have to provide ventilation. Place a thermometer in the shade near the middle of your greenhouse and monitor the temperature at different times during sunny and cloudy weather. If the temperature is reaching 80 degrees-90 degrees or higher and the plants you are growing need a moderate range of 60 degrees-70 degrees then you will have to compensate by ventilating. The temperature readings you record should be used to determine what plants you can grow, when.

Ventilation

Adequate ventilation is achieved when air can freely circulate among the plants. Spread your plants evenly throughout the greenhouse, rather than jamming them all onto one bench, so the air is distributed evenly. Greenhouses overheat easily, and in the middle of summer in the southern part of the US, you're more likely to cook your plants than to nurture them if you don't have a way to get rid of the excess heat. Choose your ventilation system by which region you live in and the size and design of your greenhouse.

The simplest option is to open up one or both doors in the morning depending on the weather report and leave them open until late afternoon. This will allow frost protection at night and some increased warming during the day.

Another alternative for cooling is the simple principle of water evaporation. Hose down your greenhouse floor and open your ceiling vents, and the entire unit will cool down quickly.

Soil And Irrigation

Commercial potting soil is good for the average home garden greenhouse, especially if you're growing veggies in large beds rather than smaller houseplant pots. These soil mixtures should include sand, peat moss, perlite, vermiculite, and fir bark for adequate drainage.

The only time you need to water is when the soil is dry. Over watering in a climate-controlled greenhouse environment has been the death of many a plant or seedling. While many greenhouse owners prefer the control of hand watering, drip irrigation systems are effective and also prevent the leaves from getting too much water on them. Drip systems are gentle on seedlings, too.

You may not need to water every day. It's wise to study the water requirements of your particular greenhouse and document your regime in a gardening notebook. This makes it easier for a friend or neighbor to take care of your plants when you're busy or out of town.

Maintenance

Each type of greenhouse will have its own maintenance requirements. One general rule is to regularly disinfect the entire greenhouse-with a scrub brush and a mixture of diluted bleach, being careful not to get any on your plants. Open up any vents to let the fumes out, scrub down all the walls and floor, then rinse with clean water.

Periodically, between disinfectings, spray the walls and corners with a hose set on the jet nozzle. This will keep the spider mites and whiteflies to a minimum.

Produce Tips

Carrots, beets, turnips, and other root crops do well in deep boxes which fit well under benches.

Tomatoes, peas, cucumbers, and pole beans need tub-type containers. Lettuce, or other low leafy vegetables may be planted in the tub with the taller vegetables.

For corn, you've never seen the likes of, plant directly in the floor of the greenhouse, in a bed prepared for it. Plant pumpkin between the rows of corn to save space.

Water your indoor plants with room temperature water, so not to injure your plants. Tap water should stand for 1 day to rid water of chlorine. This will avoid brown tips on plants.

For good drainage, use any of the following in the bottom of your boxes or pots: broken clay pots, cracked walnuts, marbles, charcoal, or gravel. Clay pots should be soaked in water a few minutes before using. This will prevent the clay from absorbing the moisture from the potting soil.

Indoor trellises can be made out of coat hangers. Bend to any shape you desire (heart, star, or other) and insert into pot.

Herbs are nature's insecticides. Be sure to include a variety of them in your garden. Make an effective and natural insecticide by adding onions and garlic to a jar of water. Let it stand for a week and then spray your plants.

Throw crushed egg shells on your garden for plant growth. To add acid to the ground, use dried coffee grounds.

Rinse vegetables and fruits outside before bringing them into your home. Place chicken wire over a wooden box that the bottom has been cut out of. Rinse the vegetables with your garden hose. The dirt and bugs will stay outdoors and your kitchen will stay clean.

WATCH FOR INSECTS AND DISEASE

The first step in disease and insect control is watchful prevention. When problems go unnoticed, the situation quickly becomes uncontrollable. Pruning off old or dead leaves, removing diseased plants, and keeping the greenhouse clean can minimize such disasters. Give your used pots, flats, and plant containers a brisk brushing in soapy water, rinse them in a 50/50 chlorine bleach-water solution, and let them dry in the sun. Isolate new plants for two weeks before bringing them into the greenhouse, and scrutinize their soil, leaves, stems, and flowers for tiny insects. A 10X field glass magnifies such minuscule creatures as spider mites, thrips, and immature whiteflies.

Hands, clothing, and shoes are common carriers of disease, so be sure to wash your hands after working with diseased plants. Never smoke inside the greenhouse, since tobacco mosaic virus can be spread by smokers onto tomatoes and peppers. If you do smoke, disinfect your hands before working with plants.

Select disease-resistant varieties. Often the name of a variety includes abbreviations for diseases that the plant has been bred to resist or tolerate. For example, Roma VF is a tomato that is resistant to both verticillium and fusarium wilt.

Periodically, inspect your indoor garden so that you can spot problems before they get out of hand. Well-balanced soils, proper nutrition (no excesses), watering, and ventilation reduce stress in plants and, in return, allow them to ward off pests and diseases.

At New Alchemy, we depend on cultural, mechanical, biological, and nontoxic chemical means for controlling such common insect pests as aphids, whiteflies, spider mites, thrips, mealybugs, and scale. Our four-step procedure should work for you, too.

STEP ONE: Since many insects assume different forms over the course of their development, learn about the insect's life cycle and become familiar with its various stages.

STEP TWO: Conduct an insect check. Even though plant feeding insects are not always*pests,* it's prudent to keep an eye out for them. Be on the offensive. Once a week, wander through the greenhouse and seek out potential foes. Flip the leaves over to check the undersides. Don't deceive yourself; once you've discovered an intruder, keep tabs on it, because you can count on more coming. People often ask, "How many are *too* many?" A general rule of thumb for vegetables is that if more than one-third of the leaf surface (underside or topside) becomes infested with herbivorous insects, additional treatment is necessary. For ornamentals, infestations over one-eighth (or in some cases even less) of the leaf area indicate a need for control.

STEP THREE: Have a control program available. Diversify strategies so that the tactics are those least disruptive to natural controls and least hazardous to human health and the environment. Never depend on only *one* control measure. Combine cultural, mechanical, physical, and biological controls.

Cultural practices that can diminish insect problems include sanitation, weed control, and using the least amount of nitrogen compatible with adequate plant growth, because nitrogen is a protein-building material for the progeny of many insect pests.

Selecting varieties that may be unappealing to pests is another cultural control. For example, tomato plants with especially hairy leaves discourage the tomato leaf miner.

Mechanical and physical controls include hand-picking (or the "squish" technique), quarantining new plants, or trapping insects with sticky yellow cards. An attractive trap plant is nasturtium, which attracts aphids, whiteflies, spider mites, and thrips.

Biological control is an approach that employs predatory and parasitic insects or other organisms to control insect pests. Natural enemies may be indigenous to your area, or you may purchase them from an insectary.

STEP FOUR: Evaluate the control program to determine the success of treatment actions. The following are suggestions for an integrated pest management program for common greenhouse pests:

Aphids are small, pear-shaped insects. The green peach aphid *(Myzus persicae) is* the most common. However, many other aphids can enter the greenhouse. Adults are approximately 1/16" to 1/5" long. Wingless nymphs vary in color, but they have the same shape as adults. Adult aphids can be winged or wingless. Green peach aphids are pale green and well-camouflaged on foliage. Favored host plants are peppers, cabbage-family members, lettuce, dill, snapdragons, and pansies.

Cultural control: Do not overfertilize. Prune off heavily infested leaves. Hose off aphids with cool water.

Biological control: Native predators include ladybird beetles, green lacewings *(Chrysopa carnea),* syrphid flies, and predaceous midge larvae called *Aphidoletes aphidimyza.* Native braconid wasps will parasitize aphids in the warn season. Ladybird beetles *(Hippodamia convergens)* can be purchased through commercial insectaries.

Chemical control: Insecticidal or household soap will kill aphids but will also kill different stages of beneficial insects. Use sparingly.

Greenhouse whitefly *(Trialeurodes vaporariorum):* Adults are white, fly-like, and 1/20" to 1/12" long. Nymphs are pale green, translucent, and have flat scales with waxy filaments. A 10X field glass is necessary to see the immature stages. Favored host plants are tomato, European cucumber, tobacco, melon, calendula, some geraniums, fuchsia, lantana, petunia, arid nasturtium.

Cultural control: Hairy plants have the best protection.

Mechanical control: Sticky yellow traps, which you can make or buy, set out by a plant's tip growth will lure adults and snag them on the gooey substance. Use the traps early in the season, and remove them once *Encarsia formosa* has been introduced into the greenhouse.

Biological control: A specific parasitic wasp, *Encarsia formosa, 1/32"* long, is available from many insectaries and is a successful biological control agent when whitefly populations are low and greenhouse temperatures are warm

(75°F). *Encarsia* is not effective during the winter months. Chemical control: You may spot-spray tip-growth areas with insecticidal or household soap, but this is harmful to *Encarsia.*

Spider mite *(Tetranychus urticae):* Adult spider mites are very small *(1/32"),* oval-shaped, and yellowish, with two black spots on their backs. A symptom of spider-mite damage is bronzish mottling on the leaves and thin webbing between the petiole and stem. Favored host plants include European cucumbers, peppers, grapes, and many ornamentals.

Cultural control: Misting the plant and increasing the relative humidity inside the greenhouse will discourage spider mites. These pests thrive under hot, dry conditions and can frequently be found in one hot spot in the greenhouse.

Biological control: A predatory mite, *Phytoseiulus persimilis is* commercially available. Introduce the predatory mites at the first sign of spider mites. The predators desiccate at temperatures of about 80°F. If your greenhouse temperature exceeds this limit, try*Amblyseiulus californicus,* which, unfortunately, does not search for spider mites as well as *P. persimilis* does. In either case, an annual stocking is usually necessary.

Chemical control: A 50/50 water-alcohol solution may reduce spider mites, but do a test spray before treating the entire crop.

Thrips *(Thrips tabaci or Heliothrips haemorrhoidalis):* These tiny, slender, rod-like insects are 1/25" long and have a hard exoskeleton. Adults are brown, and nymphs are creamy white; both hide under leaf veins, flower buds, and petals. Favored host plants are European cucumbers, melons, peppers, marigolds, gladioli, African violets, and many ornamentals.

Cultural control: Maintain good sanitation. Prepupal and pupal stages rest in leaf litter on soil beds. Eliminate any highly infested leaves, or remove the entire plant.

Mechanical control: Mist leaves and dust with diatomaceous earth if the thrip population is low. Scrape the top 1/2" of the soil away from the infested plants.

Biological control: The predatory mite *Amblyseiulus californicus* will prey on thrips at a slow rate. Both green lacewings and *Orius insidious*, the minute pirate bug, will also help control this pest, and both are indigenous to North America.

Mealybugs: There are many different kinds of these white, soft, segmented, oval insects. Between 1/5" and 1/3" long, they are usually covered with a whitish, powdery, waxlike material. Females and nymphs are wingless and are found most frequently on tropical plants. Favored host plants are banana, bamboo, ginger, citrus, and many ornamental houseplants, especially orchids.

Cultural control: Dislodge mealybugs by hosing them down with water. Quarantine new plants and discard any infected plants.

Biological control: A predatory beetle, *Cryptolaemus montrougieri,* is available at commercial insectaries. This Australian lady beetle is 1/4" long, with a black body and orange head. The larvae look like mealybugs. They prefer warm temperatures (75°F). A commercially available wasp, *Leptomastix dactylopii,* will parasitize the citrus mealybug.

Scale: There are several species of both soft scale and armored scale. Scale insects, like mealybugs, are plant suckers that distort and yellow afflicted leaves. Females are found on the undersides of leaves and stems. A female and her young live under a protected, waxy covering. Favored host plants are tropical fruit or ornamentals, especially philodendrons, palms, and orchids.

Cultural control: Dislodge scale with a forceful spray of water. Peel off any loose sheath tissue that scale could hide behind. Prune off damaged leaves.

Biological control: Green lacewings and Australian beetles *(Cryptolaemus montrougieri)* will feed on scale. A parasitic wasp, *Metaphycus helvolus,* provides variable control of several soft-scale species. All three biological-control agents are commercially available.

Chemical control: Insecticidal or household soap can be applied if beneficial insects are not being used.

3

Regulating the Greenhouse Environment

HOW DOES A GREENHOUSE WORK SCIENTIFICALLY

The greenhouse works by collecting light and converting it to heat. That is a simplistic view of how a greenhouse works. In addition to capturing light, the greenhouse also stores thermal energy and releases that energy properly. It can help moderate temperature and produce a controlled environment for plants to grow and thrive in. Further, a greenhouse offers protection from wind, rain, snow and other weather elements while also keeping your fruits from invading pests and animals.

SOLAR COLLECTION

The main task of a greenhouse is to collect solar energy. The greenhouse captures light through its walls and converts it to heat. The effect is similar to that of a vehicle with the windows up. It takes only a few minutes for light coming in a window to warm up the vehicle to a temperature significantly higher than the outside temperature. Greenhouses work the same way. The darker material within the greenhouse helps to store heat, keeping the surrounding air warmer.

The greenhouse is a closed-in environment, which means there are no breezes to push the heat away. The structure is often made of glass, or glass-like material that helps to attract the sun's rays. Without a breeze, the air within the greenhouse heats up quickly and remains warm. This creates the ideal area for plants to grow.

RELEASING THERMAL ENERGY

As the greenhouse draws in and collects sunlight, it warms the air within. This occurs naturally. The process is releasing thermal energy. The matter within the greenhouse, such as the soil and water, will absorb the heat drawn in. Even when the sun goes down, the warmth in the soil and water continue to protect the plants because these materials release the warmth slowly.Another important factor in protecting your plants is the way greenhouses regulate temperature. The thermal mass within the greenhouse helps to keep the temperatures moderate. If your greenhouse is larger and has thermal mass within it, such as the iron found in soil, it will heat up slowly and will cool down slowly. Rather than high heat in the daytime and cold temperatures at night, the thermal mass within the greenhouse regulates the temperature evenly throughout the day and night. This provides a better atmosphere for plants to grow.

PROTECTION FROM THE ELEMENTS

Another way in which greenhouses work is by providing protection from the elements. In this manner, greenhouses function much as a house does for humans. Protection from the elements is critical, especially when you are gardening in the fall or winter months. Consider some of the ways a greenhouse protects.

- The greenhouse prevents strong winds from pulling up roots or blowing seeds.
- It allows you to control how much water your plants receive. Rain, hail and snow are unable to get in.
- Pests, including vegetable eating pests, are kept out. You do not have to spray harsh chemicals on your plants. You control the types of insects or other pests allowed into the garden. It may not be possible to keep all pests out long term, but you will minimize the number.
- A greenhouse keeps excess heat and cold from affecting plants. When the temperature gets too high, the fogging or misting systems within some greenhouses can help to cool down the temperature. Other systems heat up the greenhouse when there is limited sunlight.

The ability to protect plants from any of these elements is critical to helping those plants to grow successfully. Greenhouses adjust the weather conditions to allow for better growth.

Fig. Popup greenhouse is an inexpensive option.

DIFFERENT TYPES OF GREENHOUSES

When you ask, "How does a greenhouse work" keep in mind there are numerous types of greenhouses. Some are, very simply, structures with glass walls. Others have complex heating and cooling systems within them to help control temperatures. When selecting a type of greenhouse to use, focus on your budget and your needs to control the climate.

HUMIDITY

Many amateur greenhouse growers — and some commercial growers — are not aware of the effects that humidity has on plants. It's very important to maintain the proper relative humidity to get the right kind of growth of fruits, flowers, leaves and roots. The relative humidity in the greenhouse should be about 60 percent. (This is much higher, by the way, than the humidity of the average home, which runs between 12 and 20 percent.)

If there is a humidity problem, it's usually because there is too much humidity, not too little. The temperatures in greenhouses are higher than the temperatures outside, and the warmer the air the more water vapor it can hold. If ventilation is poor, greenhouses will be like "steaming jungles," with the high moisture content encouraging vegetative or leaf growth at the sacrifice of fruit and flower production. It also invites plant diseases like damping-off and botrytis, which thrive in excessively damp and humid areas.

Of course, some growers do have problems with too low a relative humidity level. This generally occurs in dry parts of the country where greenhouses are over-ventilated. Too little humidity hastens the development of roots, flowers and fruit. If your problem is overall too low a humidity, hose down your gravel, sand or cement aisles frequently, reduce ventilation and mist those plants that need a lot of moisture.

HEATING THE GREENHOUSE

Since fuel oil, electricity, natural gas, bottle gas or coal are all satisfactory fuels for use in greenhouse heating, choose the one most likely to be available during the heating season. Low operating cost is another factor to consider in selecting a fuel.

EXTENSION OF THE HOME HEATING SYSTEM

If the BTU capacity of your home heating system is large enough to heat only your home, do not burden it by also trying to heat the greenhouse with it. On the other hand, if the system is oversized, there is no reason why you cannot extend it to the greenhouse. This is particularly true if the greenhouse is small or is attached to the home.

Unless you're a heating expert, secure advice from a heating contractor, mail-order house or greenhouse supplier about installing an additional zone for heating the greenhouse. Generally, this is not an expensive job to do with hot water or steam systems. It's a simple matter of extending the heating pipes to the greenhouse. For hot air systems, cold and warm air ducts can be extended into the greenhouse, providing it's not located too far from the home. With either of the three systems, a thermostat located in the greenhouse can control temperatures without interfering with the home heating requirements. Locate the thermometer at plant growing height and not for your own convenience. It is best to use alcohol-filled thermometers. Thermometers filled with mercury will damage certain plants, such as roses, with vapors given off if broken.

SIZE OF HEATING SYSTEM

Since most heating systems state their output rating in British thermal units (BTUs), you should know the BTU requirements for your particular greenhouse. These ten guidelines indicate why greenhouses of the same size may require vastly different heating systems:

1. The minimum inside temperature desired.
2. The lowest anticipated outside temperature.
3. Amount of exposure to winds.
4. Nature of the greenhouse surface area.
5. Double or single layering of side walls.
6. Double or single glazed greenhouse.
7. Amount of straw or other material used to cover the roof (not to the point of blocking out too much sunlight) during extremely cold weather.
8. Desirability of maintaining maximum temperatures during extreme periods of cold weather.
9. Attachment of greenhouse to heated building (as with a lean-to greenhouse).
10. Excellent, good or poor operating and maintenance schedule.

Some Final Thoughts on Heating

Consider these guidelines while planning the greenhouse heating system:

1. Choose a heater that is automatic in operation and requires minimum maintenance.
2. Select a heater large enough to heat the greenhouse. Check with your local weather bureau to find out the coldest day during the past twenty-five years. Use the lowest temperature as a criterion when establishing BTU requirements for a heating system to do the job.
3. A windy location results in a greater heat loss, so provide a windbreak as previously described to help cut heating costs; otherwise order a heater one size larger than necessary.
4. When installing a central heating system, give thought to additional

capacity if you plan to add a workshop later, enlarge the greenhouse, or have one plant heat greenhouse and home.

5. Take heed when using any type of vented heater. Use every precaution to prevent downdrafts.
6. Never use a heating system that requires manufactured gas as a fuel, it is injurious to plants.
7. Be certain the heating system is equipped with adequate controls, such as safety pilots and an automatic shut-off switch.
8. Locate several accurate thermostats, positioned at plant height, throughout the greenhouse to provide a check on heat distribution.
9. Place shades above thermometers and thermostats to avoid false readings caused by sun rays.
10. Install a temperature alarm to warn of dangerously low temperatures. Be sure to set the temperature warning high enough to give time to remedy heating or power failure before the plants are killed.

1. Provide for emergency heat. Position portable kerosene heaters and/or gasoline or propane catalytic heaters throughout the greenhouse. Perhaps a better way is to install a standby electric generator of sufficient wattage to meet power failure or brownouts.

VENTILATING

Whether building a greenhouse yourself or selecting one already constructed, give special attention to the design and the way in which it is ventilated, since ventilation and temperature are key issues in greenhouse management. In fact, a close relationship exists between ventilation and temperature.

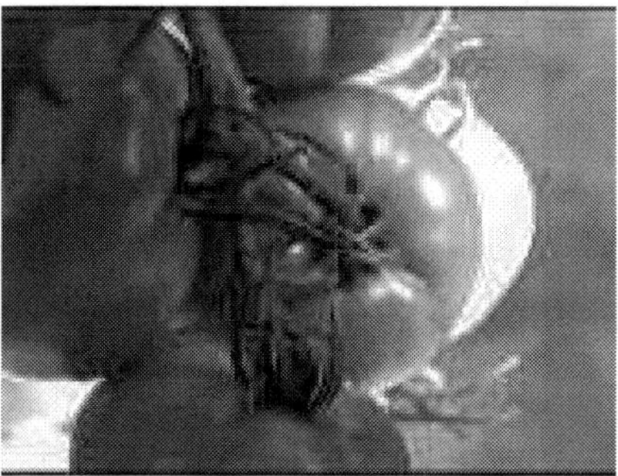

No matter how small the greenhouse, there should be some provision made for ventilation at the highest point, usually near the ridge of the roof, where hot air rises to collect.

The best arrangement for good ventilation is to alternate the vents on each side of the roof adjoining the ridge. This is not necessary for small greenhouses where there is only need for one roof vent. Vents should be built into the vertical sides of the greenhouse either at or below bench level. The purpose is to supply incoming fresh air. The combination of ridge vents and side vents provide desirable air currents inside the greenhouse.

Every ventilation system should meet these objectives:

1. To exchange inside air for fresh outside air. Such an exchange is just as important for plants as it is for people when several are closed up hour after hour in an unventilated room.
2. To control temperatures by allowing hot air to escape from a high point, to be replaced by cooler, fresh air entering at a lower level.
3. To be able to exchange air of high humidity, caused by plant transpiration, with fresh, drier air which is capable of absorbing more moisture.
4. To ensure against attacks from plant diseases and pests, which are more prevalent in unventilated quarters.

MECHANICAL VENTILATORS

For the reader who has little time, or who does not care for hand-operated vent lifting equipment — or who just desires better temperature control — an automatic, motorized vent system should be considered.

Cooling

Adequate ventilation provides some cooling for the greenhouse, though generally not enough for profitable, comfortable gardening. Additional cooling is helpful during hot weather.

Shading

The temperature inside the greenhouse can be reduced by a good shading system.

The greenhouse gardener will find this most advantageous in his operational program. Shading, coupled with moisture from wet soil or from a humidifier, will sometimes lower temperatures as much as 15°. Shading has little effect, if any, on plant growth, because summer sunlight is generally in excess of its requirements.

Slat, roll-up shades installed on the outside of the greenhouse provide cooling of the inside temperature. An evaporative cooling system installed outside the greenhouse adds to temperature reduction by pulling in fresh air through wet pads.

Shading can be provided by painting or spraying specially formulated compounds on the glass: either a concentrated material that only needs water added for immediate application, or a powder, ready to mix with water and use immediately.

Generally, the shading materials can be removed with a brush or hose, yet they remain on through a rain.

ENVIRONMENTAL CONTROL SYSTEMS

LIGHT

Photosynthesis is the key to good growth and high yields. If photosynthesis is decreased, due to low light conditions, high humidity (which closes stomates and reduces gas exchange), or water stress, then the production of sugars will decline and the fruit quality, shelf life, and size will all diminish.

Because of the critical role of photosynthesis in plant growth, a one-percent decrease in light can translate to a one-percent decrease in yield. Shading from outside topography and trees, the greenhouse structure itself, or taller plants in the greenhouse can significantly reduce the amount of light reaching the crop. Both the greenhouses and the rows of plants in the greenhouse should be oriented north and south so the light is evenly distributed across each plant. Some growers reflect light back into the crop using white floorcoverings or paint. Clean white paint is more reflective than metallic or foil, although there is some indication that foil tends to "confuse" insects and slightly decrease insect pest damage.

During long periods of cloudy weather, tomato leaves become low in sugars, and may become pale and thin. Excess nitrogen at that time can be detrimental.

Some growers prefer to shade tomatoes, while others do not. Theoretically, shading will reduce photosynthesis, and therefore total yield, however, this has not always been shown in controlled studies. In fact, in some studies, total yield was improved using 30% shadecloth. Shading can improve fruit quality, since direct sunlight on fruit can cause yellow or green shoulders, cracking, and russeting. Alternatively, older leaves can be left in place to shade the individual fruit trusses. In areas of high summer temperatures and humidity, shading may be necessary to keep temperatures within a reasonable range. Ultimately, however, the decision to shade or not depends on the location of the greenhouse, the cultivar of tomato grown, the season and the overall management system employed by the grower.

Historically, the greenhouse industry has traditionally measured light in foot-candles and lumens. Foot-candles are the amount of light received on the surface and lumens are the measure of light emitted by a light source. Natural sunlight and artificial light falling on a plant are measured in foot-candles (f.c.) while the light emitted by sources such as the sun and electric lamps are rated in lumens. A clear, sunny day may measure 10,000 f.c. and an overall winter day as low as 500 f.c. To read comfortably requires about 20 f.c. The light of the full moon measures less than 1 f.c. A light meter with a scale in direct foot-candle readings is manufactured by the General Electric Company and is sold by most greenhouse supply companies.

Supplementary artificial light, from cool white, high output fluorescent or high intensity discharge sodium vapor lamps is beneficial to plants when sunlight is unavailable but is not a complete substitution. Intensity of supplementary lighting should be about 800-1000 foot-candles at the plant surface.

Today, plant scientists are primarily interested in that light which is responsible for photosynthesis. The portion of the light band most responsible for photosynthesis measures 400-700 nanometers. This band is often termed the Photosynthetically Active Radiation (PAR). Within this range, intensity is the most critical factor along with light period. Within the PAR region light is measured as the Photosynthetic Photon Flux (PPF) and is expressed in μmol/m^2/s. Daily total of PPF, expressed in mol/m^2 have been shown to relate to total photosynthesis for the day.

In the southwestern region of the United States, the winter light readings are three times higher than in the northern regions such as the states of New York and Ohio. This is why the greenhouse tomato industry is growing so rapidly in Arizona and surrounding states.

Supplemental lighting is generally not economical for vegetable crops, with the exception of seedling production. However, for backyard or hobby situations, full-spectrum lighting can be effective in increasing yields by increasing the daylength to 18 hours during winter months.

TEMPERATURE

Both day and night temperatures influence plant vigor, leaf size, leaf expansion rate, and time to fruit development. Under low night temperatures, the rate of leaf growth is slower, and leaf size is reduced in young plants. Day and night temperatures should be carefully monitored. A general rule of thumb for most horticultural crops is for night temperatures to be approximately 5.5° C (10° F) lower than day temperatures. For tomatoes, day temperatures should be 21° -26° C (70° -79° F) and night temperatures around 16° -18.5° C (61° -65° F), although many new varieties do best with little difference between day and night temperature (check with your seed company for recommended growing temperatures). For seedlings, the temperatures should be constant, 20° -22° C (68° -72° F), then gradually acclimate the plants to the diurnal temperatures before transplanting.

High temps in excess of 30° C to 35° C will cause many different types of damage to the plants, such as inhibition of growth and even death. The physiological nature of heat damage is thought to involve a denaturation of some protein component of plant cells. Fruit abortion may occur at these temperatures as well. Temperatures lower than optimum will alter the plant metabolic systems to slow growth and again hinder fruit set.

Fogging systems can be an alternative to evaporative pad cooling. They depend on absolutely clean water, free of any soluble salt, in order to prevent plugging of the mist nozzles. Like fan and pad cooling, fog cooling is only really efficient in low humidity environments.

In hobby greenhouses, temperatures can be measured easily with a minimum/maximum thermometer. Several thermometers should be placed throughout the greenhouse, and should be calibrated against each other and a quality thermometer at least twice per year. In large commercial operations, computer controlled systems are common. Such systems can provide fully-integrated control of temperature, humidity, irrigation and fertilization, carbon dioxide, light and shade levels.

AIR CIRCULATION AND VENTILATION

Good circulation is necessary for proper cooling, heating, CO_2 replenishment, and removal of undesirable gases, such as ethylene. Your circulation system must work together with your heating, cooling, and CO_2 systems in order to obtain peak efficiency.

Many different methods of circulating air have been developed. The vent-tube system is used quite a bit, and consists of a fan-jet connected to a perforated plastic tube running the length of the greenhouse at ceiling height. The fan forces air through the tube, which moves the warm air in the roof space downward to displace the cooler air at the floor level. This design is not very efficient. A horizontal airflow system is more efficient, and can move a larger amount of air around the plants. Large fans, hanging above the crop, are set up facing one direction in one section of the greenhouse, and in the opposite direction in the adjacent section of the greenhouse. A more complicated system is a vertical airflow system, which uses fan-jets to move air along the roof, downward at the end walls, then along the floor through the crop. This system provides the best mixing of air and brings warm air down into the plants. Various types of alternative ventilation systems have been proposed, such as up-draft and down-draft chimneys. However, it will be some time before these systems are thoroughly tested and refined.

In the tropics, natural air exchange to the outside of the greenhouse can be achieved simply through the sides of the greenhouse structure. For active or mechanical ventilation, low-pressure propeller blade fans are used for greenhouse ventilation. They are placed on the end of the greenhouse opposite the air intake, which is often covered by evaporative cooling pads and louvers. The cooling pads used in combination with fans (*fan and pad cooling*) can be made from a number of materials, most often they are made of a cellulose material, usually aspen wood, or a multi-celled/honeycombed material called "kool-cel". The ventilation fans for larger greenhouses (100-120 feet in length), are normally sized to allow a maximum air exchange once per minute. Small hobby greenhouses, which have a large greenhouse surface area to floor area ratio may require an air exchange of up to 2.5 times per minute.

Humidity

In order for a plant to actively grow, it must be allowed to transpire freely during photosynthesis; this means plenty of available water, low to moderate humidity, and good air circulation. Humidity influences calcium uptake and hormonal distribution by controlling transpiration, ion pumping, and stomatal opening and closing. High humidity coupled with low air movement reduces transpirational cooling, and can lead to heat overload for the plant.

People tend to think of humidity in terms of *relative humidity*, which is the ratio of the amount of water vapor in the air to the amount of water vapor the air could hold at that temperature, expressed as a percent. Plants, on the other hand, perceive humidity in terms of *vapor pressure deficit (VPD)*. VPD is the difference between the vapor pressure in the air and the vapor pressure inside the leaf. Water moves by diffusion from the roots through the plant and out the leaves as transpired vapor, thereby being "pumped" up the plant as the vapor moves from the higher pressure inside the leaf to the lower pressure in the surrounding air. Low VPD (high humidity, greater than 90%) is often responsible for nutrient deficiency symptoms, such as blossom end rot (calcium deficiency) because the plant is not transpiring, therefore it is not drawing water, or nutrients, into the roots. High VPD (low humidity, less than 50%) can also lead to the same symptoms, because water and nutrients are pumped too quickly through the plants, depositing nutrient ions in the leaves rather than properly in the fruit.

Greenhouse humidity can be measured with a sling psychrometer. Other equipment such as a humidistat can measure relative humidity to an accuracy within 4%. Most greenhouse supply companies sell equipment to measure humidity.

Most plants can function adequately in relative humidities of between 55 and 95%, which corresponds to VPD's of 1.0 to 0.2 kPa. For tomatoes, the ideal humidity should be between 65 and 75% during the night and 80 to 90% during the day. Tomato yields and fruit quality are lower at lower VPDs (higher humidity). Leaf size can also be reduced, and flower and fruit abortion can be significantly increased under high humidity conditions. Glassiness and "gold fleck" in tomato fruit is also attributed to high atmospheric humidity. Misting and fogging systems are used by some growers to increase humidity and decrease temperatures. However, if used improperly, these systems can greatly increase the incidence of mildews and plant diseases, not to mention corrode metal greenhouse structures.

PROPAGATION

Seeds

Several tomato varieties have been specifically developed for hydroponic production in controlled environments. All varieties have indeterminate morphology; meaning vegetative growth of the plant is continual and does not stop once flowering begins. This creates long tomato "vines" which must be trained up strings hanging from the greenhouse structures to maximize space and manage the crop. Some of the more popular varieties are Apollo, Belmondo, Caruso, Dombito, Larma, Perfecto, Trend and Trust. These are hybrid varieties, and the seed can be rather expensive. This may lead some novice growers to consider germinating seed from mature fruit, but those successive generations will not necessarily have the same characteristics of the parent plants. Some hobbyists prefer to grow successive generations from vegetative cuttings, producing genetic clones from the original plants. This is okay on a small scale, however, the high risk of perpetuating a latent disease or pest problem on a large scale outweighs the cost of new seed.

Starting Media and Nutrients

Any propagation medium must be thoroughly soaked before seeds are sown to assure uniform distribution of moisture. There are many different propagation media available.

Seeding trays can be filled with a soilless mix, such as peat and perlite. Peat pellets are also popular starters. Seedlings grown in a soilless mix may have enough nutrients available to them from the media that they would not need any additional nutrients for the first few weeks of growth, and therefore could be watered with fresh water only. However, seedlings in an inert medium, such as rockwool or oasis, will definitely require nutrient solution at all times.

Rockwool blocks are available in several sizes, and are designed so that seeds can be placed directly into seeding cubes, then, as the plants develop, the cubes can be nested inside larger blocks, for a "pot in a pot" system. This minimizes transplant shock, since the larger block consists of the same material as the germination cube. Oasis horticubes are similar to rockwool cubes in that they are inert, sterile blocks with excellent drainage. Other cubes made of urethane foam and paper fiber are also available.

Tomato seeds should be sown $^1/_4$ to $^3/_8$ inch (0.6 to 1 cm) deep. Sprinkle a thin layer of vermiculite over the seeds or cover the germination cubes or pots with a large piece of clear plastic to conserve moisture at the surface. Avoid the use of plastic if the cubes receive direct sunlight, as the temperature may get too hot for good germination. The plastic must be removed as soon as emergence begins.

SEEDLING SYSTEM DESIGN

Overhead watering is the most common method used for germinating seedlings. It is important for the seedlings to be in full sun and at the proper temperature as soon as germination occurs. When watering, the water must be sprinkled uniformly over all seedlings to avoid uneven growth. The plants must be checked often to assure they do not become water stressed.

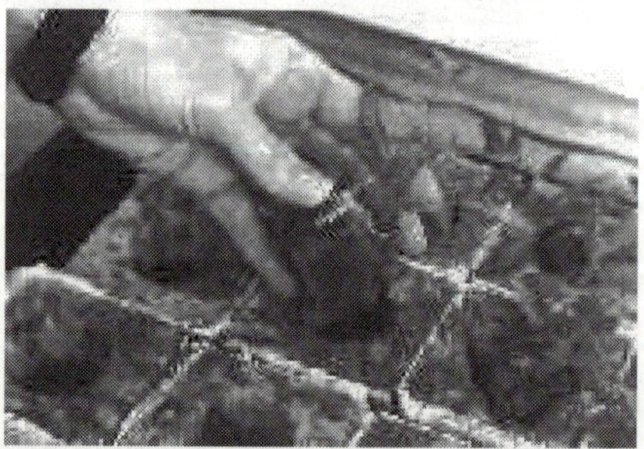

Flood and drain (ebb and flow) systems can also be very effective for germinating seedlings. Nutrient solution or water floods a shallow tray containing the sown cubes or pots, providing moisture from the bottom, which will diffuse throughout the propagation block by capillary action. Once the blocks are evenly moist, the tray is drained, which allows the cubes or pots to drain and assure aeration of the roots. This process will need to be repeated often throughout the day, but may not need to be done at all during the night. The advantages of this system are even moisture, no physical beating of the leaves and tender plants, and low labor costs (especially if timers are used).

In any event, the temperature of the irrigation solution should be at least 18° C (64° F). Irrigating seedlings with colder water will result in slower growth. During winter months, especially in Northern latitudes, supplemental light may be required for strong growth of seedlings. The lights should operate 14 to 18 hours per day.

Transplanting

The three stages of early development are germination, post-emergence, and transplant. Germination should occur within one week of seeding, post-emergence is generally 5 to 12 days, and transplanting should be done between 12 and 14 days from seeding. Once true leaves appear (during post-emergence), seedlings should be transferred into larger growing blocks (pots) from the original seedling cubes, then evenly spaced to maximize light to each plant, without any crowding or shading. The transplants must be spaced so as not to touch one another, and may need to be spread several times during their growth. If crowded, the plants will become spindly. A good transplant is one that is as wide as it is tall. If plants are somewhat "leggy", with long stems, they can be transferred into the larger blocks with their stems bent 180°, so the original cube is upside-down inside the larger block, and the main stem forms a "U" shape, emerging vertically upward from the block. Tomato plants readily grow adventitious roots from the stems if given the opportunity, producing a stronger plant with more roots. Adventitious roots will grow from the bent stem inside the block.

Transplanting into the final growing media should be done before any flowering. The final growing media should be properly leached and moistened and be at the proper temperatures before plants are brought in. Plants should be irrigated with nutrient solution immediately after moving. The spacing of tomatoes in hydroponic systems can be much denser than in soil. As little as two square feet per plant (0.2 square meters per plant) have been used with good yields and quality under high light conditions. Spacing is a function of sunlight, so in areas of lower light wider spacing should be applied.

Indeterminate tomatoes must be trained up support strings immediately after transplanting. The strings should be hung from horizontal wires, which are connected to the frame of the greenhouse. These wires will need to support hundreds of pounds of weight, as each mature plant with fruit may weigh 20 to 30 pounds (7 to 14 kilograms). Additional vertical poles can be added to help support the horizontal wires.

The wires and strings should be put in place before any other paraphernalia is brought into the greenhouse, and should be at least 10 feet (3 meters) above the ground.

The strings should not be re-used, however, a variety of clips are available which can be sterilized and re-used. As the plants grow, the strings are unwound from their hangers and moved along the horizontal wire, effectively "lowering" the plants without breaking them. Mature indeterminate tomato plants may be 40 feet (12 meters) in length, and can grow much more.

Double cropping

Some growers prefer to grow two crops of tomatoes in the growing media before tearing the system down, cleaning and sterilizing, and starting again. In this management system, young plants would be planted in the media between the older plants, just as the older plants are reaching their maximum economic life span. This effectively overlaps the crops, increasing total annual yield. However, the older plants must still be completely removed to prevent buildup of disease and excessive shading of the new crop, and care must be taken to work around the younger plants. In high light regions of the world, such as deserts and equitorial latitudes, the first crop is generally planted in midsummer and lasts through to the end of the year. The second crop can be planted in January and continue through the end of June. Alternatively, one long crop planted in late summer or fall can be grown until July.

GROWING MEDIA

Various growing media can be used in hydroponic systems. However, any system must have the following four qualities:

- sufficient support for the plants
- appropriate distribution of air, since roots need oxygen and respire other gasses, such as carbon dioxide
- maximum water availability for the plant roots
- accessible nutrient solution with consistent chemical characteristics

LIQUID (NON-AGGREGATE) HYDROPONIC SYSTEMS

Deep Flow Hydroponics

The classic hydroponic system, where plants are supported so that their roots hang into a nutrient solution, is generally called "deep flow hydroponics". This system is appropriate for hobbyists and large scale production of leafy vegetable crops. The system consists of horizontal, rectangular-shaped tanks lined with plastic. The nutrient solution is monitored, replenished, recalculated, and aerated. Commercial facilities are now quite popular in Japan. The rectangular pools act as frictionless conveyor belts where large, moveable floats of plants (lettuce) can be transported from transplant to harvest.

NUTRIENT FILM TECHNIQUE

A modification of the deep flow system is called "nutrient film technique", where a thin film of nutrient solution flows through plastic lined channels, which contain the plant roots. The walls of the channels are flexible; this permits them to be drawn together around the base of each plant, excluding light and preventing evaporation. For lettuce production, the plants are planted through holes in a flexible plastic material that covers each trough. Nutrient solution is pumped to the higher end of each channel and flows by gravity past the plant roots to catchment pipes and a sump. The solution is monitored for replenishment of salts and water before it is recycled. Capillary material in the channel prevents young plants from drying out, and the roots soon grow into a tangled mat. This method is mainly used for tomatoes.

Aeroponics

Aeroponics is another technique, where nutrient solution is sprayed as a fine mist in sealed root chambers. The plants are grown in holes in panels of expanded polystyrene or other material. The plant roots are suspended in midair beneath the panel and enclosed in a spraying box . The box is sealed so that the roots are in darkness (to inhibit algal growth) and in saturation humidity. A misting system sprays the nutrient solution over the roots periodically. The system is normally turned on for only a few seconds every 2-3 minutes. This is sufficient to keep roots moist and the nutrient solution aerated. Systems were developed by Dr. Merle Jensen at the University of Arizona, for lettuce, spinach, and even tomatoes, although the latter was judged not to be economically viable. In fact, there are no known large-scale commercial aeroponic operations in the United States, although several small companies market systems for home use.

AGGREGATE HYDROPONICS

In aggregate hydroponic systems, a solid, inert medium provides support for the plants. As in liquid systems, the nutrient solution is delivered directly to the plant roots. Aggregate systems may be either open or closed, depending on whether surplus amounts of the solution are to be recovered and reused. Open systems do not recycle the nutrient solutions; closed systems do.

In most open hydroponic systems, excess nutrient solution is recovered; however the surplus is not recycled to the plants, but is disposed of in evaporation ponds or used to irrigate adjacent landscape plantings or wind breaks.

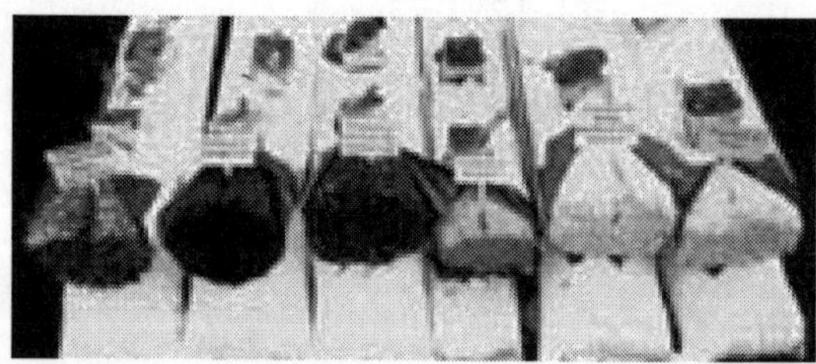

Because the nutrient solutions are not recycled, such open systems are less sensitive to the composition of the medium used or to the salinity of the water. These factors have generated experiments with a wide range of growing media and the development of more cost-efficient designs for containing them.

There are numerous types of media used in aggregate hydroponic systems. They include peat, vermiculite, or a combination of both, to which may be added polystyrene beads, small waste pieces of polystyrene beads, or perlite to reduce the total cost. Other media such as coconut coir, sand, sawdust, are also common in some regions of the world.

For growing row crops such as tomato, cucumber, and pepper, the two most popular artificial growing media are rockwool and perlite. Both of these media can be used in either closed or open systems (gravel is not recommended as an aggregate in either system). Both media are lightweight when dry, easily handled and easier to steam-sterilize than many other types of aggregate materials. Both can be incorporated as a soil amendment after crops have been grown in it.

Rockwool, or stonewool, is produced from basalt rock, and can come as spun wool, resembling fiberglass, or it can be granulated, offering an alternative to perlite and vermiculite in terms of water holding capacity and aeration. Stonewool has a high pH, generally greater than 8.0, however, it has essentially no buffering capacity, meaning it will not affect the pH of the nutrient solution nor will it affect any other media it is mixed with, such as peat moss (which has a pH of 3.8 to 4.5). Stonewool can be purchased in prepackaged "slabs"(commonly 15 x 7.5 x 100 cm long), ready to use, or as bulk granules for those growers who wish to mix their own soilless media.

Perlite is usually bagged in opaque white bags with drip irrigation tubes at each plant and drainage slits in the bags. Perlite is an inert media providing excellent aeration and water holding capacity. As in rockwool, it can be steam sterilized, rebagged and reused several times.

When both perlite and rockwool are used as closed systems, great care must be taken to avoid the buildup of toxic salts and to keep the system free of nematodes and soilborn diseases. Once certain diseases are introduced, the infested nutrient solution will contaminate the entire planting. In addition to the common practice of sterilizing the recirculating solution, there is current research exploring the use of surfactants to control certain root diseases. Such systems can be capital intensive because they require leak proof growing beds as well as subgrade mechanical systems and nutrient storage tanks.

MANAGING CARBON DIOXIDE IN YOUR GROW SPACE

If you are green to gardening you might not know that carbon dioxide, the gas we all exhale, is critical to plant growth and development. Photosynthesis, the process through which plants use light to create food, requires carbon dioxide. CO2 concentration in ambient air ranges from 300-500 parts per million (ppm), with a global atmospheric average of about 400 ppm. If you are growing in a greenhouse or indoors, the CO2 levels will be reduced as the plants use it up during photosynthesis. Increasing the CO2 levels in these environments is essential for good results. Additionally, there are benefits to raising the CO2 level higher than the global average, up to 1500 ppm. With CO2 maintained at this level, yields can be increased by as much as 30%!

Fig. Commercial greenhouse growing hydroponic tomatoes with CO_2 enriched air.

Commercial greenhouses are aware of this and commonly use CO_2 generators to maximize production. One thing to keep in mind while designing a CO_2 system is that yields will only increase if CO_2 is your 'limiting factor'. This means that if all your other variables are not optimal (light, fertilizer, temp/ humidity, pH, etc.) you will not achieve the benefits of increased CO_2 levels.

Now that we know the benefit of adding CO_2 to your indoor growing environment, one thing to note is that CO_2 enrichment will not be as effective if your grow area is not sealed since it will be exhausted before the plants can use it. Ideally, air should not be exchanged in an out of your grow room. If you have an air-cooled reflector, the air drawn through the fan to cool the bulb must enter and exit the grow area without coming in contact with the air in the grow room. Sealing your grow space allows plants to more completely use the CO_2 that you enrich the environment with.

Another thing to note is that during the night cycle plants actually give off CO_2. This causes a gradual increase during the night, until the lights come on and the plants resume absorbing CO_2; you can save CO_2 by waiting an hour or so into your daylight cycle to cut your CO_2 device on.

Lastly, CO_2 is notably heavier than air, so it is essential that your CO_2 be dispensed from above your plant canopy. Oscillating fans in the grow space, particularly around the CO_2 dispensed, will help distribute the CO_2 around the area.

Now, let's look at the various ways you can increase CO2 levels:

Homegrown CO_2's Exhale bags are a great option if you would like to see what CO_2 can do for your garden on a budget and without a lot of equipment (i.e. timers, regulators and monitors). Exhale bags are filled with mycelium (non-fruiting mushrooms) that give off steady amounts of CO_2 as a byproduct of their metabolism. These bags end up costing less and can save you a ton of hassle compared to the infamous fermentation and dry ice methods. For $32.99 you can buy an Exhale bag (available in-store only) that covers a 4×4 area for 6 months. After hanging your Exhale bag above the canopy you can use a CO_2 test kit to see how much it raises CO_2 levels.

Fig. Exhale bag CO_2 system

If you are ready to move up to a longer term, more efficient CO_2 delivery system, then the next system involves using a pin timer (Apollo 8), a CO_2 regulator and either a CO_2 tank (available for purchase or refill) or a CO_2 generator. Tanks are typically the better option for smaller spaces for ease of use whereas generators tend to be the better option for larger spaces since they run off of propane and can generate large volumes of CO_2 at low cost. Now, with either source, set the pin timer to turn the regulator on for 15 minutes every 90 minutes or so. A CO_2 calculator like this one, available from Greentrees Hydroponics, will help you determine how much CO_2 you need to release to achieve optimal concentrations for plant growth. You can also use a CO_2 test kit to dial in your system so that 1500ppm level is maintained. As your plants grow and the garden changes, retesting your CO_2 levels monthly can help you tweak your system to maintain optimum levels. Note, if you are using a Titan CO_2 Regulator, a ¼" dispensing tube is included. Hang this line above your canopy in a circle with small holes every couple of inches (to allow the CO_2 to 'rain').

Finally, for gardeners that want to achieve constant optimal growth conditions without ever wasting extra CO_2, a CO_2 monitor is a great device. These monitors, such as the Titan Atlas-3, completely automate your CO_2

system by constantly measuring the CO_2 in the area. If the ppm level falls lower than what you set on the monitor, it will automatically open the regulator and dispense CO_2. These monitors also come equipped with a photocell to ensure that you never dispense CO_2 during the night cycle.

THE GREENHOUSE ENVIRONMENT AS MINI-ECOSYSTEM

In the early 1970s, when energy costs first began their upward spiral, accelerating fuel prices drove many commercial glasshouse vegetable producers right out of business. This inflationary upswing also started a modest new trend in American gardening.

With the price tag on winter tomatoes and other warm-weather crops on the rise, many people equipped their homes with attached greenhouses, which ranged from expensive, custom-built models to low-budget, low-tech structures composed of plastic-covered frames.

We've now become accustomed to seeing such food- and flower-producing add-ons everywhere. There's no longer any reason to limit a passion for vegetables and flowers to the outdoors. Even those gardeners new to greenhouse management can be successful at indoor horticulture by following four basic rules.

KNOW YOUR GREENHOUSE ENVIRONMENT

Each attached greenhouse has its own environment, which is created by its location, design, construction, glazing, thermal mass and interior layout.

A solar greenhouse, more than any other type, is sensitive to its surrounding environment. In many ways, this type of greenhouse is analogous to a living plant cell: The sun is its primary energy source, and its glazing acts as a membrane between the inner and outer world, allowing an exchange of heat, light and air. A greenhouse can, in fact, become a mini-ecosystem if the adept gardener can manage the interaction between abiotic factors (such as wind, snow, oxygen, carbon dioxide) and the biological community.

At New Alchemy Institute, we call our greenhouses "bioshelters," because our biotic residents include more than just green plants. The bioshelter grower manages soil that's alive with tiny microorganisms and other animals that break down organic matter into humus. Plant-feeding, plant-pollinating and plant-predaceous insects stake out their own niches. Most of the flora is edible, but a small percentage of space is reserved for herbs, flowers and woody plants. Even the heat storage acts as a substrate for living organisms, since we use transparent water columns laden with green algae and stocked with phytoplankton-feeding fish, or bank huge masses of compost against the north wall. Any grower can become proficient at this type of biological management when treating the greenhouse as an ecosystem. The key is to let nature be your guide.

As the seasons blend one into another, milder versions of the world outside unfold inside the greenhouse. Since each structure is unique, keeping a record of the pilot year is the best way to learn about your under-glass environment. At the very least, enter minimum and maximum air and soil temperatures (6 inches underground) for each week. Other information such as plant vigor, future harvest dates, or insect and disease problems will guide you as you make your seed selection.

Light, temperature, humidity, carbon dioxide, ventilation, water and soil compose the atmosphere within a greenhouse and are interrelated. For example, as the temperature rises, the relative humidity drops. Likewise, under the best lighting conditions, low levels of carbon dioxide will restrict the rate of photosynthesis, limiting plant growth. You must be aware of such interactions and be prepared for some give-and-take in the environmental management of your indoor garden.

LIGHT. All plants require light for photosynthesis, and this essential gardening ingredient can be analyzed in two ways: by quantity and by quality. Quantity is scientifically measured in foot-candles (FC). One foot-candle is a unit of illumination equal to the direct illumination on a surface one foot from a standardized source called an international candle. You can, however, obtain a "thumbnail" measure of the amount of light striking a surface in your greenhouse by using a light meter in a 35mm camera.

The quality of light is defined descriptively—bright or direct, diffuse, partial, or shady. Within the greenhouse, different locations afford varying light levels. The greenhouse's southern section receives plenty of direct sunlight, whereas areas along a northern wall may be shaded. Light beams passing through a translucent glazing (such as fiberglass) scatter, resulting in diffused light without shadows. In front of the greenhouse, deciduous or evergreen trees may obstruct incoming light, creating the same effect. This arrangement is helpful during warm summer months. Partial light occurs when a plant receives only part of a day's sunlight.

Maximizing light and minimizing condensation and shading will improve plant growth during the winter months when light levels are lowest. In greenhouses with partial or shaded light conditions, the gardener's best strategy is to match the right plant with the available light. It's nonsense, for example, to attempt to grow tomatoes in a dimly lit greenhouse in January. Plants that are victims of low light conditions show slow growth, elongated stems, yellow lower leaves, weak and floppy leaves, and phototropism (plants' bending drastically toward the light source).

The amount of light a greenhouse receives will depend on its location, design, and type of glazing. Two or three layers of glazing material will reduce heat loss but will also reduce light levels. Greenhouses with insulated, opaque walls should use as much reflective light as possible. Plenty of white paint on these walls will bounce the light back into the structure. Supplementary light or artificial light can be used at your own discretion. I'd suggest using this kind of lighting when starting warmweather transplants such as tomatoes, European cucumbers, or peppers early in the year. Whatever the day length at that time, boost it up to 16 hours of light.

In the warmer months, it's equally important to shade the greenhouse, reducing both the amount and intensity of light entering it. Gardeners often overlook this critical step in climatic management. You can apply a commercially available liquid shading compound to glass at various concentrations for the coverage you desire. Eventually, the rain will wash it off: Such compounds are usually nonabrasive, nontoxic, and easy to apply with a spray tank, but shade cloth may be better suited for plastic or polyvinyl glazing. Greenhouse supply companies offer cloth that provides different amounts of shade. For a biological screen, plant vining crops — grapes, melons, cucumbers, and runner beans, for example — in or outside the greenhouse along its southern wall. When the time comes for brighter light, simply pull the crop out. But make sure that you choose vining perennials or shade trees that will be mature during the seasons when the greenhouse requires shading.

TEMPERATURE: Temperature controls a plant's rate of photosynthesis, cell division, and water and nutrient uptake. Each vegetable or flower flourishes when its optimum day- and nighttime temperatures are met. Unfortunately, that hardly ever happens inside a solar greenhouse. What's more, managing the environment for plants will limit the efficiency of a home greenhouse as a solar collector.

Plants prefer a moderate temperature fluctuation of 11° to 18°F in one day-to-night cycle. When the sun shines in the winter, the daytime temperature inside an unheated greenhouse can soar to 104°F, while at night — when heat loss through the glazing is more than the daytime heat gain and the greenhouse is closed off from the house — the temperature can plummet. Plants cannot survive under these circumstances. Therefore, if the purpose of your solar addition is to grow plants, you must be willing to sacrifice some of the free, supplemental heat you could use to warm your house. '

A greenhouse's ability to hold the heat of the day is dependent on its design, and you can control air temperature better if you follow certain recommendations when building your indoor garden.

1. Surround the perimeter of the building's foundation with two inches of closed-cell foam insulation. The north wall and roof should also be insulated.
2. Use double glazing, with a 1", tightly sealed air space between glazings, for all light-transmitting surface areas.
3. Provide thermal storage (water, cement, rock, soil, or compost) to absorb the daytime heat.

4. Install night curtains along the glazing to prevent heat loss at night. Many different types are commercially available.
5. Use tight construction to prevent air leaks and unnecessary air exchanges. Pay particular attention to vents and doors.
6. Provide for proper ventilation, drawing off hot air into the house and circulating cool air from the house back into the greenhouse. In addition, top and side vents should be large enough to bring in fresh air from the outdoors.
7. It's optional (but still a good idea) to install a low-powered fan to improve air flow and to circulate trapped hot air around the thermal mass.

There's a direct relationship between nighttime temperatures and the rate of plant growth. Higher nighttime temperatures give the grower higher vegetable yields and superior flowers.

On the other hand, greenhouse temperatures should never exceed 86°F, because an overheated greenhouse is as unproductive as one that's too cold. In fact, inadequate ventilation is the number one downfall of many solar greenhouse designs. The vent area should equal one-sixth of the glazing area, and the vent's placement is critical.

Ideally, top vents should span the entire growing area, and bottom vents should be placed as close to the ground as possible. With this pattern, natural convection forces hot air out of and fresh air into the greenhouse.

Shading, too, can prevent overheating, while small fans and evaporative cooling systems can augment ventilation and improve air circulation. A simple method involves hosing down pathways, terraces, and walls to reduce temperatures and to elevate relative humidity during the warm months.

Soil temperature is another key to a productive greenhouse, especially for organic gardeners. Most of the microorganisms that gobble up organic matter and turn out plant nutrients require soil temperatures above 55°F. A drop below this level results in no nutrient release, cold plant roots, and a slower metabolism for both plants and microbes.

Soil temperatures can be improved by using insulated growing containers and boxes, hot-water systems sunk below the growing beds, or hot air forced through a subterranean duct system. Root zone heating with electric heating cables or tapes can also ensure the proper soil temperatures. But talk to the manufacturers, and a few of their customers, before buying any of these products.

HUMIDITY: In the winter, if the air in the house is dry, the extra humidity from the attached greenhouse will be welcome. Most plants prefer a relative humidity of 55% to 60%. Excess moisture, however, can cause problems, because many pathogenic fungi germinate when the relative humidity rises above 80%. High humidity can be controlled with proper ventilation and air circulation. Sometimes a small fan inside the greenhouse can speed up the air exchange between home and garden. Watering in the morning and applying the water to the *soil* — not to the leaf surfaces — will minimize the symptoms of excess moisture. Providing proper spacing between plants and avoiding overwatering will further reduce the possibility of fungal diseases.

Condensation can also become a problem as more and more moisture is held in the air. Moreover, condensed water on the glazing scatters and reflects incoming light, reducing the amount that passes into the greenhouse by as much as 30%. A few glazings are coated with a film that beads up condensed water so that it quickly runs of the glazing. (The 3M product- Sun-Gain is one of the best for reducing condensation.) Low humidity is a summertime condition. Unless managed properly, the warm air will rob the greenhouse soil of its moisture, promoting physiological stress on plants. Shane Smith describes "A Homemade Burlap Swamp Cooler" in his excellent book *The Bountiful Solar Greenhouse*. This cooler is a backyard version of the commercial pad-and-fan system.

CARBON DIOXIDE: Normally, fresh air, exhaled breath, and a biologically active soil should provide enough carbon dioxide in an attached greenhouse. Keep in mind, though, that the hours of daylight, light intensity, temperature, and amount of carbon dioxide available affect the rate of photosynthesis and are interrelated. Within limits, higher levels of one environmental factor can compensate for a deficiency in another. For example, high concentrations of carbon dioxide (1,000 ppm) can increase lettuce yields when temperatures are lower than the optimum. Depending on the stage of plant development and all of the environmental factors mentioned, increased levels of carbon dioxide *can* improve yields and hasten plant maturity. Higher levels of carbon dioxide are particularly beneficial to many fruiting vegetables and to flowers.

4

Greenhouse Soil and Cultivation System

Organic Gardening Under Glass states that the ideal greenhouse soil (a good, sandy loam) consists of 50% solid matter—dirt particles plus organic material—and half air and water. Few native soils meet these conditions. But, by adding various combinations of sand (coarse particles that aid drainage), clay (a fine material with good mineral holding capacity) and manure, compost, or peat moss (to add humus), you *can* add enough aeration and drainage to keep your plants' roots healthy.

Once the soil's physical makeup is properly balanced, the greenhouse gardener must remember to keep it that way by fertilizing the earth in his or her hothouse. And there's nothing mystical about this periodic enrichment of greenhouse growing mediums. Just "do what comes naturally."

In other words, organic gardeners may add fish emulsion, blood meal, manure, granite dust, potash rock or any other "organic" sources commonly used to enrich the soil, while less organically minded folks may prefer to stick to the commercially produced water-soluble fertilizers in, say, a 16-16-16 formula. With either method, just ensure that plants are supplied with sufficient quantities of nitrogen, phosphates, potash and other needed micronutrients, and that the soil's humus content is maintained.

Bear in mind, too, that the warm and humid environment of a greenhouse tends to raise the acidity of soil and that this pH change may affect plant growth. Most flowers and vegetables grow better in earth that is *slightly* acid, so alkalizers (lime, wood ashes, gypsum) or acidifiers (such as sulfur) may be needed to maintain the optimum pH. Be sure to test your soil, however — either with your own pH tester or by sending a sample of the dirt to your state agricultural extension service — before applying any additives.

Salts buildup — brought on by too much fertilization (especially with chemicals) — is another serious problem to avoid in the greenhouse. White, crusty deposits on the surface of the earth or on the outside of clay pots indicate that too many nitrogen, phosphate, potash and calcium salts have accumulated in the growing medium. These substances can damage roots, yellow or wilt foliage, cause leaf burn and actually kill plants. Avoid the imbalance by watering greenhouse soil *thoroughly* to flush out excess salts. And remember: Many authorities suggest fumigating all soil used in a greenhouse with either heat and steam or with chemicals to kill pathogenic fungi, viruses, bacteria, nematodes and insects in the growing medium. For the small-scale grower who sets many plants out in pots, however, the Abrahams' pasteurization methods (outlined below) may be the most practical ways to rid earth of potentially harmful organisms:

Fill a baking pan with three or four inches of the dirt, cover it with aluminum foil, and insert a meat thermometer into its center. Then bake the container on low heat (higher oven temperatures will destroy organic matter and some beneficial organisms) for 30 minutes or until the thermometer reads 180°F. Or process the soil in a pressure cooker for 20 minutes at 5 pounds pressure.

You can also pasteurize your greenhouse growing medium with hot water. Fill a bench with earth, level it off (don't pack the dirt down), insert a meat thermometer into the flat and pour enough boiling water into the soil to bring its temperature up to 180°F. Allow the earth to dry for at least one day before you sow seeds in it.

GREENHOUSE CULTIVATION

Fig.1 Basic greenhouse plant care begins with good soil.

A lot of folks are confused by the complexities of greenhouse growing. Well, if an unsure understanding of the many published "rules and regulations" is keeping *you* from trying greenhouse cultivation, just *forget* them! All you really have to do to turn your plant palace into a dynamic package of productivity is to put *real* soil in the pots and benches; give your greenery plenty of light, air, and space; administer water wisely; and feed your hungry charges with nourishing manure "tea."

Besides — by doing without the often-recommended chemical fertilizers, sterile soil mixes, sprays, fumigants, systemics, and such — you'll find that you have a good bit of spare cash left for more *essential* items ... such as plants and pots. You'll also discover that disease and insect infestations, weak growth, and subnormal performance are (more likely than not) merely symptoms of improper culture, which shouldn't trouble the greenhouse gardener who zeroes in on the basics!

THE SOIL, AIR, LIGHT AND SPACE IN YOUR GREENHOUSE

First of all, grow only those plants that are proven stalwarts or have been bred for vigor, productivity, and resistance to disease (in many cases you'll have to do some experimenting to *find* such varieties, but other greenhouse growers can often give you "best bet" advice). Species that don't do well unless they're constantly fed — or plants that tend to succumb to aphids in spite of good growing conditions — should be classified as "unfit" and removed from your list.

In order to provide your chosen vegetables and flowers with good soil, make up a half-and-half mixture of rich garden loam and compost, or one consisting of one-third each of loam, compost, and peat moss. Then, to each prepared bushel, add a six-inch potful of well-aged manure and a four-inch potful of bone meal or wood ashes. If there's clay in your loam, put some sand in the mixture, too. (Cacti like a soil composed of one part loam, one part organic compost, and two parts sand.)

Next, be sure to give your greenhouse tenants a breath of fresh air . . . often! Insect pests — as well as fungi, mildew, and diseases — just love to attack plants that suffer from a close atmosphere, so make sure that your greenhouse is well ventilated (while, of course, maintaining the desired temperature) and you'll keep trouble at bay.

Remember, too, that full sun on your greenhouse means full production, and can cut down on the need for supplemental winter heat. (The structure can always be shaded with netting, film, paint, etc. to *limit* sunlight ... but you can't bring sun to it once it's been situated in the shade.)

Space is equally important. Vegetation needs room to grow, so if you notice the leaves of adjacent plants touching, it's best to move them away from each other. (Of course, folks who grow their greenhouse plants only in pots will find the task easy, but people who plant directly in the bench will have to either thin or plan ahead.)

GREENHOUSE GROWING TEMPERATURES

One of the main concerns of *any* greenhouse gardener is to avoid extremes and sudden changes of temperature in the growing area. So watch for those still, clear winter days that can make your greenhouse thermometer reading soar in minutes! On such occasions you may have to ventilate, even if the*outside* temperature is below freezing. *Warm* weather always calls for maximum ventilation, with all vents wide open, exhaust fan on full (if your greenhouse is equipped with one), and the door ajar, if necessary.

During the winter months, a minimum night temperature of 45 to 50 degrees Fahrenheit is best, unless you're growing tropical plants. Even then, the usual 6o degrees minimum may not be necessary, because a gardenia, for instance, will winter perfectly well in a cool greenhouse (it will simply go dormant and wait for the return of warmer weather before blooming again). Besides, cooler temperatures *favor* a wide range of flowers and vegetables, such as lettuce, herbs, geraniums, cyclamens, and many annuals.

FOOD AND WATER FOR YOUR GREENHOUSE CROPS

Don't let your plants go dry (unless you're growing succulents or cacti), but don't try to maintain a regular watering schedule, either. The variables that affect the loss of moisture from the soil (including weather, the size of the container, the kind of plant, etc.) are just too many to cope with routinely. Instead, simply check the pots *often* : When the surface soil is dry to the touch, water them thoroughly. (Dormant or inactive plants, on the other hand, should be kept barely moist.) It's simple, it's pleasant, and your indoor crops will reward you for the individual attention by growing bigger and better!

I've found that supplemental feedings aren't necessary for any plant that's been *recently*potted in good soil. In already established plants, weak or slow growth that's not attributable to winter doldrums or dormancy — or a yellowing of the leaves during a period of active development — means one of two things: The roots have filled the pot and require more room, or the plant needs additional nutrients. If evidence points to the latter problem, offer the patient a "spot of tea." Here's how: Fill a large, leakproof, rotproof pail with water, and add a generous quantity of manure. After the mix has been allowed to soak for several days, pour the liquid into your watering container through an old strainer. Dilute it — if necessary — until it's the color of weak tea, and give your plants a normal watering of this "super soup." (Be sure to periodically feed plants that *like* to be potbound, such as specimen jasmines or geraniums.)

If possible, it's best to give your hothouse residents "tea" on the morning of a bright day. Skip such feedings in the middle of long spells of dull or cold weather, and *don't* feed a dormant or ailing plant (that would be akin to asking a sick person to eat a big meal).

Attitudes and Insects

Most of the six- and eight-legged creatures, and *other* so-called pests, that inhabit your greenhouse are simply living out their life cycles and aren't really all that interested in your plants. No doubt you'll spy aphids now and then, but — if you're sticking to the basic rules — you aren't likely to be faced with an aphid buildup or takeover. Should a plant suddenly become infested, just remove it to other quarters and rinse the bugs off (assuming the specimen is worth the trouble). Keep it isolated and watch it carefully.

If the problem returns, get rid of the plant, because you can be sure there's *something wrong* with it. (But *don't*discard it, or any diseased greenery, right outside the door. In fact, it's a good idea to eliminate weeds-both inside and outside the structure-so wind and people won't be so likely to bring problems in with them.)

White flies, I've discovered, detest an organically managed greenhouse. Slugs, too, seek plants that are feeble from want of good growing conditions. (The latter pests' territory is usually confined to the dingy areas under the benches. Search such hiding spots and destroy the "enemy" wherever you find it.) Earwigs may be trapped underneath several strategically placed rags, where you'll find the little pests hiding during the day and can drown them.

Tiny creatures that hop when disturbed are harmless springtails. If you have an infestation of thrips, spider mites, or sow bugs, chances are you haven't been heeding the rules. And if you don't bring mealybugs and scales *into* the greenhouse, you won't *have* any of them! So when you buy *woody* plants (especially gardenias), make absolutely certain they're clean.

Don't, however, expect that your greenhouse will be 100 percent pest-free! It's not a sterile habitat, and it would be both unreasonable and *unnatural* to strive toward such a goal. If your plants are free from the handicaps of poor culture, pests will automatically fall under control, and your efforts will be reduced to maintaining a watchful eye, a vigilant hand-picking schedule, and — otherwise — a general attitude of loving laissez faire.

Summer Greenhouse Cleanouts

When summer comes, it's a good practice to empty the greenhouse, so that — in the process of the enclosure's complete evacuation and drying out — any lingering insects will leave. This cleaning will provide you with a fresh start come fall (you should, of course, double-check everything you bring back in). Also, with the building empty you have an excellent place to dry herbs: Choose a sunny day, spread your plants out on clean sheets or towels, and see how fast they're ready for storage! And, that's really all there is to the "science" of greenhouse growing. When you rely on nature, you'll have healthy, eager plants that are not easily fazed by changes in growing conditions. They'll have more normal development of roots, stems, and leaves, better fruiting and maturation, and stronger flavors and colors. And one of the *joys* of such greenhouse productivity is the fact that there's nothing tricky about it at all!

DESIGNS AND CLASSIFICATION OF GREENHOUSE

Greenhouses are frames of inflated structure covered with a transparent material in which crops are grown under controlled environment conditions. Greenhouse cultivation as well as other modes of controlled environment cultivation have been evolved to create favorable micro-climates, which favours the crop production could be possible all through the year or part of the year as required.

Greenhouses and other technologies for controlled environment plant production are associated with the off-season production of ornamentals and foods of high value in cold climate areas where outdoor production is not possible. The primary environmental parameter traditionally controlled is temperature, usually providing heat to overcome extreme cold conditions. However, environmental control can also include cooling to mitigate excessive temperatures, light control either shading or adding supplemental light, carbon dioxide levels, relative humidity, water, plant nutrients and pest control.

CLASSIFICATION OF GREENHOUSE BASED ON SUITABILITY AND COST

Low cost or low tech greenhouse

Low cost greenhouse is a simple structure constructed with locally available materials such as bamboo, timber etc. The ultra violet (UV) film is used as cladding materials. Unlike conventional or hi-tech greenhouses, no specific control device for regulating environmental parameters inside the greenhouse are provided. Simple techniques are, however, adopted for increasing or decreasing the temperature and humidity. Even light intensity can be reduced by incorporating shading materials like nets. The temperature can be reduced during summer by opening the side walls. Such structure is used as rain shelter for crop cultivation. Otherwise, inside temperature is increased when all sidewalls are covered with plastic film. This type of greenhouse is mainly suitable for cold climatic zone.

Medium-tech greenhouse

Greenhouse users prefers to have manually or semiautomatic control arrangement owing to minimum investment. This type of greenhouse is constructed using galvanized iron (G.I) pipes. The canopy cover is attached with structure with the help of screws. Whole structure is firmly fixed with the ground to withstand the disturbance against wind. Exhaust fans with thermostat are provided to control the temperature. Evaporative cooling pads and misting arrangements are also made to maintain a favourable humidity inside the greenhouse.

As these system are semi-automatic, hence, require a lot of attention and care, and it is very difficult and cumbersome to maintain uniform environment throughout the cropping period. These greenhouses are suitable for dry and composite climatic zones.

Hi-tech greenhouse

To overcome some of the difficulties in medium-tech greenhouse, a hi-tech greenhouse where the entire device, controlling the environment parameters, are supported to function automatically.

Cost involved

1. Less expensive greenhouse without fan and pad Rs.300 to 500/m2
2. Medium cost greenhouse with pad and fan system without automation Rs.800 to Rs.1100/m2
3. Expensive greenhouses with fully automatic control system Rs.2000 to Rs.3500/m2

Other classifications

The greenhouse can also be classified based on type of structures, type of glazing, number of spans, environmental control etc. The various types are as follows.

Classification as per type of structure

a. Quonset type
b. Curved roof type
c. Gable roof type

Classification as per glazing

a. Glass glazing
b. Fiberglass reinforced plastic glazing
   i. Plain sheet
   ii. Corrugated sheet
c. Plastic film
   i. Ultra violet stabilized low density poly ethylene
   ii. Silpaulin

Classification based on number of spans

a. Free standing or single span
b. Multispan or ridge and furrow or gutter connected

Classification based on environmental control

a. Naturally ventilated
b. Passive ventilation

Poly house

The crops grown in open field are exposed to vivid environmental conditions, attack of insects and pests, whereas the polyhouse provides a more stable environment. Polyhouse can be divided in to two types

(a) Naturally ventilated polyhouse: These polyhouse do not have any environmental control system except for the provision of adequate ventilation and fogger system to prevent basically the damage from weather aberrations and other natural agents..

(b) Environmental controlled polyhouse: This type of polyhouse helps to extend the growing season or permits off-season production by way of controlling light, temperature, humidity, carbon-dioxide level and nature of root medium.

Fig. Carnation under high-tech greenhouse

Shade house

Shadehouses are used for the production of plants in warm climates or during summer months. Nurserymen use these structures for the growth of hydrangeas and azaleas during the summer months. Apart from nursery, flowers and foliages which require shade can also be grown in shadehouses. E.g. Orchids, These shade structures make excellent holding areas for field-grown stock while it is being prepared for shipping to retail outlets. Shadehouses are most often constructed as a pole-supported structure and covered with either lath (lathhouses) or polypropylene shade fabric. Polypropylene shadenets with various percentages of ventilations are used. Black, green, and white coloured nets are used, while black colours are the most preferred as it retains heat outside.

Orientation of greenhouse / polyhouse

The design of greenhouse should be based upon sound scientific principles which facilitates controlled environment for the plant growth. Controlled environment plant production systems are used widely throughout the world to produce plant materials and products at a time or place, or of a quality that can not be obtained outdoors. Controlled environment agriculture requires far more capital investment per unit area than field agriculture and thus must essentially be correspondingly more intensive to justify investment costs. The greenhouse is a structure covered with a transparent material for admitting natural light for plant growth. The main components of greenhouse like structure, covering/glazing and temperature control systems need proper design for healthy growth of plants.

Under Indian conditions, Quonset type, multispan greenhouse is most suitable, because of its low cost and ease of fabrication. Ultra violet resistant low density polyethylene (UVLDPE) single film cladding of 200 micron thickness is sufficient for Naturally Ventilated (NV) greenhouse and fan and pad (FP) greenhouses. This should be fully tightened by stretching on the structure to avoid fluter and tearing. It should not be nailed or screwed to the structure as it gives the chance for tearing. The T-Lock of LLock should be used for fastening the sheet at structure, as this does not tear the sheet and sheet replacement is easy.

Design

The structure has to carry the following loads and is to be designed accordingly.

(a) Dead load: weight of all permanent construction, cladding, heating and cooling equipment, water pipes and all fixed service equipments to the frame.

(b) Live load: weights superimposed by use (include hanging baskets, shelves and persons working on roof). The greenhouse has to be designed for a maximum of 15 kg per square meter live load. Each member of roof should be capable of supporting 45 kg of concentrated load when applied at its centre.

(c) Wind load: The structure should be able to withstand winds of 110 kilometer per hour and at least 50 kg per square meter of wind pressure.

(d) Snow load: These are to be taken as per the average snowfall of the location

The greenhouse should be able to take dead load plus live load or dead load plus wind load plus half the live load.

The greenhouses are to be fabricated out of Galvanized Iron Pipes. The foundation can be 60cmx60cmx60cm or 30 cm diameter and one meter depth in PCC of 1:4:8 ratio. The vertical poles should also be covered to the height of 60 cm by PCC with a thickness of 5cm. This avoids the rusting of the poles.

Orientation

Orientation of the greenhouse is a compromise for wind direction, latitude of location and type of temperature control. Single greenhouses with latitude above 40°N should have ridge running east to west to allow low angle light to enter from side rather than ends. Below 40°N the ridge of single greenhouses should be oriented from north to south, since the angle of sun is much higher. This orientation permits the movement of shadow of the gutter across the green house.

The location and orientation of the greenhouse should avoid falling of shadow on the adjacent greenhouses. To avoid the shading effect from one green house to another greenhouse these should be oriented East to West. However, the wind direction and latitude are also to be considered.

Wind effects

If the greenhouse is naturally ventilated, the advantage of natural wind direction has to be taken to the maximum possible. The maximum dimension (length) of greenhouse should be perpendicular to the wind direction especially in summer. For fan and pad greenhouse the natural wind direction should be same as the air blown by fan.

Size of the greenhouse

The dimension of NAV GH should not be more than 50m x 50m. Bigger the greenhouse, more will be the temperature build up due to poor ventilation. The length of evaporatively cooled greenhouse should not be more than 60m.

Spacing between greenhouses

The spacing between naturally ventilated green house should be 10 to 15 m so that the exhaust from one greenhouse should not enter the adjacent greenhouse.

Height of greenhouse

The maximum height can be up to 5m for 50m x 50m green house and this can be reduced as per the reduced size of the green house. Higher is the greenhouse more is the wind load for structure and glazing. The side ventilation can be of 2 m width and roof ventilation is 1m in width.

Structural design

The greenhouses are to be designed for necessary safety, serviceability, general structural integrity and suitability. The structure should be able to take all the necessary dead, live, wind and snow loads. The foundation, columns and trusses are to be designed accordingly. The greenhouse structures are to be designed to take up the loads as per design loads prescribed by the National Greenhouse Manufactures Association (NGMA of USA) standards –1994.

Components of greenhouse

Roof: transparent cover of a green house.

Gable: transparent wall of a green house

Cladding material: transparent material mounted on the walls and roof of a green house.

Rigid cladding material: cladding material with such a degree of rigidity that any deformation of the structure may result in damage to it. Ex. Glass

Flexible cladding material: cladding material with such a degree of flexibility that any deformation of the structure will not result in damage to it. Ex. Plastic film

Gutter: collects and drains rain water and snow which is place at an elevated level between two spans.

Column: vertical structure member carrying the green house structure

Purlin: a member who connects cladding supporting bars to the columns

Ridge: highest horizontal section in top of the roof

Girder: horizontal structure member, connecting columns on gutter height

Bracings: To support the structure against wind

Arches: Member supporting covering materials

Foundation pipe: Connection between the structure and ground

Span width: Center to center distance of the gutters in multispan houses

Green house length: dimension of the green house in the direction of gable

Green house width: dimension of the green house in the direction of the gutter

Cladding material

Polythene proves to be an economical cladding material. Now long lasting, unbreakable and light roofing panels-UV stabilized clear fiber glass and polycarbonate panels are available. Plastics are used in tropical and sub-tropical areas compared to glass/fiberglass owing to their economical feasibility. Plastics create enclosed ecosystems for plant growth. LDPE (low density polyethylene) / LLDPE (linear low density polyethylene) will last for 3-4 years compared to polythene without UV stabilizers.

Comparison of different kinds of covering materials

Sl. No.	Type	Durability	Transmission		Maintenance
			Light	Heat	
1.	Poly ethylene	One year	90%	70%	Very high
2.	Poly ethylene UV resistant	Two years	90%	70%	High
3.	Fiber Glass	Seven years	90%	5%	Low
4.	Tedlar coated Fiber Glass	Fifteen years	90%	5%	Low
5.	Double strength Glass	Fifty years	90%	5%	Low
6.	Poly carbonate	Fifty years	90%	5%	Very low

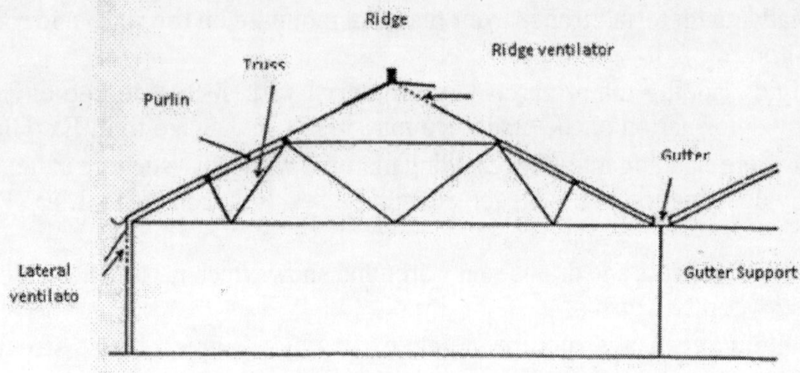

Components of typical greenhouse

Plant growing structures / containers in greenhouse production

The duration of crop in greenhouse is the key to make the greenhouse technology profitable or the duration of production in greenhouses should be short. In this context, use of containers in greenhouse production assumes greater significance. The containers are used for the following activities in greenhouse production.

- Raising of seedlings in the nursery
- Growing plants in greenhouses for hybrid seed production of flowers
- Growing plants for cutflower production.
- Growing potted ornamental plants.

Advantages of containers in greenhouse production

- Increase in production capacity by reducing crop time.
- High quality of the greenhouse product
- Uniformity in plant growth with good vigour.
- Provide quick take off with little or no transplanting shock.
- Easy maintenance of sanitation in greenhouse
- Easy to handle, grade and shift or for transportation.
- Better water drainage and aeration in pot media.
- Easy to monitor chemical characteristics and plant nutrition with advanced irrigation systems like drips.

Selection of suitable containers depends upon the crop to be produced in greenhouse, plant characteristics like crop stage, duration, vigour, growth habit, root system, etc. Generally long duration, deep rooted and vigorous crop plants require bigger containers compared to short duration, shallow and less vigorous ones. The containers provide optimum condition for germination of seed and growth and development of transplants.

Advantages and disadvantages of plant growing containers

Containers	Advantages	Disadvantages
Clay pot	Low cost Easy water management	Slow to work with pots and dry out fast They are heavy to handle
Fiber block	Easy to handle	Slow root penetration Short life
Fiber tray	Minimum use of space	Hard to handle when wet
Single peat Pallet	No media preparation Low storage requirement	Requires individual handling Limited sizes can be handled
Prespaced Peat pallet	No media preparation Limited to small sizes	
Single peat	Good root penetration	Difficult to separate
Pot	Easy to handle in field Available (square / round) in large sizes	
Strip peat pot	Good root penetration	Slow to separate
Protrays	Easy to handle Reusable	May be limited in sizes
Plastic pack	Easy to handle	Roots may grow out of container
Plastic pot	Reusable Good root penetration	Requires handling as single plant
Polyurethane foam	Easy to handle Requires less medium Reusable	Requires regular fertilization
Soil band	Good root penetration	Requires extensive labour
Soil block	Excellent root penetration	Expensive machinery
Perforated	Easy to handle	Requires regular fertigation
Plastic tray	Requires less medium Available in many sizes reusable	Roots may grow out of the container
Perforated	Less expensive	Less durable
Polyethylene	Reusable bags	Requires less storage space

Environmental factors influencing greenhouse cultivation

Plants need an optimum temperature for maximum yield and quality. The greenhouses in plain and coastal region of India needs cooling. The greenhouses in mild climates and coastal region can be naturally ventilated.

The greenhouses for hot summer climates of northern plains have to evaporatively cooled or with fan and pad (FP).

The greenhouses for northern plains may require both cooling and heating depending on the crop.

Natural ventilation

The greenhouse has to be thoroughly ventilated for control of temperature. It should be noticed that the temperature built up in the greenhouse is not exceeding 2°C throughout the year. Further during hot months the temperature in the greenhouse was same as the ambient temperature.

Unconventional method of heating and cooling

(a) Hot and cold water can be sprinkled on the greenhouse covered externally with the shadenet
(b) Use of earth tunnel for cooling in summer and heating in winter
(c) Construction of greenhouse in a trench for heating in winter cooling in summer
(d) Circulating the borewell water in pipes laid on the floor of the greenhouse

Heating of greenhouse

The heating of greenhouses in cold climates like winter in North India or Himalayan Region at high altitudes is advisable for getting better produce. Double covering of glazing with an air cushion of 2 cm to 10 cm reduces the heating load considerably.

Heating systems

These can be of the following types

a. Boiler
1. With hot water tube
2. With steam pipes
b. Unit heaters
c. Infrared heaters
d. Solar heaters

Boiler

This system is used for very big greenhouses and is a centralized system of heating. The boiler of necessary capacity is provided in the greenhouse. The fuel for boiler can be coal or fuel oil. The heating of the greenhouse is generally done through hot water at 85°C or steam at 102°C. Water or steam pipes are installed above the beds of crop and along the side wall. The steam system is cheaper than hot water system. To reduce the length of pipe to be used a number of hot water or steam pipe coils can be used and green house air circulated over them by blower for heating.

Unit heaters

These are localized system of heating and a number of unit heaters are to be provided in the greenhouse at a height of about 3 meter to distribute heat evenly in the greenhouse. In a unit heater the fuel is combusted in the chamber at bottom. Hot fumes rise inside the heat exchanger tubes, giving heat to the walls of the tubes. Smoke exists at the top. A fan forces cool air of the greenhouse over the outside of heat exchange tubes, where it picks up heat.

Infra-red heaters

The fuel gas (LPG) is burnt and the fumes at a temperature of about 480°C are passed in 10 cm diameter pipes kept overhead at a height of 1.5m above plants. Reflectors are provided over the full length of pipe to radiate the infra red rays over the plants. The plants and soil only get heated without much heating of air. The infra red heating pipes can be provided at 6 to 10 meters interval all along the length of greenhouse. The temperature of fume gases at exist is about 65°C and exhaust fan is provided for maintaining the flow of fumes.

Solar heating

Flat plate solar heaters are used to heat the water during day time. The hot water is stored in the insulated tanks. The hot water is circulated in pipes provided along the length of the greenhouse during night. Supplementary or emergency heating systems are provided for heating the greenhouse during cloudy or rainy days.

ENVIRONMENTAL CONTROL

Temperature control

The thermostat can be coupled to water circulating pump or exhaust fan for controlling the temperature inside the greenhouse. However, the lowest achievable temperature in fan and pad greenhouse is not below the wet bulb temperature in any case.

Relative humidity control

The humidistat coupled to water circulating pump or exhaust fan to control the relative humidity inside the fan and pad greenhouse. The maximum achievable relative humidity is 90% only in fan regulated (FR) greenhouse. The RH in Non ventilated (NV) GH can be increased by providing foggers.

Light intensity control

In certain areas where natural illumination is absent or very low, illumination for plants may be provided by artificial sources. Incandescent bulbs generate excessive heat and are unsatisfactory in most instances. Fluorescent tubes are useful as the sole source of light for African violets, gloxinias and many foliage plants which grow satisfactorily at low light intensities. Excessive light intensity destroys chlorophyll even though the synthesis of this green pigment in many plants is dependent upon light. Chrysanthemum is a classic example for a short-day plant., however, flower buds will not form unless the night temperature is high enough. Chrysanthemum is flowered on a year-round basis as a cut flower or potted plant simply by controlling the length of day and temperature.

Quality of light

Quality of light refers to its wave-length composition. Light in the orange-red portion of the visible spectrum from either sunlight or artificial illumination is most effective in causing the long-day response in plants. Far-red radiation appears to have the opposite effect. It is probable that the wave lengths activate some hormonal mechanism within the plant which brings about the specific effect of light on growth or flowering.

FAN AND PAD

Selection of fan

The fans should deliver the required air at 15mm static pressure. The maximum center to center spacing between the tow fans should be of 7.5m. The height of the fans is to be determined based on the plant height which is proposed to be grown in the greenhouse. The fan blades and frame are to be made of non-corrosive materials like aluminium/stainless steel.

Design

The cross fluted cellulose pad is preferred. These are available mostly in 100mm thickness. One meter of pad height is given for every 20m of pad to fan distance.

How ever, the fan to pad distance should not exceed 60m. The air flow rate should be of 75 cubic meter/minute/sq.m of pad. The water flow rate should be of 9 litres per minute/linear meter pad. The uniform distribution of water on pad is to be maintained.

Maintenance of pad

The algae will grow and salts will deposit on pads if these are not maintained properly. Good control of algae can be obtained without using chemicals by the following methods.

1. By shading the pads and sumps
2. By drying the pads daily
3. By avoiding nutrient contamination
4. By draining and disinfecting the sump regularly
5. By replenishing 20% of circulating water each time to avoid scaling of minerals.

Maintenance of fan

1. The lubrication of bearings should be done regularly
2. The v belt should be tightened as per requirement
3. The levers should be properly lubricated.

Media preparation and fumigation

Soil mixes used for greenhouse production of potted plants and cut flowers are highly modified mixtures of soil, organic and inorganic materials. When top soil is included as a portion of the mixture, it is generally combined with other materials to improve the water holding capacity and aeration of the potting soil. Many greenhouses do not use topsoil as an additive to the soil mixes, but rather use a combination of these organic and inorganic components as an artificial soil mix. When managed properly as to watering and fertilization practices, these artificial mixes grow crops that are equal to those grown in top soil.

Media preparation for greenhouse production

The media used in greenhouse generally have physical and chemical properties which are distinct from field soils.

- A desirable medium should be a good balance between physical properties like water holding capacity and porosity.
- The medium should be well drained.
- Medium which is too compact creates problems of drainage and aeration which will lead to poor root growth and may harbour disease causing organisms.
- Highly porous medium will have low water and nutrient holding capacity, affects the plant growth and development.
- The media reaction (pH of 5.0 to 7.0 and the soluble salt (EC) level of 0.4 to 1.4 dS/m is optimum for most of the greenhouse crops).
- A low media pH (<5.0) leads to toxicity of micronutrients such as iron, zinc, manganese and copper and deficiency of major and secondary nutrients while a high pH (>7.5) causes deficiency of micronutrients including boron.
- A low pH of the growth media can be raised to a desired level by using amendments like lime (calcium carbonate) and dolomite (Ca-Mg carbonate) and basic, fertilizers like calcium nitrate, calcium cyanamide, sodium nitrate and potassium nitrate.
- A high pH of the media can be reduced by amendments like sulphur, gypsum and Epsom salts, acidic fertilizers like urea, ammonium sulphate, ammonium nitrate, mono ammonium phosphate and aqua ammonia and acids like phosphoric and sulphuric acids.
- It is essential to maintain a temperature of the plug mix between 70

to 75°F. Irrigation through mist is a must in plug growing. Misting for 12 seconds every 12 minutes on cloudy days and 12 seconds every 6 minutes on sunny days is desirable.

- The pH of water and mix should be monitored regularly.

Gravel culture

Gravel culture is a general term which applies to the growing of plants with out soil in an inert medium into which nutrient solutions are usually pumped automatically at regular intervals. Haydite (shale and clay fused at high temperatures), soft- or hard-coal cinders, limestone chips, calcareous gravel, silica gravel, crushed granite and other inert and slowly decomposing materials are included in the term "gravel". The more important greenhouse flowering crops include roses, carnations, chrysanthemums, gardenias, snapdragons, lilies, asters, pansies, annual chrysanthemums, dahlias, bachelor buttons and others.

Desirable nutrient level in greenhouse growth media

S. No.	Category	Concentration (mg/l)			
		NO3	N	P	K
1.	Transplants	75	125	10-15	250-300
2.	Young pot & foliage plants	50	90	6-10	150-200
3.	Plants in beds	125	225	10-15	200-300

Media ingredients and Mix

Commercially available materials like peat, sphagnum moss, vermiculite, perlite and locally available materials like sand, red soil, common manure/ compost and rice husk can be used in different proportions to grow greenhouse crops. These ingredients should be of high quality to prepare a good mix. They should be free from undesirable toxic elements like nickel, chromium, cadmium, lead etc.

Agent	Method	Recommendation
Heat	Steam	30 min at 180° F
Methyl bromide	10 ml/cu. ft. of medium	Cover with gas proof cover for 24-48 hr. Aerate for 24-28 hr before use.
Chloropicrin	(Tear gas) 3-5 ml/cu. ft. of medium	Cover for 1-3 days with gas proof cover after sprinkling with water. Aerate for 14 days or until no odour is detected before using.
Basamid	8.0 g/cu.ft. of medium	Cover for 7 days with gas proof cover and aerate for atleast a week before use.
Formalin	20 ml/l of water (37%)	Apply 2 l/cu.ft. cover for 14 to 36 hr and aerate for at least 14 days.

Disinfection of the growing media can also be achieved by fungicides or bactericides

Pasteurization of greenhouse plant growing media

Greenhouse growing medium may contain harmful disease causing organisms, nematodes, insects and weed seeds, so it should be decontaminated by heat treatment or by treating with volatile chemicals like methyl bromide, chloropicrin etc.

Fungicides and their effect on a few fungi

Chemical	**Rate of application**	**Effect against**
Captan	2 g/l of water	*Pythium, Fusarium, Rhizoctonia and Phytophthora. Some extent to root and stem rot, white mold,black rot, crown rot and damping off.*
Metalaxyl + Mancozeb (Ridomil MZ 72 WP)	1 g/l of water	*Pythium, Phytophthora, Fusarium* and other soil borne pathogens

Temperature necessary to kill soil pests

- 115°F for water molds (*Pythium* and *Phytophthora*)
- 120°F for nematodes
- 135°F for worms, slugs and centipedes
- 140°F for most plant pathogenic bacteria
- 160°F for soil insects
- 180°F for most of weed seeds
- 200°F for few resistant weed seeds and plant viruses

Fumigation in greenhouse

Physical propagation facilities such as the propagation room, containers, flats, knives, working surface, benches etc. can be disinfected using one part of formalin in fifty parts of water or one part sodium hypochlorite in nine parts of water.

An insecticide such as dichlorvos sprayed regularly will take care of the insects present if any. Care should be taken to disinfect the seed or the planting materials before they are moved into the greenhouse with a recommended seed treatment chemical for seeds and a fungicide –insecticide combination for cuttings and plugs respectively. Disinfectant solution such as trisodium phosphate or potassium permanganate placed at the entry of the greenhouse would help to get rid off the pathogens from the personnel entering the greenhouses.

Drip irrigation and fertigation systems in greenhouse cultivation

The plant is required to take up very large amounts of water and nutrients, with a relatively small root system, and manufacture photosynthates for a large amount of flower per unit area with a foliar system relatively small in relation to required production.

Watering system

Micro irrigation system is the best for watering plants in a greenhouse. Micro sprinklers or drip irrigation equipments can be used. Basically the watering system should ensure that water does not fall on the leaves or flowers as it leads to disease and scorching problems. In micro sprinkler system, water under high pressure is forced through nozzles arranged on a supporting stand at about 1 feet height. This facilitates watering at the base level of the plants.

Equipments required for drip irrigation system include

(i) A pump unit to generate 2.8kg/cm2 pressure

(ii) Water filtration system – sand/silica/screen filters

(iii) PVC tubing with dripper or emitters

Drippers of different types are available

(i) Labyrinth drippers

(ii) Turbo drippers

(iii) Pressure compensating drippers – contain silicon membrane which assures uniform flow rate for years

(iv) Button drippers- easy and simple to clean. These are good for pots, orchards and are available with side outlet/top outlet or micro tube out let

(v) Pot drippers – cones with long tube

Water out put in drippers

a. 16mm dripper at 2.8kg/cm2 pressure gives 2.65 litres/hour (LPH).

b. 15mm dripper at 1 kg/cm2 pressure gives 1 to 4 litres per hour

Filters: Depending upon the type of water, different kinds of filters can be used.

Gravel filter: Used for filtration of water obtained for open canals and reservoirs that are contaminated by organic impurities, algae etc. The filtering is done by beds of basalt or quartz.

Hydrocyclone: Used to filter well or river water that carries sand particles.

Disc flitersL: Used to remove fine particles suspended in water

Screen filters: Stainless steel screen of 120 mesh (0.13mm) size. This is used for second stage filtration of irrigation water.

Fertigation system

In fertigation system an automatic mixing and dispensing unit is installed which consists of three systems pump and a supplying device. The fertilizers are dissolved separately in tanks and are mixed in a given ratio and supplied to the plants through drippers.

Fertilizers

Fertilizer dosage has to be dependent on growing media. Soilless mixes have lower nutrient holding capacity and therefore require more frequent fertilizer application. Essential elements are at their maximum availability in the pH range of 5.5 to 6.5. In general Micro elements are more readily available at lower pH ranges, while macro elements are more readily available at pH 6 and higher.

Forms of inorganic fertilizers

Dry fertilizers, slow release fertilizer and liquid fertilizer are commonly used in green houses.

Slow release fertilizer

They release the nutrient into the medium over a period of several months. These fertilizer granules are coated with porous plastic. When the granules become moistened the fertilizer inside is released slowly into the root medium. An important thing to be kept in mind regarding these fertilizers is that, they should never be added to the soil media before steaming or heating of media. Heating melts the plastic coating and releases all the fertilizer into the root medium at once. The high acidity would burn the root zone.

Liquid fertilizer

These are 100 per cent water soluble. These comes in powdered form. This can be either single nutrient or complete fertilizer. They have to be dissolved in warm water.

FERTILIZER APPLICATION METHODS

Constant feed

Low concentration at every irrigation are much better. This provides continuous supply of nutrient to plant growth and results in steady growth of the plant. Fertilization with each watering is referred as fertigation.

Intermittent application

Liquid fertilizer is applied in regular intervals of weekly, biweekly or even monthly. The problem with this is wide variability in the availability of fertilizer in the root zone. At the time of application, high concentration of fertilizer will be available in the root zone and the plant immediately starts absorbing it. By the time next application is made there will be low or non existent. This fluctuation results in uneven plant growth rates, even stress and poor quality crop.

Fertilizer injectors

This device inject small amount of concentrated liquid fertilizer directly into the water lines so that green house crops are fertilized with every watering.

Multiple injectors

Multiple injectors are necessary when incompatible fertilizers are to be used for fertigation. Incompatible fertilizers when mixed together as concentrates form solid precipitates. This would change nutrient content of the stock solution and also would clog the siphon tube and injector. Multiple injectors would avoid this problem. These injectors can be of computer controlled H.E. ANDERSON is one of the popular multiple injector.

Fertilizer Injectors

Fertilizer injectors are of two basic types: Those that inject concentrated fertilizer into water lines on the basis of the venturi principle and those that inject using positive displacement

A. Venturi Principle Injectors

1.Basically these injectors work by means of a pressure difference between the irrigation line and the fertilizer stock tank.

(a) The most common example of this is the HOZON proportioner.

(b) Low pressure, or a suction, is created at the faucet connection of the Hozon at the suction tube opening. This draws up the fertilizer from the stock tank and is blended in to the irrigation water flowing through the Hozon faucet connection.

(c) The average ratio of Hozon proportioners is 1:16. However, Hozon proportioners are not very precise as the ratio can vary widely depending on the water pressure.

(d) These injectors are inexpensive and are suitable for small areas. Large amounts of fertilizer application would require huge stock tanks due to its narrow ratio.

Positive displacement injectors.

1. These injectors are more expensive than Hozon types, but are very accurate in proportioning fertilizer into irrigation lines regardless of water pressure.
2. These injectors also have a much broader ratio with 1:100 and 1:200 ratio being the most common. Thus, stock tanks for large applications areas are of manageable size and these injectors have much larger flow rates.
3. Injection by these proportioners is controlled either by a water pump or an electrical pump.
4. Anderson injectors are very popular in the greenhouse industry with single and multiple head models.
   a. Ratios vary from 1:100 to 1:1000 by means of a dial on the pump head for feeding flexibility.
   b. Multihead installations permit feeding several fertilizers

simultaneously without mixing. This is especially significant for fertilizers that are incompatible (forming precipitates, etc.) when mixed together in concentrated form.

5. Dosatron feature variable ratios (1:50 to 1:500) and a plain water bypass.
6. Plus injectors also feature variable ratios (1:50 to 1:1000) and operates on water pressure as low as 7 GPM.
7. Gewa injectors actually inject fertilizer into the irrigation lines by pressure.
   a. The fertilizer is contained in a rubber bag inside the metal tank. Water pressure forces the fertilizer out of the bag into the water supply.
   b. Care must be taken when filling the bags as they can tear.
   c. Ratios are variable from 1:15 to 1:300.
8. If your injector is installed directly in a water line, be sure to install a bypass around the injector so irrigations of plain water can be accomplished.

General problems of fertigation

Nitrogen tends to accumulate at the peripherous of wetted soil volume. Hence, only roots at the periphery of the wetted zone alone will have enough access to Nitrogen. Nitrogen is lost by leaching and denitrification. Since downward movement results in permanent loss of NO3 –N, increased discharge rate results in lateral movement of N and reduces loss by leaching.

Phosphorous

It accumulates near emitter and P fixing capacity decides its efficiency. Low pH near the emitter results in high fixation.

Potassium

It moves both laterally and downward and does not accumulate near emitter. Its distribution is more uniform than N&P.

Micronutrients

Excepting boron, all micronutrients accumulates near the emitter if supplied by fertigation. Boron is lost by leaching in a sandy soil low in organic matter. But chelated micronutrients of Fe, Zn can move away from the emitter but not far away from the rooting zone.

COST ESTIMATION FOR GREEN HOUSE CONSTRUCTION

A model project proposal for floriculture industry

A. Title of the project: Title should be brief and apt. It should be indicate clearly the main business activity. Eg. Production of Rose cut flowers for domestic and export market.

B. Introduction: Give a line of introduction of the proposed business. Justification for starting the business, scope and competition should be clearly stated.
C. Production technology: Give detailed account of the entire production process along with the scientific basis for each step.
D. Project components: For cut flower production
    1. Land
    2. Greenhouse
    3. Planting material
    4. Irrigation
    5. Fertilization system
    6. Grading and packing room
    7. Refrigerated van
    8. Office equipment
    9. Import of technology
    10. Labour charge
    11. Technical manpower
    12. Pesticides, Fertilizers, preservatives

Give the costing for each of the major components and classify them into

A. Fixed cost –Permanent items
B. Recurring cost –planting, cultivation, maintenance, storage, packing and transportation costs.
E. Project yield: Estimate the total production expected in different years and the realization expected through sales.
F. Margin money: 25% of the total cost that has to be invested by the entrepreneur.
G. Repayment: Principal and interest are to be repayable in seven years with a moratorium for the first year on interest and for 2 years on principal.

Budget requirement

Total investment for the project = Fixed cost + Recurring cost = 76.5 + 166.2 in first year= 242.7.

Project yield

No. of rose plants per hectare of greenhouse = 60,000

No. of flowers expected per plant = 100 to 150

No. of exportable quality flowers /plant = 60 to 100

Price per flower in international market = Rs. 6 to 11

Total exportable flowers /ha @ 100 flowers /plant = 60 lakhs flowers

Gross income through exports @ 50 flowers/plant = 300 lakhs (minimum).

For a one hectare greenhouse to produce Rose cut flowers.

A. Fixed cost

S. No.	Item	Amount in lakhs
1.	Land and development	4.0
2.	Green house	13.0
3.	Cold storage	10.0
4.	Grading and packing room	5.0
5.	Office area	2.5
6.	Refrigerated van	1.0
7.	Generator set	2.0
8.	Fax, telephone, Computer	1.0
9.	Furniture	0.5
10.	Power supply installations	1.5
11.	Water supply system, drip irrigation and misting liners	6.0
12.	Planting material and planting	30.0
	Total fixed cost	**76.5 lakhs**

B. Recurring costs

S. No.	Item	Amount in lakhs
1.	Electricity charges / year	6.0
2.	Manures and fertilizers	1.0
3.	Plant protection	1.0
4.	Preservatives	3.0
5.	Packing material	2.0
6.	Air freight	125.0
7.	Labour charges	3.0
8.	Commission / duty/ insurance	15.0
9.	Salaries	5.0
10.	Overhead costs	0.5
11.	Maintenance cost	1.0
12.	Miscellaneous	3.7
	Total recurring cost	**166.2**

Problem management in greenhouse cultivation

The troubles which arise in the culture of crops in the greenhouse may be divided into several groups a) failure to supply the essential factors for optimum growth such as light, moisture, carbon dioxide and heat in amounts necessary for each individual crop b) fertilizer deficiencies c) fertilizer excesses d) toxic gases e) attacks by insects, animals, and allied pests and f) susceptibility to fungus, bacteria and virus troubles.

Fertilizer deficiencies

Symptoms of deficiencies of various fertilizers have been studied over a period of years with plants in greenhouses.

Chlorosis

This is a term used to denote the loss of normal green colour from the foliage whether it is on the older, more mature leaves or the younger foliage. The entire leaf may be affected, or just areas between the veins, in which case the yellowing is most usually in irregular patches shading into the green colour. Sometimes only the margin of the leaf or leaflets may be yellow, while the centre of the foliage is almost a normal green.

Necrosis

This refers to the death of the area severely affected by chlorosis. Necrotic spots or areas can also be caused by spray or aerosol damage, sunscald and other such factors which may have no relation of fertilizer.

Nitrogen deficiency

Generally the entire plant becomes lighter green, but the effect will be most noticeable on the older foliage. Gradually the oldest leaves loose their green colour, and most plants become yellow. The flowers are smaller and may lack well-developed colour.

Phosphorus deficiency

A purplish coloration developing first on the underside of the petiole, or leaf stem, which spreads to the main veins of the leaf is characteristic of this deficiency.

Potassium deficiency

The margins of the leaves of the older foliage become yellow, and the chlorosis progresses toward the mid-portion of the foliage as this deficiency increases in severity. The older leaves may drop in extreme cases of deficiency. Certain fumigants may cause marginal burning or chlorosis, and sometimes droplets of spray or fumigant may result in spots or blotches of chlorotic or necrotic nature.

Calcium deficiency

In sand culture, a typical symptom is the development of short clubby roots followed in a matter of several weeks by their death. In many cases insufficient calcium is associated with a low pH of the soil.

Iron deficiency

This is a rather common trouble although an actual lack of iron may not be the primary cause. As iron deficiency becomes more intense, necrotic areas appear on scattered portions of the yellow coloured leaves and the affected foliage may drop. Iron can become deficient in soil, but often the symptoms of this deficiency are induced by other causes from injury to the roots by over-watering or over fertilization. Nematodes, or other soil pests interfering with root growth can also induce iron chlorosis symptoms.

Boron deficiency

The number of cases where this is a limiting factor are few, and most of them are with certain rose and carnation varieties. The new foliage is thick or leathery and quickly becomes chlorotic. The rose flowers are usually very malformed. The stem tip dies, giving rise to growth of shoots immediately below, which in turn die at the tip, and a 'witches broom' effect is observed. Because deficiency symptoms can sometimes be confused with the effects of some other environmental factor of cultural practice, a thorough review of fertilizer application, soil testing, soil type, watering practices, and other procedures is warranted before hasty conclusions are reached.

Fertilizer excesses

An unfortunate belief among many growers is that when a plant does not grow under apparently favorable conditions, the trouble can be overcome by applications of fertilizer. This practice has resulted in untold damage or loss of crops, as more often than not the original trouble could have been too much fertilizer in the soil. If additional fertilizer is applied when no more is needed, the results can be very injurious. Sometimes the difference between a high but safe nutrient level and an injurious nutrient level is not very great and the margin of safety may be extremely small. Therefore, it behaves the grower to test the soil in case of doubt to determine the advisability of fertilizer application.

Nitrogen excess

The plants exhibit heavy, rank growth, with large, dark green leaves that are often crisp and break easily. Additional nitrogen may inhibit root action, causing typical symptoms of iron chlorosis. If the root system is killed, the plants wilt excessively and never recover. This yellowing of the top foliage is very common in chrysanthemums and snapdragons. Over 75 ppm of nitrates is not safe.

Phosphorus excess

Over doses of phosphorus precipitate the iron from the soil solution and make it insoluble and unavailable, causing iron chlorosis to develop. Over 25 ppm may cause trouble.

Potassium excess

Up to a certain point, excessive potash apparently is not injurious. Greater amounts inhibit root action and may cause chlorosis, wilting, or immediate death of the plant. Over 60ppm is dangerous.

Calcium excess

Usually the pH of the soil will rise when there is excessive calcium. This causes iron chlorosis in many plants and has been called over liming injury. Over 300 ppm is high.

Iron excess

In the normal pH range of soil, there is little danger of excessive iron since phosphorus or calcium will precipitate it from the soil solution. At ph 5.0 or lower, iron becomes very soluble, and on hydrangeas brown dots appear on the leaves, indicating iron is being precipitated as water vapor is lost by transpiration.

Sulfate excess

A low pH may often be characteristic of soils high in sulfates. Sometimes high sulfates are encountered at pH 6.5. Over 600 ppm is toxic to most plants.

Boron excess

This trace elements is often found in soil to which unleached cinders have been added or where boric acid has been applied indiscriminately. Certain water supplies may have rather high amounts of boron. On roses, the serrations on the margin of the leaflets of the lower leaves turn black and the remaining leaves turn yellow and drop.

Aluminum excess

This is not troublesome except on hydrangeas that are being blued. Roots are burnt, and the plants wilt.

Soluble salts excess

Too much fertilizers in the soil injures or kills roots, and plant growth is severely reduced.

Remedial measures for excess fertilizer

When fertilizer levels rise to the point where they become toxic, immediate steps must be taken to remove the excessive materials. Excessive nitrogen leaching with heavy waterings and application of of straw mulch Excessive phosphorus can not be leached. Only by addition of lime or iron sulfate Excessive potassium leaching may wash some quantity, but in clay soils removal may be almost impossible.

Excessive calcium Acidifying the soil excessive iron Raising the pH or by addition of phosphorus excessive sulfates Leaching and avoiding the use of sulfate forms of fertilizers excessive boron Water glass, or sodium silicate can be dissolved in water at the rate of 100 cubic centimeters per gallon and applied to the soil. Excessive aluminum raising the pH or by adding phosphorus excessive soluble salts leaching.

INJURY BY TOXIC GASES

Natural gas

This gas usually contains 95 per cent methane and 4 to 5 per cent ethane and frequently causes injury to greenhouse plants. The common source of injury is from corroded or leaky gas pipes inside or outside the greenhouse. This injuries usually occur during winter when the ventilators kept closed. Very small concentrations of gas are sufficient to cause damage to plants, its detection is difficult by sense of smell. One part to 350 will cause a headache after 2 hours, whereas 1 part of natural gas in 10,000 to 100,000 of air will injure many plants. The best method of detection is through the use of tomato plants. In the pre

sence of gas the leaves of tomato turn downward, because of epinastic response, which causes petioles of leaves to grow more rapidly on the upper side.

Carnations exposed to low concentrations will develop long stigmas, but this may also occur in bright weather in unshaded greenhouses. In case of prolonged exposure of young buds even 1 part to 100,000 may kill the buds and flowers fail to develop. Rose foliage on the upper shoots exhibits epinasty, or a bending downward of the petiole. Severe leaf drop may follow and the flower colour often fades. Bulbous plants usually develop twisted foliage and the flowers do not open properly.

Ethylene gas

This gas apparently is a by-product of metabolic processes and is given off in very small quantities by plants or their parts. Dropping of flowers after pollination is thought to be associated with ethylene vapors. The carnation flowers close or may appear "sleepy", that is, the ends of the petals curl inward due to ethylene gas.

Sulphur dioxide

In very low concentrations this gas is toxic to plants. Sulphur dioxide enters the leaf through open stomata and kills the cells nearby, thus showing patches of dead tissues scattered over the leaf and frequently affecting the margins. Middle-aged leaves are more susceptible than young leaves.

Damage from sulphur dioxide is commonly found in localities where coal is burnt in large quantities. Foggy days are particularly dangerous. The common practice of using sulphur on heating pipes in rose houses to control mildew is responsible for leaf drop on some varieties.

Mercury damage

Many plants are quickly damaged by vapors from metallic mercury. This damage is manifested in roses by peduncles of young buds turning yellow and later black. The color of flowers turns dark and leaves are scorched. Breaking of mercury thermometers or the use of bi chloride of mercury on beds as a disinfectant is the usual way in which mercury may be released. Control measures consist of removing all possible traces of mercury and covering the areas where mercury was spilled or applied with a 2-inch thickness of iron filings. Paint containing mercury as a fungicide should not be applied to rose houses.

2,4-D

The fumes of 2,4- dichlorophenoxy acetic acid and related compounds used as weed killers cause bending, curling, and other malformations of leaves, stems, flowers or bracts. Fumes or 'drift' from a spray applied along the side of a greenhouse may enter through the doors or side vents cause trouble. Therefore, it is well to prevent trouble by keeping such sources of potential damage out of the greenhouse, boiler room, potting shed, or any place where the fumes could conceivably enter a greenhouse.

Phenol compounds

Many materials containing phenol or its derivatives are toxic to plants. Tar, carbolic acid, pentachlorophenol and many others of similar nature should never be used under glass. Treatment of wooden bench members with wood preservatives containing phenol compounds results in severe damage to the plants.

SPECIAL HORTICULTURAL PRACTICES IN GREENHOUSE PRODUCTION

The aim of greenhouse cultivation is to obtain high yield and good quality flower with in a short period. Several methods for forcing flowers can be used successfully to obtain high yield and quality.

Rose

Deshooting

Sprouting of buds just below flower, from the point between shoot and leaf lead to smaller bud size. So these shoots should be removed regularly.

Dead shoot removal

In the old plants the dead shoot or dried shoots on plants are observed which will be the host for fungi. So regulary these have to be removed.

Soil loosening on beds

After 6 months or so, there is every chance that the soil become stony and it has to be loosened for efficient irrigation.

Bending

Leaf is a source of food for every plant. There should be balance between source (assimilation) and sink (Dissimilation).

Mother shoot bending

After planting 2 to 3 eye buds will sprout on main branch, these sprouts will grow as branches and these branches in turn form buds. This is don't to initiate bottom breaks or ground shoots which will form main framework of plant structure. The mother shoot is bend on 2nd leaf or nearer to the crown region. The first bottom break or ground shoot will start coming from the base. These ground shoots form the basic framework for production and thereon the ground shoots should be cut at 5th five pair of leaves and medium ground shoots should be cut at 2nd or 3rd five pair of leaves.

Defoliation

The removal of leaves is known as defoliation. It is done mainly to induce certain plant species to flower or to reduce transpiration loss during periods of stress. Defoliation may be done by removal of leaves manually or by withholding water. The shoots are defoliated after pruning.

CARNATION

Support system (Netting)

Good support material is metal wire mesh width of 7.5 x 7.5 cm to 15 x 15 cm. The cheapest support material is net with nylon. Minimum at every 3 meters, the wires should be supported with poles. The poles at the beginning and the end of each bed should be strong enough and be in cast concrete. For an optimal support of the crop, an increasing width of meshes may be used. Eg. The bottom net of 7.5 x 7.5 cm, then 12.5 x 12.5 cm and the upper nets 15 x 15 cm.

Pinching

Pinching refers to breaking out the tip of shoot with few leaves and encouraging growth of side shoots. There are three types of pinching

a) single b) one and half and c) double pinches

Pinching is done at a stage when the plants are young and between of 7-15cm height. Since very tender shoots are usually pinched, no special tool is required. It is done by snapping the shoot tip manually. A sharp knife or blade may be used for pinching. When the plant attains 6 nodes, the first pinch is given. This is referred as 'single pinch'. This would give rise to six lateral shoots. With a ' one and half pinch', 2-3 of these lateral shoots are pinched again. For the 'double pinch' all the lateral shoots are pinched off. Other than carnation, pinching is also practiced in marigold, Gomphrena (single pinch), and spray types of chrysanthemum (double pinch).

Disbudding

Disbudding refers to removal of side shoots so that the central/terminal bud receives maximum food for the full development. In standard carnations, side buds should be removed where as in spray carnations, the terminal bud has to be removed.

CHRYSANTHEMUM

Pinching out the apical bud

As soon as the bud stems begin to elongate in other words as soon as the buds have just separated from one another, it is used to pinch out the central bud, this improves the spray shape. If pinching out is done too early, damage may be caused to the side buds, so it is carried out between 2nd and 3rd weeks before harvesting.

PHYSIOLOGICAL DISORDERS

Plant disorders may be either due to nutritional deficiencies or unsuitable growing storage conditions. In appropriate temperature atmospheric or erratic water or food supply, poor light, unsatisfactory atmospheric conditions may also cause deficiencies of the mineral salts that are essential for healthy plant growth.

Rose

Blind wood

The normal flowering shoot on a greenhouse rose possesses fully expanded sepals, petals, and reproductive parts. The failure to develop a flower on the apical end of the stem is a common occurrence-such shoots are termed blind. The sepals and petals are present, but the reproductive parts are absent or aborted. Blind wood is generally short and thin, but it may attain considerable length and thickness when it develops at the top of the plant. This may be caused by insufficient light, chemical residues, insect, pests, fungal diseases and other factors.

Bull heads or malformed flowers

The center petals of the bud remain only partly developed and the bud appears flat. They are common on very vigorous shoots, particularly bottom breaks, and it is possible that there is a lack of carbohydrates to develop the petals. The cause of bull heading is as yet unknown, how ever, thrips infestation will also cause malformed flowers.

Colour fading

Off- coloured flowers present a problem with some yellow varieties in that the petals may be green or a dirty white instead of a clear yellow. Raising the night temperature several degrees will reduce the number of off-coloured flowers. Occasionally the pink or red varieties develop bluish-coloured flowers. This is very often associated with use of organic phosphate and various other kinds of insecticides.

Limp necks

The area of the stem just below the flower "wilts" and will not support the head. Sometimes this is due to insufficient water absorption; cutting off the lower 1 to 2 inches of stem and placing the cut stem in water at 37°C will revive the flower.

Blackening of rose petals

This is caused by low temperature and high anthocyanin content. GA3 treatment causes accumulation of anthocyanin in petals of Baccara roses. This effect was more pronounced at low temperature (20°C at day and 4°C at night) than in higher temperature (30°C at day and 20°C at night).

Nutritional disorders

Iron deficiencies can cause pale foliage. Adjusting the pH of the soil may solve this problem

Carnation

Splitting of calyx

The calyx may split down either half or completely. The petals are deprived of their support, which results into bending down of petals. Thus, the regularity of shape and structure of the flower destroyed. Splitting is associated with weather, particularly where light and temperature fluctuate. Some reduction in splitting can be obtained by keeping the night temperature at 5°F. High plant density per unit area caused more calyx splitting. Increasing doses of N reduced the number of split calyces while increase in potassium rates enhanced it. Varieties tolerant to calyx splitting are Epson, palmir etc.

Curly tip

This disorder affects the growing tips which curl and become distorted.

Tips of the young shoots fail to separate and continuation of growth results in a characteristic curvature. Poor light and other adverse conditions are thought to be the causes of the disorder. Water stress and potassium deficiency are suspected causes for a physiological curly tip and die-back of carnation flowers.

CHRYSANTHEMUM

Blindness

It occurs when the night temperature is too low and the days are short at the time when flower buds are forming. A rosetted type of growth is indicative of this difficulty. Center petals that fail to develop can be due to excessive heat; or in dark weather some varieties apparently lack enough food to open the flower. Chlorosis, or yellowing of the upper foliage, is generally associated with over watering, excessive fertilizer in the soil, or insects or diseases attacking the root system. Continued growth of shoots and failure to form flower buds when short days are started the mean night temperature was too low. Sunscald is prevalent on standards in flower in very warm weather. The petals turn brown and dry up.

GERBERA

Bushiness

An abnormality characterized by numerous leaves, short petioles and small laminae, which gives some cultivars of gerbera a bushy appearance known as bushiness. Nodes are not clearly distinguished and no internode elongation is seen.

Stem break

It is common post harvest disorder in cut gerberas. This is mainly caused by water imbalances. It could be ethylene controlled and associated with early senescence associated with water stress.

Yellowing and purple margin

Nitrogen deficiency causes yellowing and early senescence of leaves. Phosphorus deficiency causes pale yellow colour with purple margin. Increase in levels of nitrogen and phosphorus were found to promote development of suckers and improve flowering in gerbera.

ANTHURIUM

Excess light

Leaves appear bleached in the centers and may have brown tips. To control this problem, shade should be given so as to reduce the light level to 1800-2500 foot-candles.

GLADIOLI

Fluoride injury

Leaf scorch of gladioli due to the presence of fluorine compounds in the atmosphere which accumulated on the tips of leaves. The injury is associated with heavy application of super phosphate.

POSTHARVEST HANDLING PRACTICES FOR CUT FLOWERS

Cut flower quality and longevity are influenced by pre and post harvest practices. Nearly 20-40% of the cut flowers produced are lost due to faulty harvesting, post harvest handling, storage, transportation and marketing. These losses can be reduced by careful harvesting, post harvest handling, temperature management, sanitation and judicious use of floral preservatives.

Harvesting

Maturity of the cut flower mainly decides its post harvest life. The flowers must reach certain stage of development before harvesting. Most of the cut flowers are harvested in the early morning or late in the afternoon. Flowers are harvested with sharp knife or secature.

Rose

Harvesting is done at the tight bud stage when the colour is fully developed and the petals have not yet started unfolding.

Gladioli

The spikes are cut in tight bud stage when colour has fully developed in the mature unopened buds leaving 4 leaves on the plant.

Carnation

Standard carnation flowers are harvested when the outer petals unfold nearly perpendicular to the stem. Spray types are harvested when two flowers open and the remaining buds show colour.

Chrysanthemum

Standard flowers are cut soon after the disappearance of green colour in the centre of the flowers and the center petals are fully expanded. Pompons are cut when they are fully developed. Spray types should be cut when the central flower is open and the surrounding flowers are well developed and the varieties which shed pollen badly will have to be cut before they become unsighty. Cutting the stem while the flowers are slightly on the "green" side is preferred because it offers a better quality product for the customer. The stems are harvested by pulling them out and breaking of the root system leaving it behind in the bed/field be ploughed into the soil when bed/field is prepared for next crop.

Orchid

Flowers are harvested when they are fully open as the flowers cut prior to their maturity will wilt before reaching the wholesaler.

Anthurium

Flowers are harvested when the spathe completely unfurls and the spadix is well developed. Harvesting the blooms, when one third of the flowers on the spadix mature, change of colour can be observed that moves from base to tip of spadix. At this stage the flowers are harvested. Harvesting has to be done during cooler parts of the day i.e.) early morning or late evening In general the cut blooms are placed in water held in plastic buckets immediately after cutting from the plant. Delay in keeping in water allows air entry into the stem and causes blockage of the vascular vessels. Cut flowers after harvest should be shifted to pre cooling chambers in refrigerated vehicles having 2-4°C temperature as they deteriorate most rapidly at high temperature. After reaching the cooling chamber, another cut is given above the previous cut in roses, whereas in orchids lower 0.75 cm of the peduncle is cut. In gladioli, 2.5 cm diagonal cut is made to expose maximum capillary tissues for absorbing more water

Pre cooling

Pre cooling removes field heat rapidly from the freshly harvested cut flowers. Precooling lowers respiration rate, water loss and ethylene synthesis. Most of the time, greatest loss occurs due to delay in precooling. Generally two methods of cooling are followed. The first one is room cooling and the other one is forced air-cooling. In room cooling, the flowers are held in buckets which are placed in a cooler. In the forced air cooling system, the flowers packed in perforated boxes are subjected to cool air blasts for a specific period in a closed room to remove field heat. The flowers take 20-30 minutes for cooling in forced cooling depending on the flower type and initial temperature in the box. Proper temperature (1.7°C to 4°C) and relative humidity (90-95%) maintenance are critical to the success of precooling, otherwise the flowers will dessicate.

POSTHARVEST HANDLING PRACTICES FOR IMPORTANT CUT FLOWERS

Rose

Roses must be placed in a bucket of water inside the polyhouse immediately after harvesting and transported to cold storage (2-4°C). The length of time depends upon the variety and quality of the roses.The flowers are graded according to the length. It varies from 40-70 cm depending on the variety and packed in 10/12 per bunch

Carnation

After harvest, the flower stems have to be trimmed at the base and should be immediately placed in a bucket of preservative solution of warm and deionized water. A good preservative solution for carnations should be acidic (pH 4.5) with 2-5% sucrose and a biocide not phytotoxic to carnations. After keeping in preservative solution for 2 to 4 hours, flowers should be placed in a refrigerated room at 0-2°C for 12-24 hours. The flowers can be stored for two to four weeks before marketing. For this, the flowers have to be packed in cartons lined with polyethylene film. These cartons should have sufficient vent holes. The full cartons should be pre-cooled with out lid. The plastic is then loosely folded on top of the stems and the lid is closed. These cartons are stored in cool chambers designed to maintained 0°C with good air circulation and a constant relative humidity of 90-95%.

Chrysanthemum

After harvest, the stem have to be cut at equal length (90 cm is the standard), bunched in five putting a rubber band at the base and sliding them into a plastic sleeve and putting the bunches in plastic buckets filled with water. Early morning on the day of shipment (or night before) the bunches can be packed in boxes.

Gerbera

Harvesting is done when outer 2-3 rows of disc florets are perpendicular to the stalk. The heel for the stalk should be cut about 2-3 cm above the base and kept in fresh chlorinated water.

ORCHIDS

Storage

Since most orchid flowers are long-lived on the plants, they should not be harvested until needed. If these are to be cut they should be stored at 5-7°C. At this temperature most orchid flowers can be stored for 10 to 14 days. Plastic film storage is attractive and can be utilized.

Packaging

Packaging is another important aspect in the flower trade. An ideal package should be airtight, water proof, strong enough to withstand handling and small in volume. Many ways are followed to pack orchid flowers. *Cymbidium* spikes are often packed 100 flowers to a box. Standard florist boxes are used for the packing of *Cattleya* floors. Hawaiin*Dendrobium* is packed in 4 dozen sprays per box. Keeping of a wet cotton at the cut end of the flower stem which is wrapped with a polythene wrapper helps to maintain humidity.

Vase- life

Immediately after arrival, the lower 0.75 cm of the peduncle is cut off, and the flower is inserted into a fresh tube of water containing preservative. In case of spray type of orchids, the basal 2.5cm of the stem is cut upon arrival, placed in warm water at 38°C with a preservative and hardened off at 5°C. Foliar application of aluminium chloride at 500ppm, ammonium molybdate at 100 ppm or boric acid at 1000ppm increased the vase-life of *Oncidium*.. Hydroxyquinoline resulted in additional bloom opening of the flowers and also increased the vase-life.

Anthurium

Flowers can be easily stored at 13°C for 2-3 weeks. The flowers, which are harvested when 3/4th of the length of the spadix colour changes, lasts longer than the other flowers which are harvested either early or late. The average vase life depends upon life of flowers range between 12-24 days depending upon the cultivars. Anthurium is packed in cartons lined with impervious polyethylene sheeting of adequate length and width so that, when packed, the sheet can be folded over to prevent the moisture of the dampened flowers and packing material from dampening the box itself. Newspaper is used to line the carton, and shredded newspaper is used to cushion spathes that are arranged in rows facing opposite directions. Each individual spathe is wrapped and tucked with un-printed newspaper or other white paper.

CROP FAILURE

Often greenhouse owners will wonder what causes blossoms to drop from their crops; they may ask why no fruit has set. Commercial growers often ask the same question. Fruitless plants and blossom drops are common among tomatoes, peppers, eggplants, cucumbers, muskmelons, watermelons, winter and summer squash, beans, and peas. Even sweet corn may drop the blossoms from its tassels. It's a common thing not only inside a greenhouse but also in the garden.

According to Dr. Leonard D. Topoleski, professor of vegetable crops at Cornell University, lack of fruit set with tomato, pepper, eggplant and other vegetables appears to be caused primarily by the lack of fertilization of the ovary, and not lack of pollination. In other words, you can have pollination, but for some reason, no fertilization. These five factors influence sexual union or fertilization and fruit set:

- Variety
- High temperature (above 90° F)
- Low temperature (below 50° F)
- Dry air
- Low soil moisture

Outdoors, the home gardener can't do much to control these factors, and all that can be done after the blossoms drop is to wait for the next cluster of flowers to develop. However, in the greenhouse you can control temperature, humidity and soil moisture content.

FLOWER DEVELOPMENT

Normally, with most vine crops, the first few flowers to develop are male flowers, called staminate flowers. These flowers develop only as a source of pollen and never become fruit. They are larger and more conspicuous than the female flower. These male flowers naturally drop early, so don't be alarmed when they do. The second flush or subsequent flower development is a mixture of male and female (pistillate) flowers. Outdoors, insects transfer pollen from male or staminate flowers to the female or pistillate flowers. In the greenhouse you can help nature along by transferring pollen with the tip of your finger or a brush. Usually fertilization occurs, and within a few days young cucumbers, muskmelons, squash, etc., start developing.

CO2 SUPPLY

Many studies have shown that plants grown in a C02-enriched atmosphere are larger and more luxuriant than those grown in a non-enriched environment. And plants raised in an "ordinary" atmosphere do better than those raised in a C02-poor environment.

If you have a sunken or an airtight greenhouse, then, you might want to improve its growing conditions by somehow increasing the CO2 in the unit's atmosphere, especially on bright, sunny days during the lengthy cold spells when the greenhouse is tightly sealed.

The most common sources of C02 for the small greenhouse owner are dry ice (just let it melt on the walks), compressed gas in cylinders (control its flow with a valve, meter and pressure regulator), and alcohol (the cheapest source, burn it in a kerosene lantern).

If you find the above sources of C02 a bit complicated, bothersome or expensive, you might try a variation of Jim DeKorne's system. By raising rabbits which inhale oxygen and exhale C02 in cages under his hydroponic tanks, the experimenter/author of *The Survival Greenhouse* managed to increase the C02 level in his greenhouse to an estimated 700 to 800 parts per million (300 ppm is the usual concentration in the atmosphere) and at the same time obtained valuable manure for his composting bin!

PHOTOPERIOD

The beginning greenhouse gardener should realize that just as deciduous trees enter dormant states as the days grow shorter, certain other plants will not flower and produce fruit year round. Not even if he or she keeps the enclosed environment warm in the winter (unless he or she finds some way to supplement the natural light those plants receive).

In *The Survival Greenhouse,* Jim DeKorne suggests that fluorescent tubes — which produce both the red and blue wavelengths beneficial to plants — can be used as artificial sources of light in a hothouse.

These energy efficient lights only need to be burned a few hours, he says, to make up the difference between the length of summer and winter days. A timing device can easily be rigged to turn the fluorescent lights on for a few minutes before sunrise and again for a brief period following the natural sunset.

SANITATION AND PLANT MANAGEMENT

No greenhouse is trouble-free, but if you want to grow crops the easiest way possible, without constantly fighting diseases and insects, remember one word — sanitation. The inside of a greenhouse is actually a "hothouse" in which disease organisms and insects can find the right temperature and humidity for rapid multiplication. The best way to control insects, bacteria, fungi and viruses is to keep them out in the first place. Once they've gotten to a plant, control is difficult.

1. Pull up and destroy diseased plants. Don't bother trying to save them; you risk spreading the disease to other plants. It's just not worth it. Don't pile them outside of the greenhouse where they can serve as a reservoir for infection. Diseased plants piled next to the greenhouse can reinfect crops inside through spores that are blown into the house through vents and windows or tracked in on your shoes.
2. Don't let weeds grow wild next to your greenhouse. Aphids, thrips, mites and flea beetles thrive on weeds and can come through ventilators or the screen door into the greenhouse.
3. Be a good greenhouse keeper. Most pests live in crops right in the house itself. Pick up bits of foliage, stems and rubbish and destroy them. Keep weeds out! Weeds such as chickweed or oxalis grow fast under the benches and are a refuge for insects.
4. Inspect plants you introduce into your greenhouse.
5. Use soil-less materials for starting seeds and rooting cuttings.
6. Fresh air circulating through your greenhouse can do a great deal to reduce disease problems.
7. Become an amateur plant doctor and check for symptoms of disease and insect troubles on your plants.

8. Don't use soil or containers in which plants have died or have gotten sick unless you pasteurize or disinfect them first.
9. In watering, avoid wetting the foliage. Water early in the day so leaves can dry in the sun.
10. Never crowd plants; they need good air circulation.
11. Hang the hose nozzle on a hook to avoid picking up disease organisms from the floor and spreading it when you water. Watch for contamination of tools, shoes, equipment.

NATURAL SOIL AMENDMENTS

Lime: Most of our eastern soils are naturally acidic (and are becoming even more so because of acid rain). Applying pulverized lime will raise the pH into the range where nutrients are available to most plants. There are two kinds of lime: calcitic and dolomitic. The latter contains both calcium and magnesium, both of which are essential for plant growth. If the soil's pH is properly adjusted and of these nutrients is deficient, gypsum ($CaSO_4$) will correct the calcium problem, and epsom salts ($MgSO_4$) will add magnesium without altering the pH.

Blood meal: Dried blood is a natural soil amendment composed of 6% to 12% nitrogen. It may contain small amounts of phosphorus. Blood meal can be applied directly to soils or be used in composting to boost the nitrogen content. Dry fish meal is another alternative and contains about 10% nitrogen.

Bonemeal: Steamed, ground bone contains phosphorus in proportions varying from 15% to 30%. It can be worked into the greenhouse soil or sprinkled on compost.

Rock phosphate: Rock phosphate contains calcium phosphate as its major ingredient, with levels varying from 28% to 32%. This material, which is ground into a powder, is insoluble and is released slowly ... even more slowly than bonemeal.

Wood ash: Burnt wood ash is an inexpensive source of potassium (3% to 7%). Mixed into the soil, it will raise the pH and provide small amounts of calcium, phosphorus, magnesium, and sulfur. I prefer to add wood ash to compost piles when the greenhouse soil's pH is ideal.

Greensand: This nutrient supplement is dredged from the ocean bottom and is rich in minerals (7% potash). Potassium in the soil will regulate the plant's water absorption and the movement of the liquid through the vascular system. Granite dust and kelp are other sources of potassium.

USE THE BEST SOIL

Never underestimate the importance of fertile soil in the greenhouse. We build our soils to provide high fertility, adequate organic matter, multiple nutrient-exchange pathways, and nutrient storage capacities. Diverse populations of bacteria, fungi, and actinomycetes digest organic material; their activity increases both soil fertility and carbon dioxide levels. Earthworms, springtails, ground beetles, and numerous soil animals excavate and aerate pockets and waterways.

More than a quarter of my indoor gardening time is spent on soil preparation or cultivation. That's understandable when you consider that greenhouse soil nutrients are tapped 12 months of the year. On the other hand, since these indoor soils are always warmer, organic matter decomposes at a faster rate.

Constructing a greenhouse garden bed requires three basic ingredients: topsoil, compost, and — depending on your region's soil types — clay. Clean topsoil should be the largest portion of your mixture. It's the basis for texture and is the best mineral source for your plants. It should contain 2% to 5% organic matter and have a slightly acid pH factor (between 6.5 and 6.8).

Compost provides many essential plant nutrients (nitrogen, phosphorus, and potassium), and it nourishes the soil's microbial population. Excess compost, however, will cause an imbalance and produce poor soil texture.

I suggest you build a compost pile while your greenhouse is under construction. When the structure is complete, the compost will be ready to work into the beds or containers. Whatever method you prefer for making the pile, let the material cook! In order to kill most pathogens and weed seeds, compost should bake at 180°F for two or three weeks. Before you mix compost into the soil, it should be screened through a 3/8"-mesh handmade cloth to eliminate any bulky material. If your topsoil has a clay base, sand will augment drainage and aeration around the plants' root zones. Use coarse, clean sand. If that isn't available, substitute perlite. If your topsoil is sandy or sandy loam, then work clay into the soil mixture.

Use the sources closest to you. Well-decomposed leaf mold, for example, can be substituted for compost or worked into the soil along with compost. The material should be black and crumbly and free from bulky debris. Be aware that undecomposed leaf litter in the soil is an invitation to scavenger pests such as thrips, leafhoppers, and pill bugs. While leaf mold is a well-balanced soil builder, it's often acidic and may need lime to sweeten it. If you are without compost or leaf mold, dehydrated cow or sheep manure is a risky third choice, but *never* use it while it's fresh. Before adding any amendments to your batch, though, send a composite soil sample to your agricultural cooperative extension service. Every state has an office to serve you, and the price for soil analysis is a modest $2.00 to $5.00. Most of the reports are easy to interpret, but the agency's recommendations for fertilization may be couched in chemical terms and may be heavy on the dosage. A private testing facility specializing in organic agriculture, Woods End Laboratory, will test your soil for nutrient levels and measure the percentage of organic matter. They'll send a *humus chromatogram,* which is a visual display of your soil's health.

If the soil is deficient in one or more nutrients, organic measures can remedy the situation. Nitrogen, phosphorus, potassium, calcium, and magnesium are taken up by the plant in larger quantities than are other elements and may be the first to become deficient. Keep in mind, however, that good soil management pays attention to *physical* as well as nutrient qualities in the soil, and that amendments will not improve soil texture or structure.

You should also practice crop rotation and *keep rotation records.* Heavy feeders — tomatoes, European cucumbers, peppers, and the like — should be replaced with legumes or root crops. Members of the cabbage family (brassicas), such as mustard, kale, broccoli, cauliflower, cabbage, and collards, should not occupy the same area more than once a year, because recropping with a brassica promotes clubroot, a disease that retards vigorous plant growth. A comprehensive textbook that can aid in understanding plant diseases is George Agrios's *Plant Pathology*(Academic Press, 1978, $23.25).

Compacted soil can be improved with the introduction of earthworms, peat moss, and leaf mold. Perlite, a volcanic material, can lighten up a nutritionally well-balanced soil.

Excess organic matter, which leads to poor soil structure, results from too much compost in the soil. In your soil-conditioning program, alternate leaf mold with compost and occasionally revitalize the topsoil. Other natural fertilizers, such as seaweed extract, fish emulsion, and manure tea, should also be used.

SPECIAL SOIL MIXES: Our sidebar on special soil mixes is a guide for producing basic potting soil. Tiny, germinating seeds need a premium mix with light texture, good water retention, and adequate drainage.

If your greenhouse has poor air circulation, consider making of buying a sterile seedling mix. Damping-off (also known as rhizoctonia, pythium seed rot, or stem rot), a devastating disease, can wipe out your best batch of seedlings. It's caused by a soilborne pathogen that attacks sprouted seeds, roots, and succulent stems. If you've ever noticed a healthy seedling suddenly flop over with a brown, withered stem at soil level, you've seen damping-off.

If your greenhouse is properly ventilated, then you could try a seedling mixture of one part compost, one part peat, one part perlite, and one part vermiculite or clean sand. Both the compost and peat moss should be screened through a 3/8" wire mesh cloth, and the soil should be thoroughly turned.

WATER: When and how much to water depends on the time of the year, the weather conditions, the type of soil, and the depth of the container or bed. For large beds or boxes, poke your finger into the soil to see if the top inch is dry; if it is, add water. Small pots and shallow beds require frequent watering, usually every day.

Most beginners tend to overwater rather than underwater, though. You should, for example, avoid watering on cloudy, rainy, or snowy days. At these times, most solar greenhouses are cool and damp, and the air and soil may be completely saturated.

Watering in the morning will allow the leaves to dry out during the day, reducing the chances that harmful fungi will grow on wet leaves. Botrytis, stem rot, and downy mildew thrive when water coats the leaf surface, and water spots are unattractive on ornamentals, so restrict the water to the soil and keep it off the leaves.

The water should be warm (ideally, 55°F) and dechlorinated. You can preheat the following day's water in your greenhouse in garbage pails or barrels. If you own a large greenhouse, you might consider a subterranean irrigation system. It saves time and puts the water where roots can find it.

Soak the soil thoroughly once — rather than administering many light watering — and use a nozzle, breaker, or rose to break up the gush of water into tiny droplets. Seed flats, in particular, need a gentle rain of clean, warm water.

Grow What You Like to Eat, Smell, or Look At

Finally, we can discuss what really counts: the green goods! Now you can appreciate how much effort is put into controlling the environmental factors to enhance the indoor garden. Before we leave physical science, though, remember that the greenhouse environment will determine which crops will thrive there. The successful gardener considers light quality and quantity, photoperiodism, heat requirements, and nutrition for*every* crop.

Planning Ahead: The next criterion for a productive greenhouse is adequate planning. Mistakes on paper are easier to correct than mistakes cast in the soil. The first year will be the most difficult, because you won't be familiar with the greenhouse's air or soil temperatures. However, with this little manual to guide you and with the listed references as a more comprehensive resource, you should be able to make intelligent guesses.

Whether your interior layout is in beds or benches, design the first season's planting with proper lighting in mind. Which areas have the brightest light, partial light, or shade? In winter, place vining or tall plants where they won't shade medium or lower-canopy ones. Two-or three-strata planting (rows placed like benches in a stadium) makes for efficient space utilization. Resist overcrowding; doing so will pay off in the long run. Cramped plants are vulnerable to diseases and may never reach full size.

Almost everything we grow in our bioshelters at New Alchemy Institute is put there as a young transplant. This practically guarantees *100%* survival. (Seed sowing and seedling development are confined to a reserved nursery area.)

After you've selected your crops, figure out how long it will take them to develop to transplant size. Then you'll know when to sow the seeds. For example, I transplant my fall crop of tomatoes in late July. Since tomato seeds germinate in three to five days and require five to six weeks to mature into hefty-size seedlings, I must sow them in mid-June.

Devise your planting schedule for a 12-month period. Account for sowing, plant development, and harvest. Select vegetables that yield for long periods. (A friend once harvested tomatoes from the same plant for 16 months!) Adjust your timetable to the climate and weather conditions in your area.

Succession Planting: Within the greenhouse's. cool and warm seasons, there's some flexibility about when you can sow your crops. Use this to your family's advantage by budgeting your planting space. For simplicity, let's say your greenhouse has three growing beds, all with similar light quality. Plant the first bed on January 1 with Burpee's Green Ice loose-leaf lettuce and Deci-Minor, a butterhead lettuce. Two weeks later, plant Grand Rapids Forcing looseleaf lettuce and a Dutch original buttercrunch, Ostinata, in the second bed. On February 1, plant the third bed with a heat-resistant loose-leaf called Oak Leaf and with All the Year Round, a slow-to-bolt English butterhead. You'll begin to reap the benefits of your labor at the end of February and continue to harvest through mid-May.

Seeds And Seedlings: Whatever crops you choose to grow, quality seeds will offer the best beginning. I often select hybrids that are bred for greenhouse culture or for disease resistance. However, many open-pollinated varieties rival these more expensive competitors. Generally speaking, most of your leafy vegetables can be ordinary garden cultivars, but you should choose specialty varieties of European cucumbers, tomatoes, cauliflower, lettuce, primula, stock, and gerbera.

When sowing seeds, *read the package!* Following the directions on such important cultural instructions as soil temperature, depth of planting, refrigeration, or light requirements can increase your crop's germination percentage. In general, lettuce, kale, Chinese greens, endive, chard, sweet peas, nasturtiums, and calendula prefer cool soils (60°-70°F).

Tomatoes, peppers, melons, European cucumbers, and most annual flowers require a warm soil (70°-80°F). Poor seed germination usually is a result of improper or inconsistent soil temperatures. A propagating mat, which provides a constant soil temperature, will speed up seed germination and reduce losses due to damping-off. Made of heating cables sandwiched between vinyl coatings and regulated by a thermostat, it's a costly investment (about $110), but it's truly worth every cent. (A simpler method of providing constant bottom heat is to rest the seeded trays or packs on top of your refrigerator.)

A few vegetable favorites for cool greenhouses are described brief ly below. Southern growers, however, may have a wide; selection to choose from and more flexibility in planting times. Lettuce, both loose-leaf and butterhead varieties, can be grown indoors from August through May, but true iceberg lettuce is strictly an outdoor crop. Lettuce varieties that have been bred for forced culture perform the best in winter months. Around the winter solstice, growth rate may be slow (regardless of variety), especially if soil temperatures drop below 55°F. The plants need proper spacing to reduce any problems with botrytis. The red-tipped varieties such as Merveille des Quatre Saisons, Ruby, and Prizehead will put color pizzazz in your salad.

Endive is a calcium-rich green that's related to chicory. Its flavor is bitter, compared with mild lettuce, so — two weeks before harvest — blanch the lower section to sweeten its taste. Endive often bolts by early February and should be used as a fall and winter green.

Pak choi (bok choy)is a favorite Chinese vegetable whose name means "flowering white cabbage." Its succulent white stem and dark foliage are relatively hairless, compared with those of other Oriental brassicas. The time from seed to harvest can be as short as 60 days. It, too, will bolt in late winter. The tiny flowerets are entirely edible. Pinch off the terminal bud to encourage bushy growth.

Chinese cabbage is the term for dozens of different varieties, which are divided into two categories: loose-heading and heading. Many are hairy plants that are best for stir-frying. The pale green, tender, blockish types are more productive but less conducive to leaf-by-leaf harvesting. In winter, this vegetable is three times as productive as lettuce. Some varieties stand 20" tall.

Swiss chard can be grown indoors year-round. Chard is a hardy green that can withstand much abuse. Dig it up from the garden in late autumn, then replant it in your greenhouse. Both the root and leaves are edible. Tender, immature beets (cousins of Swiss chard) can be brought in from the outdoor garden, too. Both are susceptible to damage from thrips.

Kale and collards are two leafy members of the cabbage family that do best as fall or winter crops. Kale can grow to two or three feet in height, but collard buds should be pinched off at the top of the plant. This pruning initiates lateral growth that creates a bushy plant. Both kale and collards are vulnerable to aphid infestation.

Summer turnips — sharp, mustardlike greens with white globe-shaped roots — can be sown directly into the soil or planted as young seedlings. They can be grown under low light conditions, unlike radishes, which require brighter light and a longer day. Tokyo Cross Hybrid, a wintertime favorite, takes only 45 days from seed to harvest.

Celery thrives in rich, sandy-loam soil. Like its cousin parsley, celery may take three weeks or longer to germinate and another six weeks for the vegetable to reach transplant size. Space the plants 10" apart with 1' between each row. One month before harvest, blanch the bottom part of the stems by mounding soil around the bases of the plants, or block out the light there with boards. Celery guzzles both water and nitrogen. Watch out for aphids. For an extended harvest, pick only the outside stems at first. From late winter on, the year races with endless greenhouse activity. Home gardeners start bedding plants for outdoors and for *indoor* spring crops of cauliflower, tomatoes, and cucumbers.

In the warm season, the use of vining or trellised crops will maximize the growing area. Keep tomatoes, European cucumbers, melons, and pole beans to manageable heights (usually no more than 6' tall). Pruning extra growth every week encourages higher productivity, better air circulation, and prettier shapes. The fruiting vegetables require plenty of water (particularly on sunny days) and a steady diet of all the essential plant nutrients. Monthly side-dressings of sifted compost protect exposed roots and replenish easily leached nutrients such as nitrogen, potassium, and sulfur.

The following notes on tomato, cucumber, melon, and pepper culture are only tips, but you can find a wealth of written information on growing such crops under glass. If you've decided to grow flowers, you'll be glad to know there's even more information available. The newly revised *Organic Gardening Under Glass* is devoted primarily to ornamental horticulture.

Tomatoes, the favorite greenhouse crop, can be grown to extend your summer harvest into fall or spring. Plant them when soil temperatures reach at least 55°F. Air temperatures should approximate 75°F during the day and 65°F at night. Select*indeterminate* tomato varieties, and have your trellis or poles ready when you set out the crop. If you suspect you already have a whitefly problem in your greenhouse, set up sticky yellow traps to lure the adult insects away from the crops. If you're using containers, provide each plant with a five-gallon pot. Tomatoes require plenty of phosphorus and potassium in order to flower and set fruit. Fertilize or top-dress each plant with compost every two weeks. At midday, gently shake each plant to encourage better pollination and more fruit, and prune off the vegetative growth called suckers. Sweet 100 and Park's Whopper VFNT perform well in solar greenhouses.

Peppers can provide an excellent late-summer crop. Sow the seeds in May, and grow them outdoors in one-gallon pots until August. In the afternoon, transplant the peppers into a bed or into a larger container. Watering with a seaweed solution helps revitalize the crop after transplant shock. Peppers prefer a well-balanced soil, proper spacing (18" apart, 18" between rows), and bright or partial light. Green bell, banana yellow, jalapeno, and sweet and hot cherry peppers can all be grown indoors. Peppers are highly susceptible to aphid infestation.

European cucumbers, "burpless" and thin-skinned, are long (14"-15") and weigh more than a pound each. They're a vining crop that doesn't require pollination to fruit. (Nearly all of the flowers are female.) The seeds are expensive ($7.00 to $8.00 for 25 seeds), so you may want to split a package with a neighbor. However, when stored under the right conditions, the seeds are viable for two or more years. What's more, one plant can easily yield 35 pounds of cucumbers! This crop requires high levels of nitrogen and frequent irrigation. (The Stokes Seed Company provides detailed cultural instructions with its seeds.) Powdery mildew and bacterial wilt are common diseases. Cucumbers also attract whiteflies, spider mites, and thrips.

Melons, a popular crop for northern growers, must have soil temperatures of 60°F and up. They can be trellised if the fruit is supported with netting (or retired panty hose) tied to the trellis with wire or cord. Higher yields are obtained by artificial pollination. (At midday, take a camel-hair, thin-tipped paintbrush, insert it into a male flower, and then transfer the yellow pollen onto a female flower.) Ambrosia Hybrid and Charantais produce four- to eight-pound, salmon-fleshed cantaloupes.

5

Greenhouse Operations and Practices

INTRODUCTION

Perhaps there is no greater joy than owning a hobby greenhouse and entering a warm, dry room filled with green plants when there may be frost, wind, or rain outdoors. For many people, tending to a greenhouse is like entering a relaxing, private world, isolated from workaday worries as well as the weather. A greenhouse can be an absorbing hobby with the satisfaction of growing fragrant flowering plants, foliage plants, ingredients for fresh-picked salads in winter, transplants for the spring garden, or bouquets of cut flowers.

Do not be fooled, however, into believing that a hobby greenhouse does not involve some work. Constant attention is required at most times of the year. This often means every day during the summer unless automatic watering and ventilation systems are installed. During the year, there are always jobs to be done. But none of these chores have to be strenuous or tedious if tasks and the materials needed to accomplish them are arranged intelligently. The purpose of this publication is to provide information about tasks that should be done to have a well-run, efficient hobby greenhouse, one that is satisfying for the owner and a joy for the entire family. Information on hobby greenhouse construction and environmental maintenance equipment can be found in Extension publication ANR-1105, “Hobby Greenhouse Construction.”

GREENHOUSE OPERATIONS

A part of Missouri Botanical Garden that the public rarely sees is the greenhouse complex, which includes a whole acre under glass!

A series of 18 greenhouses are connected to a large central hallway called the Head House. This is where much of the hard work takes place. Staff and volunteers busily propagate new plants from seeds or cuttings, and pot and transplant other plants at workstations designed specifically for these tasks. But the work doesn't end in the Head House. Each greenhouse has routine maintenance tasks, which include watering, fertilizing, pest control, repotting, pruning, and even weeding the gravel floors in some greenhouses.

The plants in each greenhouse have different environmental needs. Temperatures, humidity levels, and light levels vary greatly from greenhouse to greenhouse. Even the soil and fertilizer used may be very different.

Three of the greenhouses are devoted solely to the Garden's extensive orchid collection. Orchids are divided into a cool house, an intermediate temperature house, and a warm house. The annual Holiday Show and the annual Orchid Show make use of the foliage plants found in three additional greenhouses. The plants range in size from knee high to tree-sized and include tropical foliage, peace lilies, ficus trees, palms, and philodendrons. Former residents of the old Desert House in this area include tree aloe, tree opuntia, bird of paradise, and a giant ponytail palm.

The Horticulture division works closely with the Research division in caring for the plants in three more greenhouses. One contains a wide variety of plants collected by researchers. The other two contain all tropical plants, including many aroids.

Representing the opposite extreme in humidity, the desert greenhouse is the temporary home of many unusual and rare varieties of cacti and succulents from around the world. The former Desert House, which was located on the south side of the Climatron , was demolished in 1994.

Built in 1913, it was no longer safe for visitors. This wonderful collection of cacti and succulents cannot be on public display until the Garden receives a generous donation to fund the construction of a new Desert House similar to the Temperate House currently on the north side of the Climatron.

In the stock house, cuttings are taken for spring and summer bedding plants used on the grounds.

The aquatic nursery occupies half of a greenhouse. Water lilies and other aquatic plants housed here bloom magnificently in summer throughout the Garden's water features. The other half is devoted to newly propagated plants. A smaller greenhouse is used as a shade house in the summer.

Four production greenhouses are dedicated to spring and summer bedding plants and flowering Holiday Show plants, including more than 2000 poinsettias, the first of which arrives in July as a rooted cutting! Heated floors are used in two of these greenhouses to encourage root growth in early spring plants, while the foliage above ground is acclimated to temperatures as low as 40 degrees.

The public is invited to take a tour of the greenhouses on a specific day in spring, usually on Earth Day. The tour is at a specific time and has limited openings.

GREENHOUSE GARDENING – GREENHOUSE OPERATIONS

We're rounding the bases and heading for home plate with this five part series designed to help you decide whether a greenhouse is right for your gardening interests. If the complexities of a needs analysis, the many choices of design and materials, and the selection of features and accessories haven't scared you off yet, then this piece on greenhouse operations shouldn't be all that intimidating. After all, this is where you get to put the gardening structure into use and reap the benefit of your investment.

Let's look at the basics of greenhouse operation, keeping in mind that specific plants may require special care beyond the basics. Also, keep in mind that your climate and weather conditions will dictate to some extent how you operate your greenhouse. Factors like sunlight, humidity, wind and soil can influence things like venting, watering and air circulation.

VENTING HEAT AND HUMIDITY

The number one task of greenhouse operations is maintaining an environment that is conducive to plant growth. That means warm, but not excessive heat, and minimizing humidity unless your specific plant variety calls for high humidity. High heat will significantly shorten the life of your greenhouse film. High humidity tends to encourage pests and disease.

If you're using manual ventilation methods, this will be a morning and evening chore. If you're using automatic devices, then you'll need to set the controls to open vents as the heat starts to reach what you'd consider an optimum temperature. Structures oriented to capture the prevailing breezes will have an easier time getting rid of excessive heat and humidity.

Taking care not to over water your plants will help reduce excess humidity. Moisture in the soil will tend to evaporate during the day, and if it's not vented out, it will linger and promote pests and disease.

Watering

To be sure, you will need to water your plants. There are several ways to water plants in a greenhouse. Oddly enough, some greenhouse gardeners prefer to water by hand, that is, with a watering can. The idea here is that the amount of water can be carefully regulated as well as placed. This is important if you're growing a wide variety of plants that have varying needs for water.

An alternative to hand watering with a watering can is to water with a hose. This can be messy as it tends to create splashing or spraying that in many cases is unwanted. Nevertheless, if you're growing plants on racks or tables, instead of in the soil, this is a good alternative. For plants grown in the soil, there are better approaches.

One helpful means of watering is to use a drip system. One common type of drip systems employs individual emitters along a line. Depending on the emitter used, the gardener can vary the amount of water that is emitted over a given length of time. Other systems use tubing with small holes that serve as an alternative to drippers.

Individual emitters are great for targeting specific plants, and they are a good choice for planting beds and permaculture in the greenhouse where the location of plants doesn't change. Although the drip system can be reconfigured, this isn't a chore that anyone would look forward to at the start of each planting season.

Drip tubing emits water every twelve inches or so along the length of the tubing. This type of drip setup is best for watering a larger bed of plants where the drip tubing can be laid in a snake-like pattern to distribute water throughout the bed. This type of dripping technique is especially useful for vegetable row crops like peppers, beans and kohlrabi, where individual plants are spaced about the same distance apart as are the outlets in the tubing.

Whether using drip emitters or drip tubing, it's best to find a way to run the supply line so it's off to the side or overhead. This will keep unnecessary lines out of the growing area. If you place the supply line overhead, it will promote draining clear and that will avoid freeze damage during times of the year when freezing is a possibility.

Air Circulation

Air circulation inside the greenhouse is essential to minimize pests and diseases. With smaller greenhouses this isn't as much of a concern since open windows, doors and vents can provide good circulation when there is a breeze outside. For large greenhouses, natural air circulation is a bit more challenging – much like trying to get air to circulate throughout your house. The use of large fans and air handling devices can help promote good air movement.

A supplement to forced air circulation can be had by orienting the greenhouse such that prevailing winds will naturally enter windows, doors and vents to provide air flow through or across the greenhouse. It should be noted that both flowers and vegetables benefit from air movement sufficient to cause plants to move. Such movement supports strong growth, blossoms and pollination.

Dealing with Animals

Even though a greenhouse is a relatively closed and controlled environment, occasionally the gardener will have trouble with critters. For greenhouses where plants are growing in the soil at grade level, burrowing animals can be especially troublesome. Ground squirrels and rabbits come to mind as animals that seem to delight in making a burrow right where you would like to grow your tomatoes, collards or zinnias. The only practical solution is to make certain the greenhouse is sufficiently buttoned up to minimize the potential for these animals to enter. Another creature that presents problems for the greenhouse gardener is the common field mouse. Mice are plentiful and always looking for a comfortable place to call home. What better place than a warm and sheltered gardening structure during cold and foul weather? Not only is there an ample supply of water, but many of the fruits, vegetables and plants growing inside can provide a nice meal. And, if there are no mature plants to nibble on, there is nothing better than finding a stash of seeds, or a flat or two of young seedlings. Mice are particularly destructive to young seedlings.

In addition to sealing up the cracks and crevices of your greenhouse, you'll need to take some steps to eradicate mice. There are repeating mousetraps on the market, and several designs for homemade versions of the same. The traditional snap type mousetraps is also highly effective. It's likely that your greenhouse troubles are only caused by a handful of mice so after you catch five or six of them, you'll likely find your troubles are nearly over.

Starting Seedlings

Seedlings are quite often started indoors. That's a nice protected location, but it can lead to a mess where you don't want it. With a little effort, even a hobby greenhouse gardener can use their unheated greenhouse as a place for starting seedlings. This is my preferred method because it keeps the mess outside, minimizes transporting seedlings, and presents seedlings to bright sunlight which is essential for good growth. If you're tired of leggy seedlings that enjoy the grow lights, but still stretch towards the window for better natural light, then use your greenhouse as a place to start seeds – it's outside where they're going to live anyway.

To start seeds effectively, you'll need at least a seedling heat mat and an enclosure that acts as a greenhouse within a greenhouse. One approach to achieving this is to use a cold frame inside the greenhouse. You can also use a clear curtain of greenhouse film to seal off a small area dedicated to seedlings. Such an approach allows you to use a small thermostatically controlled electric heater to warm up the area surrounding your flats of seedlings.

For table top seedling starts, one could even do something as simple as using a clear covering over the table that holds your seedlings (under their own clear cover). This simple cover could make use of a frame to hold it away from your seedling trays, or it could simply be draped over the top of your seedling tray covers.

Just make certain that you monitor your seedlings frequently because a covered seedling tray will accumulate excessive moisture quickly. Also, remember that a clear covered seedling tray, inside of a clear covered enclosure, inside the greenhouse can multiply the effects of the sun – even in the dead of winter – and this can kill seedlings quickly if they're left unmonitored during the day. Also, you might need to cover the whole operation at night with an old comforter or other such insulating blanket. This will help capture warmth from the seedling heat mat, and minimize temperature swings experienced by the seedlings.

Pots, Raised Beds or Soil

There are three approaches to growing plants in a greenhouse: planting in pots; using fixed raised beds; and, planting in the soil at grade level. The choice is largely dependent upon your intended use of the greenhouse. Let me highlight the reasons why one might choose one or more of these methods for their greenhouse operation.

Pots are a good choice if you're going to sell individual plants. Having them in a pot makes them easy to load up for sale at a marketplace. Pots are also a good choice if your greenhouse is something more akin to a living space, as you'll likely want to rearrange things every now and then. Pots are also a good choice if you expect to transplant seedlings to another place within the greenhouse, to a traditional outdoor garden space, or to a place within your home.

Raised beds are an excellent way to multiply the warming effect of the sun on the soil. This allows you to get a head start on the growing season. They also provide a large amount of thermal mass above ground and this helps keep the interior of the greenhouse warmer during the night. Raised beds also clearly define the growing space, and they can make gardening a little less back-breaking as well. One of the drawbacks of a raised bed is that it cools rather quickly at night and during a cooler day, so they're not the best choice for overwintering various plants.

Planting directly in the soil of the greenhouse is perhaps a more traditional approach, but it provides a number of benefits. First, planting directly in the soil allows the gardener complete freedom in terms of configuration. Second, it allows for easy large scale rototilling and amending of the soil. Third, plants at grade level make best use of the natural soil warmth, so this is a good choice for bringing cold hardy varieties into the winter months.

Occasional and Winter Season Operations

My last suggestions with respect to greenhouse operations involve occasional use, and winter season greenhouse gardening.

As an example of an occasional operation, think of a very small greenhouse dedicated to sprouting and caring for seedlings. It could be a sort of "incubation station" that feeds the main open sun garden beds used during the summer. This could be the best possible use of a very small greenhouse simply because it gathers lots of light, it can fit just about anywhere, it's easy to keep warm with a small portable heater, and the structure doesn't allow sufficient room for much else. Some that I've seen allow you to walk in a few feet and turn around – a one person operation at best. If you have a very small greenhouse, this might be the best use of that "sun space."

A large greenhouse, with or without a source of heat could be put to use as a protected gardening area during the winter, especially if you enjoy vegetable gardening. If you have a source of heat or a good way of capturing solar energy, you might think about this aspect of greenhouse operations – a year round vegetable garden. Even if you don't have heat generation or collection resources in abundance, off-season gardening is still possible if you grow cold hardy cultivars and get them started during the regular growing season so they're freshly matured plants as winter arrives.

With winter season greenhouse gardening, you won't be digging carrots out from under the snow; you'll simply lift off row covers or open the cold frames inside your greenhouse and harvest your crops. The best part of winter season greenhouse gardening is that it makes good use of your greenhouse as a year round asset, not simply a part-time season extender. Anytime you can get more use out of an asset you have, you're increasing its value. That makes it a much more cost-effective asset right from the start.

DEALING WITH THE HIGH COST OF ENERGY FOR GREENHOUSE OPERATIONS

Increased fuel costs and colder than normal winters make heating costs a significant burden on many greenhouse operations. So, how can growers deal with high energy costs in the greenhouse? The problem can be addressed in several different ways. Growers can conserve energy in the greenhouse, evaluate alternative or additional fuel sources or heating systems, evaluate growing temperatures and other production practices, consolidate operations into less space, critically evaluate when to bring the next greenhouse into production, and streamline operations.

Regardless of what a grower does to reduce his energy use, he still has to examine how to pay for increased costs related to higher fuel prices. Growers have suffered increases in the prices of pots and plastic as well as peat, pesticides and fertilizers over the last few of years. In addition to the increased direct costs of heating, growers will be faced with higher transportation costs as well - not just for the products they are delivering - but also for those they receive. So, in addition to reducing costs in the greenhouse, how can growers adjust their production and pricing to remain profitable?

CONSERVING ENERGY IN GREENHOUSES

The Greenhouse Structure

The first line of defense in efficient heating of a greenhouse is the structure itself. Losses vary depending on the greenhouse covering and the age of the structure. In general, newer structures will have better seals around the coverings and openings than older houses.

Double poly - Double polyethylene (poly) coverings reduce heating costs about 50% compared to single poly coverings. Most greenhouses in Virginia that are used for winter production are inflated double poly houses. Different polyethylene films vary from 35% to 60% heat loss. Ask your supplier about the film's thermal value. Selecting films that reduce water condensation will enhance light transmission and improve heat retention. Maintaining proper inflation between double poly layers is critical to maximizing the insulation value of the covering.

Retrofitting - A glass greenhouse can be covered with one or, preferably, a double, inflated layer of poly for extra insulation during the winter. A single layer of film over glass can reduce annual heating costs by 5% to 40% whereas a double (inflated) layer can reduce costs 40% to 60%. Remember that there is a tradeoff between increased energy efficiency and reduced light transmission with additional layers of poly.

Winterize openings - A tight greenhouse with few air leaks around vents, fans or doors will cost less to heat. Repair any holes in the plastic, glass or doors. Keep doors closed and caulk or weatherstrip door frames and other openings.

Maximize the Insulation

Endwalls - Insulate the endwalls of the greenhouse, especially the north endwall. In most parts of Virginia, the north endwall provides very little light for crop production. This wall can actually be constructed of a solid material like wood. Plywood (1/2-inch thick) will lose about the same amount of heat as a double poly wall. At least, insulate this wall for winter production. Reflective (foil backed) insulation boards provide better insulation than other rigid foam boards. Place them with the reflective side facing into the greenhouse. If possible, add windbreaks outside the greenhouse along the north wall. These may be conifers planted for screening or a temporary fence material to divert the wind over the greenhouse. The south endwall can be insulated with an extra layer of plastic.

Foundations on new construction - On new construction, foundation heat loss can be reduced by half through the installation of 1 to 2 inches of polyurethane or polystyrene insulation. This insulation should be installed 1.5 to 2 feet deep around the foundation wall with care given not to leave gaps or openings. This is especially important when installing any type of floor heating system.

Existing foundation and side walls - If the foundation of the greenhouse was not insulated during construction, make sure that all gaps or holes below the foundation board are filled or repaired. If the greenhouse has a concrete kneewall, insulating the inside of it with insulation board can significantly reduce heat loss. Reflective insulation boards can be added to the inside of any flat greenhouse wall but should not extend above the crop or bench height. Leave a small airspace between the insulation and the sidewall to prevent freezing of the greenhouse wall. Be sure that the reflective surfaces are not in contact with perimeter heating pipes. Sidewall insulation can reduce annual heating costs 5% to 10%.

Fans and vents - To reduce other air leaks, insulate secondary fans and vents to reduce heat loss through unused areas during the winter. Do not cover all of the vents; remember that winter ventilation is required for humidity control and to restore the oxygen/carbon dioxide balance in the greenhouse. Keep these vents in good working condition so that they close tightly when not in use.

Add a Thermal Blanket

Up to 85% of the heat loss from a greenhouse occurs at night. Using a thermal blanket to retain heat at night can be a cost efficient investment. These blankets are easier to install and create less shading in gutter-connected houses than in a quonset house. Remember to use a porous curtain material so that condensation from the underside of the roof of the greenhouse will not pool above the plants. Use a flame-resistant material or, for growing structures, a thermal blanket that alternates flame-resistant and non-flame-resistant material. For greenhouse structures where an internal curtain cannot be installed, external curtains are available that can reduce radiation loss from the greenhouse at night.

Reductions in heat loss - Blankets offered primarily for heat retention can reduce energy use by up to 50%, whereas blankets offered as combination thermal blanket and summer shade protection can reduce winter energy use

25% or more. Recouping installation costs - With purchase and installation costs running \$2.00 to \$2.50 per square foot, these systems pay for themselves in one to two years- or less under high fuel prices.

Installation details - Make sure that the blanket fits the greenhouse walls tightly to reduce heat loss above the blanket. Heating or water lines should be located below the blanket or be well insulated to reduce heat loss.

Open slowly - Take care not to open the blankets too quickly over a chill-sensitive crop. On 10°F to 20°F nights, the temperature above the thermal blanket could be 30°F in a 60°F greenhouse. Open the blanket 6 to 12 inches for about 30 minutes to allow mixing of the air before opening it completely. Some growers wait until the sun has risen and warmed the air above the blanket before opening it and allowing that air to mix with the rest of the greenhouse air. That may be dictated by the light requirements of the crop.

Keep it open during snowstorms - In the case of snow storms, the blanket should be left open to allow the heat to reach the roof to prevent snow accumulation on the roof of the greenhouse.

Heating System Efficiency

Maintaining maximum heating efficiency of the existing heating system is critical to reducing heating costs in the greenhouse.

Annual maintenance - Examine the equipment for physical damage to any parts of the system. Check the vent pipe and air inlet or discharge pipes for obstructions (i.e., bird nests).

Furnaces should be cleaned and adjusted at least once per year. Check that the boiler, burner and backup systems are operating in peak efficiency. Clean the soot from inside the furnace. A 1/8-inch layer of soot can increase fuel consumption by as much as 10%.

Fuel choice - Use the proper fuel for the system for maximum efficiency.

Insulation - Insulate boiler or distribution pipes in areas where heat is not needed.

External air for combustion - Install an air inlet pipe for direct fired heaters to provide fresh air for combustion from outside the greenhouse.

Clean radiation surfaces - Clean heating pipes or other heat radiation surfaces frequently.

Motors and pumps - Keep all motors and pumps properly maintained for maximum efficiency.

WARNING: Do not inhibit the fresh air supply to the greenhouse heater. If you are using a heater that requires greenhouse air for combustion, be sure to leave about 1 square inch of opening for each 2,000 Btu/hr of heater output. If possible add an inlet pipe from outside air to serve the burner.

Add Horizontal Air Flow (HAF) Fans

Reducing air leaks and heat loss in the greenhouse will make the house "tighter" which will also tend to increase the relative humidity. Regardless of the type of heating system used, install a sufficient number of horizontal air flow (HAF) fans to adequately circulate the air inside the greenhouse. Good air circulation will improve temperature and humidity uniformity in the greenhouse, which reduces the incidence of cold pockets in the greenhouse and improves plant quality and uniformity. Monitor the humidity level in the house, generally keeping it below 80% to minimize disease incidence, and vent when necessary.

Air speed - Air circulation by the HAF fans should be maintained at 2 to 3 cubic feet per minute over the floor surface of the greenhouse. For example, a 28-foot x 96-foot greenhouse requires an airflow of 5,376 cubic feet per minute (28 x 96 x 2 cubic feet per min per square foot = 5,376 cubic feet per minute). This greenhouse would require four HAF fans capable of moving air at 1,440 cubic feet per minute. This could be provided by four 16-inch fans with 1/15-

horsepower motors at 1,600 revolutions per minute. Horizontal air flow fans are generally available in two air flow capacities, but check the fan specifications to determine that they meet the calculated needs.

Fan location - The HAF fans should be located 2 to 3 feet above the plants and aligned parallel to the sidewalls of the greenhouse so that the air is circulated around the house in a rotational pattern.

Winter operation - The HAF fans should be run continuously during the winter to improve temperature and humidity uniformity in the greenhouse.

Environmental Control

Use aspirated thermostats - Thermostats should be aspirated with greenhouse air and be placed near the plant canopy in locations representative of the rest of the greenhouse (not near sidewalls, fans, or doors). Aspirated thermostats save 2% to 3% of the total fuel bill by improving fan and heater operation.

Electronic thermostats - Switching to solid-state electronic thermostats can also improve efficiency by reducing the differential between the on and off modes, usually down to 1°F instead of the 3°F to 4°F of mechanical thermostats.

Calibrate sensors - Calibrate the sensors regularly to maintain proper environmental temperatures. If you are lowering greenhouse growing temperatures, sensors must be accurate to avoid chilling damage to the crop.

WHAT ABOUT OTHER FUEL SOURCES AND HEATING SYSTEMS?

Most Virginia growers use unit heaters in individual greenhouses, most often fueled by liquid propane (LP) gas. Conversion to alternate fuel sources is not a ready option; therefore, compare the costs from different fuel providers in your area and choose the best deal available. Maximize greenhouse efficiency in terms of space utilization and energy conservation practices. Consider upgrading the combustion equipment in existing unit heaters. The increased efficiency may pay for itself.

Alternative Fuels

With significant increases in the per unit cost of natural and LP gases, many growers evaluated alternative fuel sources. Some growers who had previously "upgraded" to natural or LP gas furnaces still had working oil, wood or coal-fired furnaces or boilers connected to their greenhouses, and switched back to those fuel sources.

Compare unit costs of fuels - When considering switching to alternative fuels, remember to compare apples to apples. In other words, look at all fuel sources on a cost per heating equivalent, e.g., dollars per million Btu's ($/MBtu). A comparison of the costs of different fuels based on $/MBtu which were calculated using the heat value and efficiency rating stated under the "assumptions." To use this chart, draw a vertical line through the price of the fuel being considered to the Heating Equivalent Cost line. This line shows the price per MBtu. For example, if the cost of LP gas is $1.30/gal, the unit cost for a 70% efficiency furnace is $21.84/MBtu.

Consider dependability of the fuel source - In evaluating alternative fuels, also consider the dependability of the source of the fuel. Make sure that sufficient quantities of an acceptable quality fuel will be available when needed.

Conversion and operation costs - In addition to actual fuel costs, calculate the cost of converting to the new heating system and the labor involved in operating the new system. Remember that coal and wood-fired boilers or furnaces require additional labor investments and you will also need a means of disposing of the ashes.

Alternative Heating Systems

Many growers also considered changing the primary heating system. Alternatively, growers should evaluate the efficiencies of different heating systems (Table 1) and consider using combinations of different types of heating systems for the greenhouse. Evaluate the newer, more energy efficient heating systems to determine the "pay-back" period for individual operations. It may be worth the investment.

Table : Estimated efficiencies of several greenhouse heating systems.

Heating system	**Estimated efficiency**
Warm insulated floor	90%
Warm uninsulated floor	80%
Hot water pipes near floor	85%
Steam pipes near floor	80%
Hot air heaters	60%

Zone for higher temperatures - Consider adding higher efficiency bench or floor heating systems in root zones of areas that require higher temperatures, such as propagation or seedling and plug production areas. These systems consist primarily of electric cable or mat systems for small scale implementation. For larger areas, hot water piping, on or under benches or in the floor, provides excellent growing conditions for roots while reducing air temperatures. In general, less than optimum temperatures have a greater effect on plant roots than on plant shoots.

Hot water boilers - Modular, low-mass, hot water boilers that are very energy efficient are now available for individual greenhouse heating. They heat smaller amounts of water combined with the more efficient heat delivery capacity of aluminum pipes, fins, and plastic tubing. Hot water heat provides more gentle, uniform heat than hot air heaters. In addition, they are very flexible by allowing the grower to zone the heat for different locations or purposes within the greenhouse.

Hot water unit heaters - Hot water, forced-air, unit heaters also are available. Improvements in efficiency in heat exchangers and low volume tubing have increased the efficiency of these units as well.

Infrared radiant systems - Infrared radiant heat systems are available that provide warming of plants, people and surfaces without heating the air. These heating systems are very economical with reports of up to 30% fuel cost savings over forced-air unit heaters. Some Virginia growers reported paying for the system in energy savings in less than two winter heating seasons.

CHANGING GROWING PRACTICES

It is logical that reducing the greenhouse temperature, especially at night, would reduce heating costs. In fact, reducing the night temperature by just 1°F can reduce a greenhouse heating bill by 2% to 3%. So, how low can we go? Greenhouse temperatures affect plant growth and flowering. In particular, they affect the time required to finish the crop. Be aware that some plants are more sensitive to lower temperatures and may cease to grow when a base temperature is met. This base temperature is lower for cool-season crops than for warm-season crops. In addition, growth is more strongly affected as the temperature approaches that base temperature.

Also, be aware that lowering the greenhouse temperatures can cause additional disease problems. You may want to run plants at optimum temperatures until the roots reach the edges of pots. Then lower the temperatures and run the plants drier to prevent root rot. Avoid overcrowding and provide horizontal air movement to ensure uniform temperatures and dry foliage. Use temperate irrigation water in the morning so the medium warms up faster and there is better nutrient uptake.

Impact of temperature on crop finish time - Table 2 shows the estimated delay in finishing bedding plants when the nighttime temperature is reduced from a normal air temperature of 68°F or 63°F. To use this table, determine the normal air temperature, 68°F or 63°F, of the greenhouse. Then, estimate the base temperature of the crop in question. The 41°F base temperature is for the more cold-tolerant, warm-season crops. Check previous records for the normal production time for the crop and determine how many days would be added by growing the crop at the lower night temperature.

Temperature reduction example - A grower normally grows his vinca (a warm-season crop, base temperature 40°F) at 68°F and finishes that crop in 12 weeks (84 days). This year he wants to grow the crop at 64°F, so he can expect to take an additional 13 days (15% of 84 days) to finish that crop, for a total of 13.8 weeks. Table 2 provides a guideline for scheduling bedding plant crops under lower energy inputs, but be aware that other factors like light level, specific crops and other environmental conditions will affect crop scheduling as well.

Utilize space wisely - Plan the spring production schedule carefully. Maximize the use of heated greenhouse space. Don't bring the next greenhouse on-line until absolutely necessary.

Group plants - Group plants according to temperature tolerances so that some houses are run cooler than others. Plan for maximum efficiency.

HAF fans - Keep the HAF fans running constantly to keep air temperatures uniform and reduce the incidences of cold pockets in the greenhouse.

RECOVERING THE COSTS

Increased fuel costs - Whereas fuel costs normally account for about 7% to 10% of the costs of production, in the 2000-2001 heating season that cost was close to 20% to 25% of the total. Most greenhouse grower profit margins are less than 10%. So how can growers recover the "loss" of this much money? First, growers must recognize that in order to stay in business, they must recover at least some of these costs. Very few growers are financially able to absorb these costs and remain in operation. This industry is traditionally one of the last to raise prices or add surcharges to their products, but it is an option.

Increased input costs - As fuel costs increase, the costs of pots, plastics, chemicals, fertilizers and media components also increase. Availability issues of some fertilizer sources also contributes to increased input costs.

Costs of production - Growers must know their costs of production. Put pencil to paper and calculate all of the costs. Develop a budget for the greenhouse operation and specific seasonal crops that will allow determination of the likelihood of making a profit and allow determination of the breakeven points. This will allow the grower to determine the relationship between the minimum volume sold and the minimum selling price per flat.

Prepare an enterprise budget - Dr. Forrest Stegelin (Extension Agricultural Economist, University of Georgia) prepared an enterprise budget for bedding plants. Based on that budget, he calculated the expected results of changes in different factors of production. For example, a 1% increase in the utility rate for heating with natural gas decreased profit by 2%. However, a 1% increase in the selling price of a flat of bedding plants will increase profit by 16%; or, a 10% increase in the selling price of a flat will increase profit by 160%. In addition, a 1% increase in the percentage of the crop sold as marketable, e.g., reducing your waste from 10% to 9%, results in a 25% increase in profit. To summarize, growers can have significant impacts on their profits by managing production to maximize marketability and by making modest increases in the selling price.

Add fuel surcharges - In many cases, growers are not comfortable adding a price increase sufficient to recover significant increases in fuel costs. In other cases, prices were set for many customers prior to the fuel crisis and growers wanted to honor those commitments. Therefore, many growers across the country added fuel surcharges to their product prices. After doing the cost of production calculations, several growers found that adding a fuel surcharge to everything they sold during the spring would reverse their losses and restore a profit. They passed the fuel charges on to their customers, who in turn passed it on to the consumer. Economists tell us that most consumers do not remember what they paid for plants last year and are not likely to notice a 50¢ increase per pot. Growers must determine their costs and plan how to recover excessive costs due to high energy costs so that they can afford to stay in business.

Recover delivery costs - Also consider delivery of greenhouse products. Most industries charge for the delivery of their products. On the whole, the greenhouse industry provides this as a free service. How long can growers afford that? Strongly consider adding delivery charges, or at least fuel surcharges, to delivery services.

Table : Estimated delay in crop finishing time for bedding plants grown under reduced nighttime air temperatures.

Crop base temperature	Cooler air temperature	Approximate delay in crop timing
Normal air temperature of 68° F		
36° F (cool-season crops)	64° F	11%
	61° F	13%
41° F	64° F	13%
	61° F	15%
45° F (warm-season crops)	64° F	15%
	61° F	18%
Normal air temperature of 63° F		
36° F (cool-season crops)	59° F	13%
	55° F	15%
41° F	59° F	17%
	55° F	20%
45° F (warm-season crops)	59° F	20%
	55° F	25%

THE PLANT ENVIRONMENT

Even though a greenhouse is an enclosed space, it is not isolated from the outside environment. Conditions within the greenhouse are constantly changing. Learn not only to see but also to feel changing conditions. Watch weather forecasts so that preemptive steps can be taken to compensate for changing outside conditions. Day length, light intensity, temperature, humidity, and precipitation frequency change hour to hour, day to day, and season to season. Greenhouse owners should be able to recognize these changes and alter environmental control equipment to keep the greenhouse environment optimum for plant growth.

Variations also exist within a greenhouse. Look and feel for patterns of light or shadow, low or high humidity, and stagnant or moving air. These patterns create microclimate differences from the greenhouse center to the walls. Take advantage of microclimate differences by placing plants in areas within the greenhouse suitable for their growth.

LIGHT

During the day, leaves of plants use the energy from sunlight combined with carbon dioxide from the air and water from the soil to manufacture sugar and oxygen in a process called photosynthesis. At night, plants burn sugar produced during the day and release the energy for maintenance and growth in a process called respiration. Photosynthesis and respiration can be viewed as opposing processes, one capturing energy, the other using it. Plants must receive enough light during the day not only to meet the needs of maintenance but also to have enough left over for growth.

Every plant species has its own requirement for light intensity. Most vegetables, cut flowers, and many flowering potted plants require high light intensity to grow well. Most foliage plants and some flowering potted plants require lower light intensity to grow. Under light intensity that is too low, plants exhibit slow growth, spindly, slender elongated stems, yellow lower leaves, and soft succulent growth. In some cases, they exhibit larger, thinner leaves and in others they exhibit smaller leaves and stem bending toward a light source (called phototropism). Under light intensity that is too high, plants exhibit smaller, light-green thick leaves, short thick stems and, in extreme cases, burned leaf margins or scorched blotches on the leaves.

Light intensity in the greenhouse is measured in foot candles (f.c.). A clear summer day may measure 10,000 f.c., while an overcast, winter day may measure 500 f.c. The amount of light needed for a person to read comfortably is about 20 f.c., while the light of a full moon is less than 1 f.c. Measuring the light available to plants requires a simple, convenient tool called a light meter. It is the only way to be sure plants are receiving the correct amount of light. Light meters can be purchased from greenhouse supply companies for $70 to $120. Recommended light intensity ranges for specific plants can be found in books under the additional reading section of this publication.

The purpose of glazing (the transparent or translucent material such as glass covering a greenhouse) is to capture sunlight as well as to separate the interior greenhouse environment from the outside environment. During the summer, high light intensity can burn low-light requiring plants and raise interior temperatures excessively. Light intensity and heat load in the greenhouse can be reduced using one of several means of shading.

Shade fabric is a woven polyethylene cloth that can be purchased from greenhouse supply companies. It comes in weave densities ranging from 20 to 90 percent. It is more effective in heat reduction to purchase a size large enough to drape over the outside of the greenhouse rather than hanging the fabric inside. One problem with draping fabric over the outside of the greenhouse, however, is that it can interfere with vent operation. During the summer in Alabama, high light requiring plants can benefit from 30 to 40 percent shade while low light requiring plants may need 50 to 80 percent shade. Purchase shade fabric with grommets along the edges so the cloth can be tied down in case of strong wind.

One simple and inexpensive alternative is to purchase shade paint from a greenhouse supply company. Mix the paint with water according to the manufacturer's directions. Shade paint is a weak- binding latex paint that is diluted and sprayed on the outside of the glazing. It is often applied in two applications, one light application in mid to late March and a second application in mid to late April. Shade paint is designed to weather off the glazing gradually over the summer and fall. However, it is frequently necessary to wash the glazing in late fall with soap and water and a long-handled brush to prevent unwanted light reduction in the winter.

Greenhouse blinds are regarded by many owners as the best shading alternative. Blinds can be purchased in a wide selection of roller types made with wood, plastic, or plastic-coated aluminum slats. Many owners mount blinds on the outside of the greenhouse that aid in heat reduction but like shade fabric can interfere with vent operation. Blinds designed to be mounted inside the greenhouse can be adjustable.

Most methods for increasing light intensity after a greenhouse is constructed are drastic, such as cutting down trees or removing other outdoor obstacles, or expensive, such as installing artificial light sources. However, plants can be spaced farther apart and objects such as hanging baskets can be taken down in the winter to reduce competition and shading. Painting as many interior surfaces as possible with white semigloss or gloss paint can also increase light intensity. Exterior latex works well but epoxy paint is even better. Paint benches, walls, doors, glazing supports, and even the floor, if possible, to reflect light. Another solution is to use a herbicide to kill all vegetation within 10 to 15 feet around the outside of the greenhouse and to spread white rock on the outside to reflect light into the greenhouse.

Temperature

Each plant species has an optimum and tolerable temperature range for growth. Plant growth and flowering are rapid within the optimum temperature range. Tolerable temperatures, which may be higher or lower than optimum, allow the plant to grow but at a reduced rate. Growth usually stops and plants may be damaged at temperatures outside the tolerable range. Recommended growing temperatures can be found in books such as those listed under the additional reading section of this publication. Generally, these recommendations are for minimum night temperatures because heating is required to maintain a minimum temperature for growth.

Most plant species grown in greenhouses are tropical or subtropical in origin and heating, when needed, to a 60 to 65 degrees F minimum night temperature works well. Exceptions to this recommendation include many cool-season plants such as primula, pansy, and some orchids. Cooler than optimum night temperatures will slow growth while warmer temperatures will speed growth. Daytime temperature should generally be 5 to 10 degrees F warmer on cloudy days and 10 to 15 degrees F warmer on sunny days than the night temperature. Excessively warm temperatures during the day or night, especially during cloudy weather, can reduce growth because respiration is increased and plants use sugars faster than photosynthesis can manufacture them.

Temperature requirements can also change with a plant's stage of growth. Generally, germinating seed and seedlings and rooting vegetative cuttings require warmer temperatures, plants growing vegetatively perform better under somewhat cooler temperatures, and flowering plants need under even cooler temperatures. With a mix of plants at different stages of growth in the greenhouse, it may be difficult to select an ideal temperature; nonetheless, provision should be made for germinating seed and rooting cuttings in a warmer setting.

Greenhouse temperature maintenance equipment (fans, heaters, etc.) is commonly regulated by installing one to several thermostats depending on the number of devices that require control. Thermostats controlling heating equipment are set to the minimum desired temperature and cooling devices are set to the maximum desired temperature. Do not depend, however, on the accuracy of commercial thermostats. Instead, install a high/low thermometer next to the thermostats and adjust the thermostat set points according to the high/low thermometer. High/low thermometers record the low temperature at night and the high temperature during the day. They have two liquid-filled glass stems and a metal bar within the glass stems that moves as the temperature changes, but stays in place at the lowest and highest temperature readings. Record the temperatures and reset the high/low thermometer daily. The thermometer is reset by moving the metal bars with a magnet or by pressing a button on the face of the thermometer.

Relative Humidity

Relative humidity (RH) is a measure of how much water is dissolved in the air at a particular temperature expressed as a percentage. Generally, growth of many plants is relatively unaffected by RH between 45 percent and 85 percent. Plants growing at RH below 45 percent may grow slowly, have smaller leaves, require watering more frequently, or develop burned leaf margins or leaf tips. Plants growing at RH above 85 percent are susceptible to fungal pathogens, especially if water condenses on the foliage.

Several conditions can occur in a greenhouse that result in problems caused by high or low RH. During the summer, high light, high temperature, and rapid air movement from fans can reduce RH to unacceptable levels. Shading to reduce light and temperature and using evaporative cooling (cooling pads) are the best solutions. RH can be raised for a short time by using a hose to wet down interior surfaces (walks, side walls, and open bench areas, but not plants). It is also advisable to keep the greenhouse full of plants because plants generate a lot of RH.

During the spring and fall, warm days followed by cool, clear nights cause rapid heat loss from the greenhouse, especially from the glazing material. Warm, moist interior air moving next to cool glazing material can drop to the dew point temperature and cause water to condense in droplets on the inside of the glazing material. These droplets run down the slope of the roof, grow larger, and then rain down on plants below creating ideal conditions for the growth of fungal pathogens. Two ways to reduce this problem is to avoid watering plants late in the day and to make sure the greenhouse floor drains well with no standing water or constant wet spots. The best way, however, to alleviate this problem is to wire a fan to a 24-hour time clock and set the fan to turn on for 30 to 60 minutes (depending on the size of the greenhouse) starting at 9:00 or 10:00 pm. The goal is to exchange the warm, moist interior air with cool, moist outside air, then allow the heating system to warm the air to its set point, thereby reducing the amount of water in the greenhouse air. Ironically, high RH and condensation are generally not a problem during the cold of winter because heating reduces the amount of water in the air.

The Root Environment

Underneath every healthy plant is a healthy root system. Although most of us know what a healthy plant looks like, few of us bother to learn what healthy roots look like. Learning the characteristics of healthy roots is one key to successful growing and diagnosing of plant problems. Drop plants out of their pots periodically and examine the roots. Roots may be thin, fibrous, and many-branched or thick and straight with few branches depending on the plant species. However, they should be more or less white, not brown or black. There should be root hair development just behind the root tip. Root hairs should be straight, not curled, discolored or absent. Roots should grow toward the bottom of the pot and, when mature, cover the entire soil volume. Disease, incorrect watering practices, poor soil, excessive fertilizer, or a combination of these factors can cause root problems.

Potting Soil

The major function of potting soil is to provide air (oxygen and carbon dioxide), plant support, and a constant supply of water and fertilizer nutrients to the roots. Roots take up oxygen and give off carbon dioxide in respiration to carry out their functions. Therefore, potting soil must have a sufficient number of large channels or pores to allow water to move through quickly and to allow air to exchange with the atmosphere. It should also have a sufficient number of small pores to hold adequate water and fertilizer between applications. In addition, potting soil should be initially low in fertilizer, free from toxins or herbicides, standardized and uniform for consistent results, and free from diseases, insects, and weed seed. Soil from the yard cannot meet many of these criteria, especially once confined to a pot. Therefore, it should not be used in a potting soil for the greenhouse.

Most of the potting soils used in greenhouse growing are called soilless mixes. As the name implies, they do not contain soil from the ground. There are two choices for obtaining sufficient potting soil, either mix your own or purchase it commercially already prepared in bags from retail sources. Commercial potting soil is convenient and inexpensive, but unfortunately, no standards exist for content or quality. There may be a high variation among brands. Look for a brand with "Professional Potting Mix" on the label, then look for a list of contents.

The potting mix should contain predominately peat moss, perlite, and/or vermiculite. Run a test in your greenhouse with several brands using different plants to see which one performs best. The advantage of mixing your own potting soil is that you have control over the content and quality. Recipes for three soilless potting soils are found in Table 1. Ingredients for mixing your own potting soil can be purchased from garden centers or greenhouse supply catalogs.

Soilless mixes are composed of two categories of components. The organic component gives potting soil the ability to absorb large amounts of water and fertilizer. Peat moss is used more than any other organic component, but composted bark or composted byproducts (leaf mold, sewage sludge, etc.) can also be used. The drainage component improves the potting soil's ability to drain water and exchange oxygen and carbon dioxide with the air. Perlite and vermiculite are widely used, but sand (washed river sand) can also be used. Chemical additives can be blended in the potting soil when the organic and drainage components are mixed.

The pH of a potting soil is a measure of the acidity or alkalinity of the mix. The pH scale ranges from 1 to 14 with 7 being neutral. Kits or meters for testing potting media pH can be purchased from garden centers or greenhouse supply catalogs. Most plants grow well in a soilless potting soil with a 5.5 to 6.5 pH. However, a potting soil using peat moss as an organic component will have an unacceptably low pH. Dolomitic limestone, which also supplies calcium and magnesium needed for plant growth, is added to the potting soil at the time of mixing to raise the pH. It is both convenient and economical to add some fertilizer to the soil at the time of mixing. Superphosphate (rock phosphate), a commercial micronutrient formulation and a source of nitrogen and potassium can be added at mixing. Keep in mind that these rates will get plants off to a good start, but additional fertilizer will be needed once plants establish. Four cubic feet is a convenient amount of potting soil to mix at a time. This amount will fit into a 30-gallon, new or clean garbage can for storage and will fill approximately 171 4-inch pots, 93 5-inch pots, or 56 6-inch pots. Begin by constructing a box from plywood with a 1-cubic foot inside dimension. Measure the organic and drainage ingredients according to Table 1 and mix them with a shovel on a clean surface to prevent contamination by root pathogens (cover dirty surfaces with plastic). Add just enough water to the mix to barely darken the color. Turn the soil as you add water. Measure the fertilizer and limestone using an accurate scale and mix them together in a bucket. Add some of the fertilizer/limestone mix and turn the soil, repeat until all the fertilizer/limestone mix is uniformly blended.

Table : Three Soilless Potting Soils for Hobby Greenhouse Culture

Type	Ingredient	per 1 cu. yd.	per 4 cu. ft.
	Peat moss (50 percent)	13-1/2 cu.ft	2 cu.ft.
High moisture	Vermiculite (50 percent)*	13-1/2 cu.ft.	2 cu.ft.
	OR		
High drainage	Perlite (50 percent) **OR**	13-1/2 cu.ft.	2 cu.ft.
Intermediate	Vermiculite (25 percent) * + Perlite (25 percent) each	6: cu.ft. each	1 cu.ft.
	Dolomitic limestone (ground)	8 to 10 lb.	19 to 24 oz.
	Superphosphate (0-20-0)	2 lb.	5 oz.
	Potassium nitrate (13-0-45)	1 lb.	2-1/2 oz.
	Minor elements (manufacturer recommendations)		

*Medium or coarce grade

Watering

Miswatering, typically overwatering, is probably one of the major causes of failure with plants in a greenhouse. Despite all that has been written, watering plants comes down to two critical decisions: when to water and how much to apply at a time. How much water to apply at a time is relatively easy as long as plants are growing in well-drained potting soil. Apply an amount of water that will saturate the entire soil volume in the container plus enough for a small amount to run out the drainage hole in the bottom of the pot.

The decision of how often to water should not be based on habit, nor should watering simply be done at certain time intervals. Always check plants to determine if they require water. One advantage to a soil containing peat moss is that it changes from dark brown when wet to light tan in color when dry. This color change can be used to determine when to water. Likewise, soil containing peat moss changes from heavy when wet to much lighter in weight when dry. With practice and experience, lifting pots periodically can help you determine when it is time to water. This method is especially useful for hanging baskets. Sticking your finger into the soil about a half-inch to feel for moisture can also be used. Many plants develop a gray-green cast to the foliage when dry. This can be used to judge when to water. The goal, however, is to water before plants wilt. Wilting damages plants, often causing lower leaf loss, stunted growth and delayed flowering.

Hand watering is probably the most common watering method used in hobby greenhouses. Hand watering should be done early in the morning so that water on the foliage dries before nightfall. A watering can with a water breaker fitting is useful for watering dry spots or an occasional water-hungry plant but for larger jobs, a hose will be needed. The hose usually has a thumb valve to control water flow, a water wand to extend reach (usually a 2-foot wand is sufficient) and a water breaker nozzle (2-1/4-inch diameter has wide application) at the end to soften the flow water impacting the soil surface. A one-half gallon per minute mist nozzle is also handy for watering seedlings.

When watering, go through the greenhouse systematically so that plants are not missed. Apply water gently so that the soil does not puddle, wash excessively, or knock-over young seedlings. This may require repeated light applications, especially to flats. When done, wind the hose close to the faucet so it is not under foot and hang the watering wand and breaker up off the floor to prevent the spread of diseases. Hoses last longer if the water is turned off at the faucet and the hose is drained after use.

Fertilizer

Fertilizer requirements for plant growth can be classified into two groups according to the amount used by plants. The macronutrients nitrogen, phosphorus, potassium, calcium, magnesium and sulfur are needed in relatively large quantities while the micronutrients iron, manganese, boron, zinc, molybdenum, copper, and chlorine are needed in very small amounts. Calcium, magnesium, and sulfur are generally supplied by adding dolomitic limestone and superphosphate to the potting soil at the time of mixing. Adding micronutrients at the time of mixing supplies plant needs for these nutrients for three to four months.

The macronutrients nitrogen, phosphorus, and potassium are highly soluble and wash from the potting soil easily. Therefore, they must be applied frequently, often in liquid form. There is a wide range of water soluble fertilizers available in garden centers and mass market outlets, but all will provide the percentage of nitrogen, phosphorus, and potassium (example: 20-20-20 is percent N-percent P-percent K) on the front label. When shopping for a fertilizer, purchase a water soluble, general plant fertilizer with the three percentages either very close or identical in value. Generally, it is more cost effective to purchase the highest analysis available (highest value for N-P-K).

Water soluble fertilizers can be applied by mixing a measured amount of fertilizer, according to the product label, with water in a watering can and drenching the potting soil. However, this method can become a time-consuming task if you have a large number of plants. A simple fertilizer injector that delivers fertilizer into the water line can be purchased from garden centers and mass market outlets. Common brands are Siphon, Siphonex, and Hozon. These units attach between the faucet and hose and have a siphon tube that is placed in a bucket filled with concentrated fertilizer solution. The concentrated solution is drawn into the hose, diluted in water, and delivered to plants during the normal watering operation. Follow the manufacturer's directions for mixing the concentrated fertilizer solution.

How often to apply liquid fertilizer depends on the growing environment, the plant type, and how rapidly the plant is growing. Plants in high light and temperature during late spring, summer, and early fall can be fertilized about once a week, especially annual flowers, flowering potted plants, and vegetables. Medium growth rate plants and plants in moderate light and temperature during early spring and late fall can be fertilized about once every two weeks. Slow growing plants and plants under shade can be fertilized about once a month. Many plants that stop growing in the winter should not be fertilized until growth resumes in the spring.

Propagation

Every hobby greenhouse owner either already has an interest in propagating plants or will soon develop one; there is something fascinating about becoming involved in starting a new life. Besides always purchasing established plants to meet your needs can be expensive.

Seed Germination

Start with good quality, fresh seed of known parentage. Seed collected from the wild or from the neighbor's yard often does not produce plants like the original. For flowering annuals and vegetables, purchase named varieties from reputable sources. Mail order sources and reputable garden centers are the best sources because they often carry the best varieties adapted to your area and they turn over their inventories fast enough so the seed are not too old. Stay away from bargain basement seed sales.

There are many different types of containers for germinating seed. They include plastic pots, paper pots, peat pots, peat blocks, multi-cell trays, and open flats. The container to choose depends on seed size. Large seed probably perform best sown individually in pots; medium and small seed perform best sown in multi-cell trays; and very small seed perform best sown in rows in open flats. Seedlings in open flats will require transplanting soon after germination. The containers should be filled with a potting soil designed for seed germination. Generally, seedling mixes are finer textured than general potting soils so they can accommodate small seed. Seedling mixes can be purchased from garden centers and mass market outlets.

Seed should be sown in moist, but not wet seedling mix. In the process of sowing, do not place seed too close together or competition for space will result in spindly, weak seedlings. Resist the temptation to sow more seed than you really need. Follow the directions on the seed package for seed spacing and sowing depth.

Large seed are placed in holes dibbled in the soil—a good rule is to make the hole no deeper than twice the diameter of the seed. Small seed are often sown directly on the soil surface and covered by sifting a small amount of fine vermiculite (fine or super fine grade) or seedling mix over the seed. A good way to water sown containers without washing the seed out of place is to submerge the container in a shallow pan of water so moisture can be absorbed by the soil through the drainage holes. Be sure to label the containers to identify what was sown. Store leftover seed sealed in labeled zip-lock plastic bags placed in the vegetable keeper of a refrigerator for future use. Note any instruction on the seed package for how long seed will remain viable under storage conditions.

Seed require a warm, moist environment to germinate. Tenting is an easy way to provide high humidity during germination and to prevent seed from drying out. On a small scale, slip the sown containers in a plastic bag (large zip-lock bags work well) and seal the open end. On a larger scale, construct a tent over a greenhouse bench from plastic pipe and clear sheet plastic. Do not expose the tents to direct sunlight. A piece of 40 to 60 percent shade fabric or cheesecloth can be used to shade the tents.

Germination temperatures vary greatly depending on the plant species, but a soil temperature of 70 to 80 degrees F works well for many seeds. Check the seed package for temperature information. Soil temperature can be monitored with a soil thermometer, which you can purchase from greenhouse supply company. Placing sown containers on an electric germinating mat (soil warming mat designed for propagation) that can be purchased from greenhouse supply companies can accelerate seed germination. Remove the tents as soon as the majority of the seedling unfold cotyledon leaves and place them at growing light intensity. Seedlings should be transplanted to larger containers before they begin to crowd, especially those sown in open flats. Seedlings with one or two mature leaves survive transplanting better than older seedlings, so do not delay transplanting!

ROOTING CUTTINGS

Growing plants from cuttings involves removing a plant part and placing it under conditions that favor development of a new root system. This is a form of cloning, often called vegetative propagation, because the new plant will be genetically identical to the parent plant. Vegetative propagation is often less expensive and faster than starting plants from seed.

Many plants are easy to root from cuttings. Some can be rooted directly in a glass of water placed in a bright window that does not get direct sun. In general, herbaceous annuals and perennials and tropical foliage plants are easier to root than woody trees and shrubs. Select a healthy disease- and insect-free parent plant, preferably one that does not have flowers. With a sharp knife, remove a 3- to 5-inch cutting from a stem tip of the parent plant. This type of cutting is called a terminal cutting. If the cutting has flowers or flower buds, remove them. Trim the larger leaves from the lower end of the cutting so that three to four smaller leaves remain toward the cutting tip. Dip the cut end of the cutting into a rooting powder (purchase from garden center or greenhouse supple company) and tap off the surplus. Rooting powders come in different formulations for different types of plants so select a formulation based on the plant type being propagated. Removing portions of the stem below the shoot tip of the parent plant can also make subterminal cuttings. However, cuttings taken from too low on the stem may be too woody and root slowly, if at all.

Cuttings can be started in any of the containers discussed for seed germination. Generally, a coarse, well-drained potting soil such as the 50 percent peat moss and 50 percent perlite mix outlined in Table 1 promotes rapid rooting. Poke a hole in the soil and insert the cut end of the cutting into the soil up to the lowest leaves. Do not stick the cuttings all the way to the bottom of the container. Stick them just deep enough to stand up. Water the cutting immediately. During this process, do not allow the cuttings to wilt. If cuttings must be transported or sticking the cuttings must be delayed, seal them in a plastic bag with wet paper towels, place them in a cooler or refrigerator and protect them from high light.

Because cuttings do not initially have roots, they must have a high humidity environment to prevent desiccation until roots form. If a few cuttings are stuck in a pot, cover the pot with a clear plastic bag, seal the bag with a rubber band and place the pot in bright, but not direct light. On a larger scale, construct a tent over the cutting containers on a greenhouse bench from plastic pipe and clear sheet plastic as discussed for seed germination. Cuttings may require from 2 weeks to 6 months to root depending on the species and plant type, so be patient.

Another method for rooting cuttings that is used by serious hobby greenhouse owners, especially for cuttings of woody shrubs and trees, is intermittent mist propagation. During propagation, a film of water is maintained on the leaves by applying a fine mist from mist nozzles attached to a plastic water line installed above the bench. A day/nighttime clock turns the system on early in the morning and off late in the evening. A cyclic timer activates an electric solenoid valve in the water line to turn the mist on for a preset time, typically five seconds, and then off for a preset time, typically 5 to 10 minutes. The key to successful rooting is to set the off time so the leaves are constantly wet without excess water soaking the soil. Therefore, the off-time interval must be adjusted for changing conditions, a longer time during cloudy weather or a shorter time during sunny weather.

f****

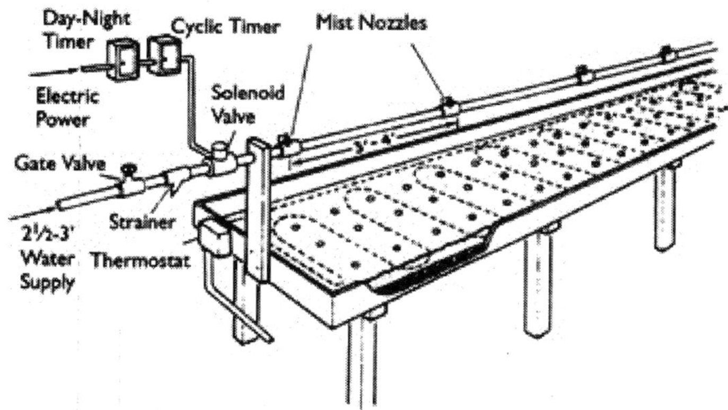

Fig. Design for an intermittent mist propagation system.

Greenhouse growing, like gardening, is both an art and a science. Many of the ideas presented here are practice applications of the science of how to grow plants. However, the artistic side of a hobby greenhouse is to choose plants that look and grow well and that please the owner. Choose a reasonable variety of plants and then arrange the plants and the interior space in a way that is pleasing, comfortable, and functional for all who visit.

6

The Multifunctional Homestead Greenhouse

GREENHOUSE BASICS

MATERIALS

Greenhouses were initially made of glass. Today, only Bill Gates buys a glass greenhouse.

Greenhouses are sometimes made of double-walled polycarbonate, a clear, rigid plastic that has excellent light-transmission properties and lasts a long time. (The service life is said to be twenty years.) Smaller polycarbonate greenhouses are available, offering the advantages of structural rigidity to resist snow load, and not having to be replaced every few years, like sheet plastic. However, it is quite expensive—the polycarbonate for just one end of my 20x48-ft greenhouse cost $500—and making a large greenhouse with it might require mortgaging your house.

Most homesteaders who want a greenhouse of any real size opt for sheet plastic over a metal frame.

I strongly recommend a proper greenhouse plastic: 6-mil polyethylene sheeting that has been treated to resist ultraviolet breakdown is best, and is readily available from any greenhouse supply. The version I use is guaranteed for four years, and in most cases can easily go five full seasons. However, it's a good idea not to push your luck and go for that sixth year, even if the cover still seems sound: Like the Wonderful One-Hoss Shay, once it starts to give way it all falls apart at once. If that happens in the middle of winter, you kiss your green beauties goodbye.

I prefer to put two layers of plastic on the greenhouse, with a small, energy-efficient blower inflating the space between. The dead-air space between the two "skins" increases the insulating value of the cover—it can make a difference of several degrees. An inflated "bubble" also sheds snow more readily, and better resists "chatter" in the wind, resulting in better wear of the cover.

Most non-professionals would do best starting with a greenhouse kit, containing all the components for assembling the completed greenhouse. I chose a Paul Boers kit (manufactured in Canada, distributed to me via Penn State Seed Company in Pennsylvania). The style is "gothic"—that is, the arches come to a rounded peak up top, better for shedding snow—and I paid more up front to get 1-½-inch galvanized steel pipe (rather than 1-inch) for added strength. If you are in an area with any snow in winter at all (or with frequent winds), make that additional investment.

FOUNDATION

Fig. Foundation Board

In his excellent *Four-Season Harvest* (*highly* recommended), Eliot Coleman has a design for a modest (12x20) greenhouse that has no foundation—the edges of the plastic sheeting are simply covered with earth. However, most larger greenhouses should have a foundation. When I initially installed my greenhouse, I installed a wooden foundation to attach the "channel lock" (into which the plastic cover is secured). Since I will not use pressure treated wood on my place, especially in close proximity to food crops, I used 2x8 pine boards, with several coats of linseed oil. Bad idea—don't repeat my mistake. Any wood in contact with the ground (even pressure treated) will eventually rot out—my less than adequately protected boards did so in five years, at which point the screws on the channel lock began popping out and the plastic cover started looking for the wind.

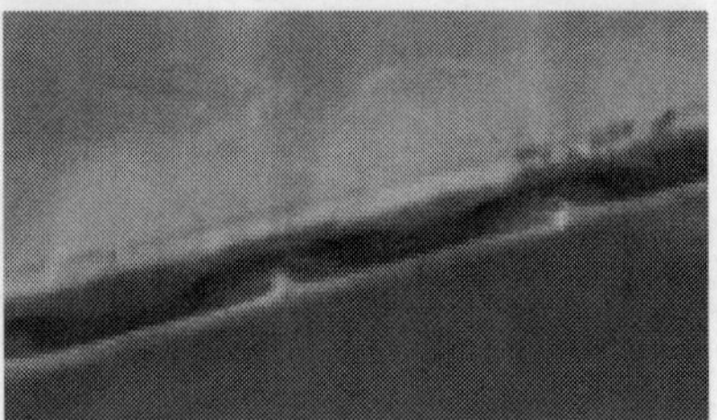

Fig. Channel Lock

I have not explored options for composite boards made of recycled plastic—they might be an option. My solution was to install (in the Fall of 2005) a single course of 4-inch hollow concrete block on a small poured footer, then lock a better grade fir 2x4, sealed against moisture, onto the top of the block foundation, using J-bolts pushed into wet concrete filling the holes in the block where needed.

The channel lock is still screwed into wood, but it is not wood that is ever in contact with earth or rain. With repeat applications of sealant as needed, it should last as long as I do. Of course, if it ever does require replacing, doing so would be much simpler this time around—I would simply remove the nuts from the J-bolts, take off the boards, and replace them.

Size

My advice to anyone thinking about installing a greenhouse: The bigger, the better. The larger the greenhouse, the more thermal mass inside in the form of soil that is warmed by the sun during the day, and the greater the moderation of overnight temperatures inside the greenhouse. Another reason to go with the largest greenhouse you can afford and have space for is that you will find more and more things to do with your greenhouse. For example, if your greenhouse has excess space beyond what you need for your own winter-greens needs, you can grow green forage crops to cut for your poultry, goats, or rabbits. You will never regret having made that additional stretch for a larger greenhouse—you will likely regret the reverse.

Be aware that most greenhouse kits are made up in stock sizes. Thus buying a larger stock size may make more sense than ordering a smaller custom size. For example, my initial idea was to erect a 20x32-ft greenhouse. I found, however, that by buying the 20x48 stock size, I picked up an additional 320 square feet of growing space (a 50 percent gain) for a mere $100.

Bracing

I know whereof I speak: In February, 2003 a snow storm predicted to grace us with two or three inches dumped fourteen instead. I went out the next morning to see my beloved greenhouse crushed, inch-and-a-half steel pipes on the ground like spaghetti. Have you ever seen a grown man cry?

Fig. Bracing the Arches

Since that sad experience, I put up 2x4 vertical braces from the earliest possible date for snow in late fall until the latest possible snow date in early spring. The top ends of the braces are drilled to engage the bolts at the gothic peak of the arches, supporting the structure as it takes on snow load. We typically have modest amounts of snow, so I place braces under every other arch. If you get a lot of snow, it might be good to brace under every arch.

KEY PLANNING QUESTIONS

Should you erect the structure yourself or hire out installation?

If your skill set includes squaring a foundation and drilling metal to receive screws, putting together a modern greenhouse kit is not difficult, and you will save a lot of money. I spent about $4000 on my greenhouse, and close to half that amount was what I paid to the crew who put it up. On the other hand, you may prefer to pay to have the job done better than you anticipate you can do yourself. For example, the last time I put on plastic sheeting I did the job myself. The result is certainly adequate, but I did not get as tight a "bubble" as when contracting that chore out to someone more experienced.

Do you plan to grow in summer?

Will yours be a cold-season greenhouse only, or do you plan to grow year-round? Since I have plenty of garden space for warm-weather crops, I use my greenhouse for vegetable production in the colder parts of the year only. I found that two solar-powered exhaust fans I installed initially were superflous, and I bartered them to a friend. If you plan to grow crops in summer, you will need heavy-duty exhaust fans. A greenhouse design incorporating roll-up sides would also be advisable.

As said, I do not grow vegetable crops in my greenhouse in the summer. There are certainly advantages to leaving the greenhouse fallow over the summer: The soil "solarizes" in the intense heat of the sun, burning off potential pathogens and dessicating even the most die-hard slug. However, last year it occurred to me that I wasn't doing anything in the summer to improve the soil in the greenhouse, equivalent to my practice of cover cropping whenever and wherever I can in the garden. So I grew a cover crop in the greenhouse over the summer. I found that such a strategy requires a lot of water, but makes a big difference in soil quality. My cover crop of choice was cowpeas, since they do well in the concentrated heat and the drier soil of the summer greenhouse.

Fig. Cowpea Cover Crop

Bench or earth grow?

In most commercial greenhouses raising bedding plants, flats of plants are grown on tables or grow benches. For homesteaders, however, growing right in the earth floor of the greenhouse is the only reasonable choice. The crop plants have more room for their roots to roam; the earth as observed earlier is a huge heat sink, and stays much warmer than the air temperature at bench level; and growing in earth beds allows improvement of the soil over time as we work with successive crops.

Fig. Winter Salads

GROWING IN THE WINTER GREENHOUSE

SOIL CARE

You should be as concerned about improving soil quality in the greenhouse as in the garden. I grow a cover crop of cowpeas in the off season to improve the soil. Another possibility is the growing of forage crops—grain grasses, mixed crucifers, peas, etc.—as cut-and-come-again forage for poultry in the winter.

The biomass of the root systems of some of these plants, especially rye, is quite large. If you rotate your forage plots over the greenhouse beds, their soil will over time increase in tilth, fertility, and humus as the spent root systems decompose.

Fig. Cowpea Cover Crop

Use of compost is of course always a good idea, especially for its boost to the microbial populations in the soil. As in garden growing, mulches help moderate the temperature in the soil, conserve soil moisture, and decompose over time, increasing soil tilth and fertility.

One caution regarding soil care in the greenhouse: It is important to avoid over-fertilizing with nitrogen. Green leafy crops can sometimes accumulate unhealthy levels of nitrates, especially in the low light conditions of the winter greenhouse. I never add nitrogen fertilizers in the greenhouse. Composts are a good source of fertility, though it is better to use plant-based rather than manure-based (higher in nitrogen) composts. I am even concerned about the nitrogen fixed by the summer cowpea cover crop, and plan to follow it with a quick mixed grain cover to "sop up" some of the nitrogen before the fall greenhouse planting season comes in.

The Moderated Winter

A homestead greenhouse can add tremendously to sustainable food production. However, adding huge amounts of artificial heat in order to grow tomatoes in January or cucumbers in March is anything but sustainable. Hence, I strongly recommend relying on the protection from winter's extremes provided by the structure itself, and on naturally cold-hardy plants, in order to bring in your winter crops. Let's look at each of those points in turn.

Most new greenhouse owners are surprised to learn that a plastic-skinned greenhouse gets quite cold at night—in fact, the air temperature will often be only a few degrees above ambient temperature outside. Upon reflection, this is not really so surprising: The translucent skin that acts as a portal for the radiant heat of the sun during the day is also no barrier to the radiation of stored heat out of the structure into the cosmos at night. How is it, then, that the greenhouse is so effective at keeping plants alive, even when winter is turning the ground to iron outside? You could think of the soil inside the greenhouse as a rechargeable battery. During the day, it charges from the heat energy of the incoming sunlight. At night, it loses that stored energy at a prodigious rate, true, but it has a huge amount of heat it can lose before the soil starts to freeze.

The other way in which the structure protects its sheltered plants is by moderating the extremes of winter. Plants which are adapted to low temperatures will still be badly stressed if the temperature plummets from a high of 40° F in the late afternoon to 18° by dark; or if sharp winds join in on the abuse ("wind chill" isn't just a problem for us humans); or if they get rained on in low temperatures. The greenhouse acts to slow the abrupt temperature changes, and to keep wind and cold rains at bay.

Remember, however, that the moderating influence of the greenhouse is effective only when we are growing naturally cold hardy plants. I have harvested lettuces, completely exposed in the garden, in mid-December in a fairly benign winter. Spinach will often survive a cold winter in the garden, and rejuvenate when encouraged by the sun come spring (here in Zone 6b). You might say that we are using the greenhouse to imitate for naturally cold hardy plants like these an unusually mild winter—not to teleport them to somewhere in the tropics.

Two factors make possible the survival of cold hardy plants through freezing temperatures. I referred above to the way the growing beds store solar heat during the day, and can lose that heat profligately before the ground starts to freeze. But by the point that the ground does start to freeze, it's morning, and the cycle begins anew. I've gone into my greenhouse many a morning after a 10° night to find only a quarter of an inch of frost on the surface of the growing beds. That quarter inch is no problem—as long as there is no freezing deep into the root zone, the plants are not unduly stressed.

Fig. Cold Hardy Lettuce

The other factor is a neat little trick the plants have learned, but which is apt to be unsettling the first time the gardener sees it. When the air temperature gets below freezing, certain plants such as lettuce have learned how to move water out of their cells into the intercellular spaces, to prevent rupture of the cell walls when the water crystallizes (freezes). In this state, the leaves become limp. When the gardener comes into the greenhouse after a deep-cold night, the sight of drooping lettuces seems to indicate a disastrous end of the winter growing effort. After half an hour of sunlight, however, the plants' cells rehydrate, and they perk up as bright and pretty as they were before their descent into the chill.

The Mirror Season

Experienced gardeners may have some difficulty adjusting to the paradoxes of winter gardening. Unlike in spring, when the season is gloriously *opening out* into greater warmth and longer days, in the fall it is *shutting down* into a time of ever-greater darkness and deeper chill. The implications for growing are tricky, and take some getting used to. This reversal in the general trend of the season is perhaps the biggest adjustment the winter gardener has to make. We have to re-learn many of our assumptions, particularly about scheduling our crops. Do remember that the biggest challenge is apt to be the reduced photoperiod, rather than the low temperatures (assuming we make appropriate choices of cold hardy crops).

The bad news: During the darkest time of winter, there is insufficient solar energy to support vigorous growth. If we have started our plants too late to make most of their growth before the short days, they will indeed survive the cold temperatures, but instead of growing actively will sit and sulk, awaiting sunnier days.

The good news: On the other hand, if we get the timing right to produce, say, a mature head of lettuce by the dark days, the window of opportunity for harvest expands enormously. That perfect head of lettuce that would demand "use it or lose it" within a matter of days in June, will sit contentedly in prime condition, awaiting your pleasure, for two or even three months in the middle of winter.

One implication of the dormancy at the heart of the winter harvest season: When you start your crops in the late summer or early fall, start far more than you think you will need. As you make your earliest harvests, you will not be able to start new crops, but if you have plenty "in the bank" at that point you can continue making generous harvests until the longer days make possible some late-winter crops.

Watering

It is best to water deeply from time to time (in lieu of frequent shallow waterings). Water in the morning, as soon as the frost is off the leaves, to give the plants time to dry before descending into nighttime cold again. Avoid over-watering, which makes plants "sappy," less able to stand the cold and other stresses (and less flavorful and nutritious as well). Test the soil with your finger:

As long as you feel good moisture half an inch or so deep, it is better not to water.

Ventilation

It is important to appreciate how hot a closed greenhouse can get on a sunny day, even if the temperature outside is quite cold. Do not stress your plants by leaving the doors to the greenhouse closed when it is sunny. I typically shut up my two large doors (one at either end) at night, then open them wide during the day. If the day is unusually cold, blustery, and cloudy, I will prop the doors partially open. However, I always ensure there is some air movement through the greenhouse during the day.

Incidentally, I found that open doors at either end of the structure provide sufficient ventilation during the winter—exhaust fans were superfluous. I know growers with 20x96-ft greenhouses who report that ventilation is adequate using open doors alone. Remember that as the air in the greenhouse heats in the sunlight, it will rise and exit the structure, and more air will be drawn in from outside, providing constant natural air exchange.

Insects

Fig. Chard with Yarrow

My approach to leaf-eating insects in the greenhouse is, as in the gardens and orchard outside, not so much about *control* as about *balance*. Hence I encourage all the flowering plants I can inside the greenhouse. I planted yarrow throughout the beds last fall, and it bloomed late into the fall and quite early in the spring.

Perhaps it was the flowering yarrow that encouraged the obvious increase in lady beetle population—in any case, I had far less trouble with aphids this spring. I also allow unharvested chicories, crucifers, and onions (grown from bulbs discarded in the kitchen because of sprouting) to flower and boost insect populations.

My impression is that the insect season gets an early start in the warmth of the spring greenhouse, then the lady beetles and their comrades migrate out into the garden as it starts to bloom, boosting earlier insect diversity there.

CROPS FOR THE WINTER GREENHOUSE

Just as for my spring garden, I prefer to start plants that are going into the greenhouse as *transplants* if at all possible. Starting with transplants is even more important in a greenhouse, actually, since the greenhouse may still be too hot to direct sow crops in the late summer, when some crops need to be started.

Salads

- *Lettuces* are quite resistent to frost, though they are not as cold hardy as some other winter garden plants. Some varieties are better adapted to cold weather and short days, so study your seed catalog descriptions. I always grow a dozen different varieties—I guess I'm easily bored with only one or two textures, colors, and tastes.
- *Chicories* are my favorite winter salad. Indeed, during the height of winter—January and February for me—you can forget your mesclun and fancy lettuces, give me chicories! And if you've been turned off to stringy, bitter, tough endives and escaroles from the supermarket, be assured that—in the reduced light and chill of the winter greenhouse—chicory's bitterness is tinged with sweet, and the stringy toughness is replaced by a delightful juicy crunch. Chicories come in many shapes, colors, and types: round heading, tall heading (sugarloaf, the chicory equivalent of a Romaine lettuce), open heading (escarole and endive), cut-and-come-again leaf types (catalogna, cardoncella), radicchio, mini-headers of which you use whole tiny heads in salads (grumolo), even chicories with edible roots—all in a riot of beautiful colors, often variegated: green, rose, salmon, red, pink, etc. (An unusually good source for chicory seeds is Seeds from Italy. Be careful, though: Last time I was on their site I ordered nineteen

varieties!)

- *Less well known salads* include mâche and edible chrysanthemum. Some are astoundingly cold hardy, such as claytonia (or miner's lettuce) and minutina (*Herba stella*). And don't forget *scallions* as an easily grown addition to winter salads.

Fig. Raab

Fig. Red Mustard

Cooking Greens

- *Spinach* is extremely cold hardy. I prefer young spinach, so I make successive sowings throughout the winter growing season. During the darkest part of winter, of course, the spinach will not make much progress. However, with the coming of longer days it will grow rapidly.
- *Crucifers*—including mustards, raab, Oriental greens such as pak choi and tatsoi, etc.—are tasty and nutritious "potherbs," and are excellent candidates for cold-weather growing.
- *Chard* (or Swiss chard) is simply a type of beet (*Beta vulgaris*) bred for its large tender leaves and rapid re-growth, rather than its roots. It is cold hardy and productive.
- *Green onion and garlic tops* make great cooking greens. When I plant my garlic crop in the garden in the fall, I use the biggest cloves only. The smaller cloves go into the greenhouse for growing "garlic scallions." We also sort out the smaller stored onions, or the ones

that have begun sprouting, and plant them in the greenhouse for their beautiful and nutritious green tops.

Herbs

Parsley, cilantro, leaf celery, dill, and other cold hardy herbs make great additions to winter salads and to the soup pot. They are easy to grow.

Brassicas

Brassicas that head (such as cabbages and broccoli) are more likely to develop large, tight heads if grown in the late-winter greenhouse rather than in the fall. (Some varieties are more suited to greenhouse production than others, so study your seed catalogs.) An exception is kale, which is an excellent crop for the fall-winter greenhouse if you make an early enough start on your transplants.

What About Root Crops?

In my experience, root crops such as beets or carrots, even though cold hardy, are also not suitable for planting in the fall greenhouse—they will grow, but do not receive sufficient energy in the shortening days to "make root." I have, however, had excellent results growing carrots, beets, potatoes, and daikon (as well as the smaller radishes) in the late winter greenhouse, harvesting these crops up to two months earlier than their siblings in the garden.

Fig. Tender Perennials

Overwintering Tender Perennials

Here in Zone 6b, certain of the "tender perennials"—such as rosemary, tarragon, and white sage—may or may not make it through the winter. In the late fall, I dig up these herbal allies and plant them temporarily inside the greenhouse. With the additional protection, they survive the winter easily, and are ready to go back out to their accustomed places come spring.

An Early Start on Warm Weather Crops

All warm-weather crops can get a much earlier start in the late-winter, early-spring greenhouse. I start tomatoes, peppers, and eggplants as early as mid-January to the end of February. (I start them under grow lights in the basement, then move them into the greenhouse when they get too big for the grow bench.) As long as I pot them on as needed to prevent their getting potbound, I have *big* plants that are growing fast and which experience no check on their growth when it is warm enough to plant them out in the garden. Using this strategy, I get ripe fruits a month earlier than I would if planting less developed plants.

Actually, I plant a few extra-early tomatoes in the greenhouse itself, to savor that first vine-ripened tomato earlier than any plant in the garden could possibly match.

Another warm-weather crop I like to start in the greenhouse is sweet potatoes. I choose a few of the tubers that have stored best of all through the winter, half-bury them horizontally in moist sand, and keep them in the warmest spot in the greenhouse until sprouts start coming up from the mother tuber. By the time the weather has warmed sufficiently to plant sweet potatoes, the "slips" have numerous dark green leaves and their own roots, and I snap them off for transplanting into their garden ridge.

GREEN FORAGE FOR LIVESTOCK

Winter Feast

Winter can be a difficult time for our livestock, especially those lucky ones whose owners have given them access to pasture during the green season—how they miss those great greens in the dormant time of the year. To offer fresh green forage in the winter (which is beneficial even in small amounts), we can reserve some of the greenhouse for growing "green chop" for our goats, cows, poultry, etc. Grain grasses (wheat, barley, rye, oats), mixed crucifers (rape, mustards, turnips grown for the leaf, etc.), and peas are excellent candidates for cut-and-come-again green forage

. Another possibility is *sprouting* some of the grains we feed our livestock.

Soak the grains, lay out in a thick layer in plant trays (or even directly on greenhouse beds), cover lightly with straw or other loose organic material, and allow to sprout. Once the shoots have grown an inch or two and "greened up," offer them to your wards and see what happens.

CHOOKS AND WORMS IN THE GREENHOUSE

CHICKENS IN THE GREENHOUSE

Greenhouse Pen

My second assumption is that the body heat of the enclosed flock will moderate the overnight chill in the greenhouse. Again, I have no control for testing this proposition scientifically, but I had 43 chickens, three ducks, and two African geese in there at the height of last winter—I'm convinced that more than 250 pounds of warm living bird has to make a difference.

Finally, I hate confining my flock in the winter. It's a necessity, since they would degrade the dormant pasture sod if on it full time.

That is, it *was* a necessity, until it occurred to me I could heavily mulch the garden area outside the flock's sleeping quarters in the greenhouse pens, net it with electronet fencing, and release the birds onto it during the day. (I used several 800-lb round bales of old hay, since a dry season did not permit a heavy fall cutting off my pasture.) The results were more than satisfactory: The mulch was deep enough (six to eight inches) to prevent freezing of the soil in my climate (Zone 6b), and the busy chickens stcratched down through it to live animal food (earthworms, slugs and slug eggs, etc.), and germinating seed in the hay—both a terrific boost in nutrition. The mulch absorbed the poops laid down and scratched in by the flock, rather than accumulating as a slick glaze on a patch of bare frozen dirt, eager to run to the nearest stream, lake, or estuary (to say nothing of the groundwater) with the first thaw. The mulch thus recaptured that manure as fertility for the soil in the coming season. The chickens, quite cold hardy if not wet, enjoyed themselves in the sun, on even the coldest days. And shelter at night, or from rain during the day, was always a few steps away inside the greenhouse pens.

By spring, the mulch hay had been shredded to something between fine mulch and finished compost, and was easy to apply in the garden, even between closely planted crops like carrots.

When you use a mulch like this, which contains pulverized droppings, it is advised that you allow 60 days—some would say as much as 120 days—before harvest. Frankly, I have not paid much attention to such "withdrawal times" when using homestead manure—an entirely different beast from manures of animals in high-confinement operations—and have never had the slightest problem with such mulches.) Finally, remember that the mulch was laid down over a *garden*, and was protective of its soil, preventing the horror of bare soil over winter.

Vermicomposting in the Greenhouse

I experimented with a 3x4-ft worm bin for several years. When I did the greenhouse renovation project, it seemed the perfect opportunity to step up to more serious vermicomposting. We put in two courses of 4-inch hollow block for the bins, dug almost 16 inches into the earth, 40 feet right down the center of the greenhouse.

Every 8 feet, we put a cross wall of block, to give five 4x8-ft bins 16 inches deep. We put two 4x4-ft lids made of ¾-inch plywood on 2x4 framing over each bin, giving in effect two 4x4 sections in each bin. (Great for management: I can empty out one section and refill with bedding. The worms migrate in and populate from the full side.) When the flock is out of the greenhouse over the summer, their two 8x8 pens are used for an additional 128 sq ft of vermicomposting bin.

Fig. Bin Lids

Since I needed access down the center anyway, I didn't lose much growing space to the new worm bins. And those substantial 4x4 lids over the bins have been a godsend. I routinely roll a fully loaded wheelbarrow over them. They are a great place to lay out work projects (the Lady of the Manor having forbidden doing so on the front porch since we re-decked it). We've even set up a table on them and had a picnic there; and I addressed a seated class of sixteen on them one raw March day.

Fig. Beginning the Cycle

Of course all the kitchen throw-offs that don't go to the flock get fed to the worms. But the scale of my operation since the expansion is way beyond the "worms eat my garbage" scale. I haul in pony poop by the pickup load from a neighbor who breeds and boards horses. I find that pure horse manure usually doesn't heat up enough to be a problem for the worms. Manure mixed with hay, straw, or sawdust will do so (as in a compost heap); but in the two-halves management I practice in the bins, the worms in the one side can back off and wait out a heating/outgassing spike in the new material before starting to nibble at the edges.

Fig. Harvesting Earthworms

The worms serve well the admirable goal of responsible manure management. In the process, they convert the manure bedding into castings (earthworm poop), one of the best of all natural fertilizers—rich not only in plant nutrients in forms easy for roots to take up, but carrying a huge load of microbes to boost the micro-life in the top inches of the soil. Last winter, the populations were finally high enough to make regular harvests of earthworms to feed the flock. To harvest, I simply shoveled out one or two five-gallon buckets of almost finished bedding at a time, and dumped it out on the mulched garden. The chickens and ducks made short work of the earthworms and worm eggs (the vegetarian geese were appalled), in the process scratching the castings into the mulch and "banking" their fertility against the coming withdrawals of spring. (Note that one should offer the bedding in a different part of the garden every day—otherwise excess, and harmful, fertility can build up in one spot.) guidance on selecting, installing and maintaining a greenhouse

vegetables, fruit, herbs and ornamental plants for growing under cover

practical advice on general care, harvesting, storage, propagation and pest control

- Designing and Building a New Greenhouse
- Glazing
- Measuring Light in the Greenhouse
- Sun Substitutes: Choosing the Right
- Lighting System
- Carbon Dioxide (CO2) in the Greenhouse
- Setting Up for Composting
- Watering Your Greenhouse Plants
- Humidity
- Air Temperature
- Soil Temperature
- Cooling and Ventilating the Greenhouse and Sunsapace
- Weather and the Greenhouse
- Gizmos for the Greenhouse

7

Vegetable Garden: Soil Management and Fertilization

In the garden, managing soils to improve *tilth* and garden *fertilization* are related but not necessarily the same process. For example, compost or manure may be added as a soil amendment to improve tilth; however, they will add nominal amount of plant nutrients. A manufactured fertilizer may be added to supplement soil fertility levels, but it will not improve a soil's tilth. For optimum yields and quality, gardeners need to pay attention to both soil management for improving tilth and soil fertilization.

Tilth is a term related to the suitability of a soil to support plant growth. Technically speaking, tilth is "the physical condition of soil as related to its ease of tillage, fitness of seedbed, and impedance to seeding emergence and root penetration".

SOIL AMENDMENT OR FERTILIZER

The term *soil amendment* refers to any material mixed into a soil. By law, soil amendments make no legal claims about nutrient content or other helpful (or harmful) properties. Compost and manure are common soil amendments used to improve soil tilth. They may also supply nominal amounts of plant nutrients.

Some of the nutrient effect seen from adding soil amendments is likely due to their effect on soil microorganisms. The organic material in soil amendments is a food source that allows microorganisms to multiply. The larger numbers increase the conversion of nutrients in the soil to plant usable forms.

Mulch refers to a material placed on the soil surface.

By law, the term *fertilizer* refers to a material that guarantees a minimum percentage of nutrients (at least the minimum percentage of nitrogen, phosphate, and potash). An *organic fertilizer* is derived from natural sources and guarantees the minimum percentages of nitrogen, phosphate, and potash.

Soil Amendments

In the vegetable garden, the routine addition of organic soil amendments such as compost will optimize potential yields and quality. The goal in soil management is to increase the organic content to 4-5%, over a period of years.

Common amendments include compost, manure, compost made with manure, fall leaves, straw, and peat moss. Home compost has the advantage that the gardener controls what goes into the compost, reducing problems with salts, weed seeds, and plant diseases.

In climates with long growing seasons, another method to add organic matter is to grow green manure crops in between the vegetable growing season. In some areas, this would be a winter crop, in hot areas of the south this would be a summer heat crop. In areas like Colorado, where the entire growing season is used for vegetable production, a green manure is less practical. For additional information, refer to *CMG GardenNotes* #244,Cover Crops and Green Manure Crops.

How Organic Amendments Improve the Soil

On clayey soil, organic matter (over a period of years) glues the tiny soil particles together into larger aggregates, increasing pore space. This increases soil oxygen levels and improves soil drainage, which in-turn increases the rooting depth, thereby allowing roots to reach a larger supply of water and nutrients.

On sandy soils, organic matter holds over ten times more water and nutrients than sand. Organic matter also encourages the beneficial activity of soil organisms and helps remediate soil compaction.

Application

General application rates for compost or other organic soil amendments are based on the salt content of the materials and soil and on the depth to which it is cultivated into the soil. Ideally, cultivate the soil amendment into the top six to eight inches of the soil. On compacted/clayey soils, anything less can lead to a shallow rooting system with reduced plant growth, lower vigor, and lower stress tolerance.

Table 1 gives the standard application rates for compost. Compost made solely from plant residues (leaves and other yard wastes) is basically free of salt problems, and higher application rates are safe.

Compost, which includes manure or biosolids as a component, has a potential for high salts. Excessive salt levels are common in many commercially available products sold in Colorado.

In compost made with manure or biosolids, the application rate is limited unless a soil test on that batch of product shows a low salt level. An amendment with up to 10 dS/m (10 mmhos/cm) total salt is acceptable if incorporated six to eight inches deep in a low-salt garden soil (less than 1 dS/m or 1 mmhos/cm). Any amendment with a salt level above 10 dS/m (10 mmhos/cm) is questionable.

Compost needs to be thoroughly mixed into the upper six to eight inches of the soil profile.

Do not leave compost in chunks, as this will interfere with root growth and soil water movement.

As the soil's organic content builds in a garden, the application rate should be reduced to prevent ground water contamination issues. A soil test is suggested every four to six years to establish a base line on soil organic matter content.

If using a green manure cover crop, till the cover crop in before it reaches four inches in height.

In the vegetable garden do not plow in woody materials such as bark or wood chips. They may interfere with seedbed preparation and may result in soil nitrogen depletion.

Table : Routine Application Rates for Compost

Site	Incorporation Depth 2	Depth of compost before incorporation 1	
		Plant Base Compost and other compost known to be low in salts3	**Compost Made With Manure or Biosolids** for which the salt content is unknown 4
Annual application to vegetable and flower gardens – **first three years**	6-8 inches	2-3 inches	1 inch
Annual application to vegetable and flower gardens – **fourth year and beyond**	6-8 inches	1-2 inches	1 inch

1. Three cubic yards (67 bushels) covers 1,000 square feet approximately one inch deep.
2. Cultivate compost into the top six to eight inches of the soil. On compacted/clayey soils, anything less may result in a shallow rooting depth predisposing plants to reduced growth, low vigor and low stress tolerance. If actual incorporation depth is not 6 to 8 inches, adjust the application rate accordingly.
3. Plant based composts are derived solely from plant materials (leaves, grass clippings, wood chips and other wards wastes). Use this application rate also for other compost known, by soil test, to be low in salts.
4. Use this application rate for any compost made with manure or biosolids unless the salt content is known, by soil test, to be low. Excessive salts are common in many commercially available products sold in Colorado. Based on soil tests of commercially available compost, this application rate may be too high for products extremely high in salts.

PRECAUTIONS WHEN USING COMPOST AND MANURE

Manure, compost made from manure, and bio-solids may be high in salts that will interfere with crop growth. Do not add more than one inch per season without conducting a soil test to evaluate potential salt build-up.

Due to a health issue (*E coli* contamination), fresh manure additions should be made at least four months prior to the harvest of any edible crops. In other words, apply fresh manure only in the fall after crops are harvested.

Fresh manure or unfinished compost products may be high in ammonia. Avoid application of products with an ammonia smell; they could burn roots and leaves. Manure and compost may be source of weed seeds.

Nutrient Release Rates from Compost and Manure

Gardeners need to understand that the nutrient release from compost and manure is slow, taking years. Adding compost or manure to improve soil tilth is not the same as fertilizing.

The typical nitrogen release rates from manure is only 30 to 50% the first year (fresh manure), 15 to 25% the second year, 7 to 12% the third year, 3 to 6% the fourth year, and so on. With compost and composted manure, the release rate is even slower, 5 to 25% the first year, 3 to 12% the second year and 1 to 6% the third year.

Since the nitrogen percentage of compost and manure products is typically only 2 to 4%, the amount of actual nitrogen release to support crop growth is very small.

- For soil with 4 to 5% organic matter, the mineralization (release) of nitrogen from soil organic matter will likely be sufficient for crop growth.
- For soils with 2 to 3% organic matter, the mineralization of nitrogen from soil organic matter will not likely be sufficient for heavy feeding vegetable crops. Supplement with 0.1 pound nitrogen fertilizer per 100 square feet.
- For the typical garden soil with 1% organic matter or less, the mineralization of nitrogen for soil organic matter will be minimal. Add 0.2 pounds of nitrogen fertilizer per 100 square feet.

FERTILIZATION

Soil fertilization is the addition of soil nutrients to support crop growth. While some soil amendments add small amounts of nutrients, amending the soil to improve soil tilth is not the same as amending the soil to provide nutrients.

Manufactured fertilizers are popular with gardeners because they are readily available, inexpensive, easy to apply, and generally provide a quick release of nutrients for plant growth. Application rates for any fertilizer depend on the content and the amount of nutrient to be applied. In products containing multiple nutrients, the application rate is always based on the nitrogen content.

Nitrogen Applications

Nitrogen is the nutrient needed in largest quantities by plants and the one most frequently applied as fertilizer. It is annually applied in the form of manufactured fertilizer, organic fertilizers, and/or organic soil amendments. Application rates are critical, because too much or too little directly affects crop growth.

The standard annual application rate for home vegetable gardens is 2 pounds actual nitrogen per 1,000 square feet (0.2 pound actual nitrogen per 100 square feet). When organic matter is supplied, adjust the rate accordingly to account for nitrogen released by the organic matter. [Table 2]

Manufactured nitrogen fertilizer can be broadcast and watered in, or broadcast and tilled into the top few inches of soil. It can be banded 3-4" to the side of the seed or plant row. Do not place the fertilizer in the seed row or root injury will occur. Some soluble types are applied in the irrigation water. "Organic" nitrogen fertilizers are typically tilled in or some can be applied in irrigation water.

Table : **Standard Nitrogen Fertilizer Application Rate for Gardens**

	Soil Organic Content		
	Typical garden soil low in organic matter (1% OM)	**Moderate level of organic matter (2-3% OM)**	**High levels of organic matter (4-5%)**
Nitrogen Fertilizer	0.2 lbs actual N per 100 sq. ft.	0.1 lbs actual N per 100 sq. ft.	0
Fertilizer examples			
Ammonium sulfate 21-0-0	1 lb. fertilizer per 100 sq. ft. approx. 2 cups)	0.5 lbs. fertilizer per 100 sq. ft. (approx 1 cup)	0
Ammonium nitrate, 34-0-0	0.6 lbs. fertilizer per 100 sq. ft. (approx. 1 1/3 cup)	0.3 lbs. fertilizer per 100 sq. ft. (approx. 2/3 cup)	0
Urea, 45-0-0	0.4 lbs. fertilizer per 100 sq. ft. (approx. 1 cup)	0.2 lbs. fertilizer per 100 sq. ft. (approx. 1/2 cup)	0

Starters Fertilizers

In setting out transplants, starter solutions often promote early growth. Because transplants have been hardened-off (growth slowed to prepare the plant for movement to the exposed, windy, outdoor environment), the nitrogen in the starter solution gives the signal to resume active growth. Because phosphorus is less available in cold soils, phosphate may also be helpful in spring and before soils have thoroughly warmed.

A starter fertilizer is any water-soluble fertilizer added to the irrigation water. Common examples include MiracleGro, Peters, Schultz Plant Food,

Fertilome Root Simulator and Plant Starter Solution, etc. They generally contain ammonium nitrate since it is readily usable by the plant. Some products claim that vitamins or hormones promote plant growth. These claims are not supported by research findings.

Nitrogen "Side Dressing"

Plant need for nitrogen varies. Beans, peas, tomatoes, and vine crops (cucumbers, squash, pumpkins, and melons) are examples of vegetables with a lower need for nitrogen. High nitrogen promotes excessive growth of the plant at the expense of fruiting.

Crops such as potatoes, corn, and cole crops (broccoli, cauliflower, cabbage, and kale) use large amounts of nitrogen and need supplemental applications during the growing season (referred to as *side dressing*). For example, home garden potatoes often show nitrogen deficiency from August into fall. Symptoms start as a yellowing of lower leaves and progress into a general browning and dieback of the vine. When nitrogen stress hits, potatoes become more susceptible to diseases, including Early Blight and Verticillium Wilt. [Table 3]

Fertilizers commonly used in the home garden for side dressing include ammonium sulfate, ammonium nitrate, and water-soluble fertilizers such as MiracleGro, Peters, etc. Phosphate and potash fertilizers are best added in the spring or fall, when they can be cultivated into the soil.

<table>
<tr><th colspan="5">Table : Nitrogen Side Dressing of Vegetable Crops</th></tr>
<tr><th rowspan="2">Vegetable</th><th rowspan="2">Timing</th><th colspan="3">Application Rate
Based on rate of 0.1 lbs. actual N per 100 square feet)</th></tr>
<tr><th>Ammonium sulfate
21-0-0</th><th>Ammonium nitrate
34-0-0</th><th>Water soluble
fertilizers</th></tr>
<tr><td>Asparagus</td><td>1. Early spring
2. At end of harvest season</td><td rowspan="6">0.5 lbs. fertilizer per 100 sq. ft. (approx. 1 cup) Sprinkle over soil and water in, OR place in furrow to side of plant. CAUTION: an over application will burn roots, stunting or killing plants.</td><td rowspan="6">0.3 lbs. fertilizer per 100 sq. ft. (approx. 2/3 cup) Sprinkle over soil and water in, OR place in furrow to side of plant. CAUTION: an over application will burn roots, stunting or killing plants.</td><td rowspan="6">See label of specific product. Water soil with fertilizer added to water. Low burn potential, but significantly more expensive.</td></tr>
<tr><td>Sweet Corn</td><td>1. At 12" tall
2. One month later</td></tr>
<tr><td>Leafy green vegetables</td><td>3-4 weeks after emergence</td></tr>
<tr><td>Onions</td><td>3-4 weeks after emergence</td></tr>
<tr><td>Potatoes</td><td>Late-July to early-August</td></tr>
<tr><td>Tomatoes, peppers, and eggplants</td><td>First fruits 1" diameter</td></tr>
<tr><td>Cole crops (broccoli, cabbage, cauliflower)</td><td>1. 2-3 weeks after transplanting
2. 4-5 weeks after transplanting</td><td></td><td></td><td>See label for specific product.</td></tr>
</table>

Phosphorus and Potassium Applications

A soil test is the best method to determine the need for phosphate and potash. With a fertilizer containing nitrogen and phosphate and/or potash, the application rate is always based on the nitrogen percentage because nitrogen is most critical to plant growth.

Phosphate and potash fertilizers are best applied in the spring or fall, when they can be tilled into the soil

Phosphorus

Phosphorus levels are adequate in the majority of established Colorado gardens. Deficiencies are most likely to occur in new gardens where the organic matter content is low and in soils with a high pH (7.8 to 8.3). Excessive phosphorus fertilizer can aggravate iron and zinc deficiencies and increase soil salt content.

Routine application of compost or manure will supply the phosphorus needs in most garden soils in Colorado.

Where phosphorus levels are believed to be low, the standard application rate without a soil test is ¼ to 1-pound triple super phosphate (0-46-0) or ammonium phosphate (18-46-0) per 100 square feet.

Potassium

Potassium levels are naturally adequate to high in most Colorado soils. Deficiencies occasionally occur in new gardens low in organic matter and in sandy soils low in organic matter. Excessive potash fertilizer can increase soil salt content.

Routine applications of compost or manure will supply the potassium needs for most garden soils in Colorado.

Where potash levels are believed to be low, the standard application rate without a soil test is ¼ to ½ pound potassium chloride (0-0-60) or potassium sulfate (0-0-50) per 100 square feet.

MANAGING SOIL COMPACTION

On clayey soils, soil compaction is a common problem limiting crop growth potential. Soils are typically compacted in the construction process. Walking on wet soils, cultivating wet soils, and the impact of rain are other common forces compacting soils.

The following are suggested to help minimize soil compaction in the garden:

- Add organic matter to clayey soils.
- Avoid cultivating or working a clayey soil when wet. To evaluate, squeeze a handful of soil. Then try to crumble it. If it will crumble, it can be worked. If it will not crumble but stays in mud balls, it is too wet to be worked.
- Avoid cultivating other than to prepare a seed bed or till in organic

matter and fertilizers. For weed control, use a mulch, hand removal, or shallow cultivation only.

- Use a raised bed with established walkways, and avoid walking on the growing bed.
- Mulch the soil, year round, to minimize the compaction forces of rain and sprinkler irrigation. Winter rains on bare soil are a major compaction force. This also helps manage weeds and reduces irrigation need.

Table : **Cool Season Vegetables**

Vegetable	Minimum Container Size*	Minimum Direct Sunlight Per day	Remarks
Beets	8″ deep	8 hours	• Best in cool temperatures, grow a spring and fall crop. • To give space for root development, thin greens to three inches". • A consistent supply of water and nutrients promotes the rapid growth essential for quality produce.
Broccoli Cabbage Cauliflower Collards Kale	10″ deep 5 gallons per plant	8 hours	• Best in fall production (e.g., plant mid July for fall harvest along the Colorado Front Range). • Minimum spacing per plant is 18 inches by 18 inches. • A consistent supply of water and nutrients promotes rapid growth and is essential for quality produce. • Heavy feeder, requiring frequent light fertilization. • Crops develop a strong flavor if the soil gets dry.
Carrots	8″-12″ deep	8 hours	• Best in cool temperatures, grow a spring and fall crop. • Use short root varieties, like Short & Sweet or Scarlet Nantes. • Roots will crack and be strong flavored if the soil gets dry. • Thin early to two to three inches apart. • Decorative foliage.
Chard	8″ deep	6 hours	• Space to six or more inches between plants in a row. • Harvest outer leaves allowing plants to continue to grow. • Makes an excellent "cut and grow again" crop. • Colored varieties are very decorative. • Responds to frequent light fertilization. • A consistent supply of water and nutrients promotes the rapid growth essential for quality produce.
Kohlrabi	8″ deep	8 hours	• Best in cool temperatures, grow a spring and fall crop. • A consistent supply of water and nutrients promotes the growth essential for quality produce. • Never allow soil to become dry. • Kohlrabi is a heavy feeder, requiring frequent, light fertilization.
Leaf Lettuce	8″ deep	6 hours	• Grow as a spring or fall crop; avoid hot summer temperatures. • Use softhead or leaf types. • As the young crop grows, thin to nine-inch spacing; crowding (competition for space, water and nutrients) reduces quality. • A consistent supply of water and nutrients promotes the rapid growth essential for quality produce. • Responds to frequent light fertilization. • Lettuce become strong flavored if the soil become dry, during hot weather, and with crowded plants.
Onions (green)	6″ deep	8 hours	• Onions require a consistent supply of water. Never allow soil to become dry. • Thin the crop by harvesting young plants. • Plant in early spring. • A consistent supply of water and nutrients promotes the rapid growth essential for quality produce.

Peas	8″ deep	Full sun	• Not well suited to container gardening. • Best in cool temperatures, grow a spring and fall crop. • Use dwarf, edible-pod or snap types for salads and stir-fry. • May be grown in hanging baskets or trellised. • Needs good air circulation to avoid powdery mildew.
Radish	8″ deep	8 hours	• Best in cool temperatures, grow a spring and fall crop. • A consistent supply of water and nutrients to promote rapid growth is essential for quality produce.
Spinach	8″ deep	6 hours	• Best in cool temperatures, grow a spring and fall crop. • A consistent supply of water and nutrients promotes the rapid growth essential for quality produce.
Turnips	8″ deep	8 hours	• Best in cool temperatures, grow a spring and fall crop. • When large enough to make greens, thin to four inches, allowing roots to develop. • A consistent supply of water and nutrients promotes the rapid growth essential for quality produce.
* Larger container sizes will make crop easier to care for, providing a bigger supply of water and nutrients.			

VEGETABLE GARDENING IN CONTAINERS

Container vegetable production is somewhat more demanding than growing flowers and other ornamentals in containers. Quality of most vegetables is based on the soil's ability to provide a constant supply of water and nutrients. Vegetables become strong flavored, stringy, and tough under dry or low fertility conditions. With the limited root spread in a container, the gardener must frequently and regularly supply water and fertilizer. In growing container flowers, minor lapses in daily care may interrupt flower production, but flowering eventually resumes with returned quality care. With container vegetables, minor lapses in daily care may significantly reduce produce quality.

COOL SEASON VEGETABLES

Table : **Warm Season Vegetables**

Vegetable	Minimum Container Size*	Minimum Direct Sunlight Per Day	Remarks
Beans	8" deep	full sun	• In a long box 12-inch wide, plant bush beans or trellis pole • Beans have a high water requirement during blossoming. • Beans drop blossoms with dry soil or excessive wind.
Cantaloupes Muskmelons	5+ gallons per plant	full sun	• May be trellised to conserve space. • Compact varieties preferred for container gardening. • With male and female blossoms, may need hand pollination. • Needs good air circulation to minimize powdery mildew.
Cucumbers	8" deep 3+ gallons per plant	full sun	• Grow bush-types in hanging baskets or on a trellis (vines grow 18-24+ inches long). • Grow strong vining-types on trellis. • Needs good air circulation to minimize powdery mildew. • Young plants are very sensitive to wind burn.
Eggplant	8" deep 4-5 gallons per plant	full sun	• One plant per container. • Requires night temperatures above 55°F for pollen development.
Peppers	8 deep 2-5 gallons per plant	full sun	• One plant per container or space to 14 to 18 inches in row. • Requires night temperatures above 55°F for pollen development. • Decorative, attractive plant with fruit.

Summer Squash (Zucchini)	8 deep 36 by 36 space	full sun	• Compact varieties more suited to container gardening. • Great in a whiskey barrel size container. • One plant will produce six or more fruit per week. • Has male and female blossoms. May need hand pollination. • Needs good air circulation to minimize powdery mildew. • Keep fruit picked for continued production.
Tomatoes	12" deep 2-5 gallons per plantdepending on cultivar (plant size)	full sun	• Cultivars vary in mature plant size from determinate bush) types to large, indeterminate vines over 6 feet tall. • Patio types (small vines) are great for container gardening and may be grown as hanging baskets or trellised. • Standard garden types require a larger container (like a whiskey barrel) and trellising. • Requires night temperatures above 55°F for pollen development. • Crowding cuts yields and increases disease potential. • Blossom end rot (black sunken area on bottom of fruit) is a symptom of inconsistent watering (too wet or too dry) or inadequate pot size.

* Larger container sizes will make crops easier to care for, providing a bigger supply of water and nutrients.

Cool season vegetables prefer the cool growing temperatures (60°F to 80°F) of spring and fall. Most are intolerant of summer heat. They do tolerate light frosts. Leafy and root vegetables prefer full sun, but are tolerant of partial shade. They are intolerant of reflected heat during the summer season.

Spring crops are typically planted two to four weeks before the average spring frost date. Along the Colorado Front Range, spring planting times are mid-April to early-May. Most are replanted in mid-July to mid-August for a fall harvest.

The quality of these vegetables is directly related to their ability to grow rapidly in a good soil mix under frequent light fertilization and a constant supply of water. Crops become strong flavored if they become dry.

WARM SEASON VEGETABLES

Warm season vegetables prefer warmer summer temperatures (70°F to 95°F) and are intolerant of frost. They are typically planted after the average spring frost date as summery weather moves into the areas. Along the Colorado Front Range, planting time would be mid-May to early June. Warm season crops need full sun.

GROWING VEGETABLES IN A HOBBY GREENHOUSE

EXTENDING THE GROWING SEASON

Off-season vegetable production in the hobby solar greenhouse is an enjoyable way for year-round gardeners to extend the harvest season of fresh vegetables. However, without the expense of a greenhouse, gardener can extend the growing season weeks to even months with cold frames and plastic tunnel gardening. For details on frost protect and cold frames, refer the *CMG GardenNotes* #722, Frost Protect and Extending the Growing Season. Winter vegetable production in a greenhouse is only cost effective with an energy efficientgreenhouse structure, a well-designed solar collector, and optimum management.

Winter vegetables have a slow growth rate due to low light intensity. Crops should be planted to obtain a near harvestable size by mid-October. The use of artificial light for vegetable production (except for starting transplants) is generally not cost effective.

A gardener's success is dependent on the greenhouse design and construction to conserve energy and on the management care given the greenhouse crops.

Before investing in a greenhouse, carefully consider your real interests in extending the gardening season. Are you only interested in adding a few weeks to the harvest season? Are you interested in year-round gardening in a solar greenhouse OR do you need a winter break from gardening activities?

PASSIVE SOLAR GREENHOUSE

For the gardener considering a passive solar hobby greenhouse, here are a few key points to consider. Refer to other greenhouse references for additional details.

For solar collectors, any area with direct sun, but not blocking solar illumination of plants, is a potential location. For a hobby greenhouse, solar collectors are typically built into an insulated north wall.

A solid brick wall on the north makes a good solar collector. Brick absorbs 30 to 35% of the solar radiation. With a brick storage wall, the greenhouse quickly heats on a sunny winter day and ventilation will be needed by mid morning.

Fig. Brick storage wall in passive solar hobby greenhouse – Thermal storage mass is a wall made with two layers of brick filled with concrete. In this well-built structure, nighttime temperatures dropped to 35°F with no supplemental heat when outside temperatures dropped to –17°F. Note young crops in raised-bed style garden with drip irrigation.

Water storage using plastic milk jugs makes a great storage system. Water jugs absorb 90% of the solar radiation, holding three times more heat than brick or rock. This increased heat storage holds night temperature higher longer into the night, resulting in slightly improved crop growth compared to brick storage.

Fig. Milk jug water storage wall in a passive solar hobby greenhouse. Disposable milk jugs on left and returnable milk jugs on right are spray painted flat black. In this well-built structure, nighttime temperatures dropped to 39°F with no supplemental heat when outside temperatures dropped to -17°F.

With milk jug storage, spray the milk jugs with flat black paint, and add one tablespoon of Clorox-type bleach per jug (to prevent algae growth in the warm water). Secure the cap back on the jug with a ring of caulk. Place the milk jug on a bookcase type frame not more than two jugs high.

Fig. Hobby greenhouse being constructed with double glazed patio door glass.

Disposable milk jugs develop leaks over time and require routine replacement. Heavier weight jugs (like returnable plastic milk jugs) last longer. Other types of containers may be used. Keep the size two gallons or smaller or water will stratify with hot water on the top and cooler water on the bottom, reducing efficiency. A passive solar hobby greenhouse is only effective when built to optimum energy specifications. Because the major heat loss is through the glazing, double-glazing (which reduces heat loss by 25 to 35%) is required. Double glazed patio door glass is great for glazing a hobby greenhouse. Glass suppliers sometimes have recycled (used) patio door glass available at minimal prices. Night curtains may add an additional 30 to 50% energy conservation. On a passive solar hobby greenhouse, the north, east, and west walls are typically insulated to an R-value of R38. The foundation and floor are insulated from heat loss to the ground.

Cold air infiltration is the second major source of heat loss. For passive solar to be effective, minimize cold air infiltration with good design and construction techniques. Insulative vent covers help reduce cold air infiltration at night, but must be removed daily to allow thermostats to maintain proper temperature.

A passive solar hobby greenhouse requires an east to west orientation. In northern Colorado latitudes, an east to west orientation receives 25% more solar energy than a north to south orientation. Sometimes the hobby greenhouse may be oriented slightly to the east for faster morning warming. An orientation 20° off east to west will cut 4 to 5% of the solar potential, while an orientation 45° off east to west will cut 18 to 20% of the solar potential. At northern Colorado latitudes in January, a north to south orientation cuts 25% of the solar potential.

A poorly constructed greenhouse cannot be retrofitted into an efficient passive solar unit.

COOL SEASON VEGETABLES

Fig. Lettuce in solar greenhouse raised bed.

Cool season vegetables do well in the greenhouse or cold frame. High temperatures are not desirable, and an occasional near freezing dip will not harm crops. High light intensity is not as critical for cool season crops as for warm season crops.

General temperatures for cool season crops

- Daytime: 50°F to 70°F
- Daytime short-term temperature extremes: 35°F to 90°F
- Nighttime: 45°F to 55° F
- Germination: 40° to 75°F
- Figure 3. Lettuce in solar greenhouse raised bed

WARM SEASON VEGETABLES

Warm season vegetables require high light intensity and moderate night temperatures. They cannot be cost effectively grown during the winter in a hobby greenhouse without solar heat collectors. Greenhouse climates control is critical for these fruiting crops to produce. Warm season crops are not compatible with cool season crops due to differing temperature needs.

General temperatures for warm season crops

Fig. Beans in solar greenhouse raised bed

Fig. Raised bed vegetables in solar greenhouse.

- Daytime – 60°F to 85°F
- Daytime short-term temperature extremes – 50°F to 95°F
- Nighttime – 55°F to 65°F
- Germination – 60°F to 85°F

TENDING A GREENHOUSE

Greenhouse gardening is similar in many ways to gardening outside. The plants still need adequate nutrients and water, and protection from insect pests and diseases. You still must tie, prune, and tend to them.

But the greenhouse environment is also very different from that of abackyard garden. The very things that make greenhouse growing more controlled and convenient also make it more demanding. In a greenhouse, you control temperature, humidity, soil aeration, soil moisture and drainage, fertility levels, and light. This degree of environmental control gives you a tremendous amount of latitude as well as some new responsibilities.

Temperature: Heaters, vents, and fans are your allies in temperature control. Even in a well-designed solar-efficient greenhouse, outside conditions are sometimes so cold and cloudy that auxiliary heat is needed to keep plants growing at an optimum rate.

Vents and fans help to cool the greenhouse. On a sunny day, even at 20°F below zero, greenhouse air can heat up well beyond healthful levels. If the greenhouse is attached, you can move this hot air into your home. But in a freestanding unit, hot air must have a way to exit, and cool air a way to enter.

Passive vents allow for this sort of movement, as do thermostatically controlled exhaust fans and intake vents. Manually operated vents are relatively inexpensive, but you'll need to check them at least twice a day, and open or close them as necessary. Automatic ventilation systems are more costly, but they save time and reduce the chances of excessive cooling or heating.

Adjust air temperature in the greenhouse according to the level of light. In general, summer crops grow best at temperatures of about 75° to 85°F in the daytime and 60° to 75°F at night. On cloudy days, these temperature ranges should be somewhat lower, since the plant is not manufacturing as many sugars as usual.

Winter air temperatures can go as low as 45°F at night without damaging most leafy green crops and shouldn't go much above 65° to 70°F during the day. Spring seedlings vary in their temperature preferences. Cool-weather crops, such as broccoli and lettuce, grow most vigorously at 50°F nights and 60° to 65°F days, while warm-weather plants such astomatoes and squash require nights at a minimum of 55°F and days of at least 65°F but no higher than 80°F.

Ornamentals typically need night temperatures no lower than 55°F, and tender tropicals can require night temperatures of 60°F or even higher.

Investigate the temperature requirements of the plants you plan to grow before installing your greenhouse and heating system so you can match the heater to your plants' needs. You can find a wide range of heater types and sizes, from freestanding propane heaters to powerful wall-mounted electric heaters. As with the greenhouses themselves, all greenhouse equipment is available through greenhouse and garden supply catalogs and Web sites.

Air circulation: Air circulation is extremely important to plant health. Good air circulation strengthens the woody tissue in stems and decreases the opportunities for fungi to attack your plants. Dense plant growth can interfere with air circulation and contribute to excessive relative humidity. Leave adequate space between plants and prune so that leaves from adjacent plants don't touch each other.

Plants use carbon dioxide from the air to manufacture sugars. In a closed greenhouse, carbon dioxide can be so depleted that plant growth is slowed. Remember to ventilate to change the air supply at least once each morning, even if you have to add extra heat.

Besides vents and fans, one low-tech way to increase air movement is by installing screened windows and doors in your greenhouse. By opening a window on one end and the door panel on the other, you'll have cross-ventilation. Positioning windows at the top and bottom of the greenhouse walls allows warm air to rise and escape from the upper windows, and cooler air to enter through the lower ones. Humidity: Greenhouses that feel like rainforests don't produce sturdy, healthy plants. Relative humidity should be close to 70 to 85 percent during high-growth periods. At levels of 90 to 95 percent, plant growth is weak, early bolting occurs, and fungal diseases become a real problem. Decrease humidity levels by venting or exhausting humid air and watering only when necessary. Growers in arid climates can increase humidity levels in the greenhouse by spraying water on the floor.

Light: Light levels in a greenhouse are partially determined by the design. When planning a greenhouse, check shade patterns from roof overhangs at the summer solstice in June and modify the plan if the shade is too great.

Fluorescent lights are very useful when you're growing spring seedlings, particularly in cloudy regions. They can also give a boost to midwinter greens and the last of the fall-fruiting crops. Ornamentals will also be healthier and more attractive with supplemental lighting. Shop-light setups suspended over raised benches are easy to install. You can choose fluorescent bulbs designed for plant growth, bulbs that mimic sunlight, or simply pair cool and warm bulbs in your fixtures. For intense light in a smaller area, another option is a compact fluorescent setup.

For plants like sun-loving orchids and tomatoes that require the equivalent of direct sunlight, you can also set up HID (high-intensity discharge) lighting systems with special bulbs. These systems are costly, though, and tend to give off a great deal of heat, so they're typically used by specialists and professionals rather than people with home greenhouses. Most plants will do fine with typical greenhouse light and supplemental fluorescent lighting.

Whatever system you choose, adding a timer will give you control over the amount of light your plants receive without having to worry about turning the lights on and off manually. Timers can also control automated watering and mist systems, fans, heaters, and other equipment.

Don't forget that plants can receive too much light as well as too little, especially in summer. Special greenhouse shade fabric panels are available in many sizes, as well as lengths you can order or cut to fit. You can choose from screening fabrics that will provide light shade to heavy shade, or protect plants from both too much light and heat buildup. Typically, you attach them over the greenhouse roof, though in areas of intense light you can choose a size that will cover the upper part of the walls.

Another option is to use shading paint developed for greenhouses. You can find paint that dries white, but becomes transparent in rainy weather to let in more light. Make sure you choose a paint specially developed for greenhouses so you can wash it off before winter.

Soils and fertility: Commercial growers sometimes amend the soils under their greenhouses and plant right in them. Home greenhouse growers usually find it easier to use benches with individual pots set on them or growing beds filled with a soil mix. Soil mixes for containers, benches, and beds should be lighter and more fertile than most garden soils. Good soil mixes drain fast, hold moisture well, contain balanced and slow-release organic nutrients, and have a slightly acid pH.

If you buy a potting mix, make sure you choose one that's organic. There are many options available in garden centers and from garden supply catalogs and websites. If you choose to make your own potting soil, a basic recipe is 2 parts soil, 2 parts finished compost, 1 part peat moss, and 1 part vermiculite or perlite. If the soil is clayey, add sand; if it's too sandy, use vermiculite instead of perlite and increase the proportion of peat moss. Test the pH and adjust it if necessary.

Add compost and other amendments such as vermiculite each spring and fall. Good mid-season fertilizers include compost tea and side dressings, earthworm castings, liquid fish emulsion, and seaweed. Foliar feed plants by spraying leaves with dilute compost tea, nettle tea, or liquid seaweed for extra nutrients and some disease resistance. Fertilize less in winter, when cool soil temperatures inhibit microbial activity.

GREENHOUSE VEGETABLE PLANTS: GROWING VEGETABLES IN A HOBBY GREENHOUSE

If you're like most gardeners, you're probably ready to get your hands on some dirt by the middle of winter. If you install a hobby greenhouse next to your home, you may be able to make that wish come true virtually every day of the year. Growing vegetables in a hobby greenhouse allows them to extend the season, sometimes by months, giving you a year-round gardening opportunity. While you can't grow all vegetables in a greenhouse 12 months of the year, you can plant cool-weather vegetables and let them grow through the worst of the winter weather with a simpleheating system installed.

HOW TO GROW VEGETABLES IN A GREENHOUSE

Greenhouse vegetable plants may end up growing faster and stronger than those grown in a traditional garden, because you will be giving them the ideal environment for growth. When it's below freezing outside, passive solar collectors and small heaters can leave the interior of a greenhouse cool but perfectly liveable for most spring vegetables. In the heat of the summer, fans and other cooling units can protect tender plants from the scorching heat of a southern climate.

You can grow greenhouse vegetable plants directly in the soil inside the enclosure, but container gardening is a more efficient use of space. You can take advantage of all three dimensions by placing planters on shelves, using trellis systems for vine plants and hanging planters for smaller vines, such as cherry tomatoes andstrawberries.

Winter Vegetable Growing

Growing winter veggies for greenhouses is possible because most cool-season plants can tolerate temperatures near freezing, as long as their soil isn't muddy. Container gardening solves that problem by giving the plants a perfect mix of potting soil.

If you're planning on winter vegetable growing whenbuilding your greenhouse, add a passive solar collector such as a wall of black-painted water jugs. This will collect solar heat during the day and reflect it into the greenhouse at night, helping to prevent freezing. Add an additional small heater, either propane or electric, for the coldest days of the year.

Once you have the greenhouse built, experiment with plant placement for the best growing conditions for each variety. Cool season plants such as peas, lettuce, broccoli, carrots and spinach all have slightly different needs, and moving them around in the enclosure is the best way to find what works best with each plant.

8

Greenhouse Growing

GREENHOUSE GARDENING

Fig. *Function* is the most important factor in determining the type and size of greenhouse you choose.

Most gardeners would love to own a greenhouse. This appeal may be strongest in cold climates, but being able to grow an endless supply of sturdy little seedlings is a pretty appealing concept no matter where you live. And what gardener isn't intrigued by the idea of having a tropical environment filled with orchids, citrus and jasmine; or wouldn't relish the opportunity to pick fresh salad greens and vine-ripened tomatoes on a cold winter day. There are now dozens of affordable, well-constructed greenhouses on the market, as well as a full range of accessories that make greenhouse gardening easier than ever.

This may seem like a simplistic question, but function is really the most important factor in determining the type and size of greenhouse you choose.

An attached greenhouse or sunroom is the right choice if you want a place to read and putter among potted plants. For starting seeds, a freestanding polyethylene-covered hoop house can probably give you everything you're looking for. If your objective is to have a nearly year-round supply of fresh greens and herbs, you may want to consider a solar greenhouse that requires little or no supplemental heat.

Can you imagine yourself tending an extensive collection of orchids, propagating begonias and experimenting with oleander and passiflora? If so, you'll want a well-insulated, professional-quality greenhouse that can be temperature-controlled year-round, with running water, a power source for supplemental lights, active ventilation and plenty of room for expansion.

Appearance may also be an important consideration. Will you be happy with a polyethylene hoop house, or is it important that your greenhouse be a more aesthetically pleasing addition to your home and your landscape?

Climate and location are crucial considerations. One reason greenhouses are so popular in England is that their climate is far more moderate than what most of us must cope with here in the U.S. Operating a year-round greenhouse in Vermont or Minnesota usually requires an insulated foundation, double glazing, insulating shades, buried power and water lines, and a serious financial commitment for heating.

In the summer, maintaining a plant-friendly environment may require shade cloth, multiple fans and a misting system. But people who do have a greenhouse, and have tasted the pleasures of being able to fuss around in their own warm, plant-filled jungle, would be quick to argue that the benefits outweigh the challenges.

WHAT SORT OF GREENHOUSE?

Custom Design or Kit?: There are now so many companies offering so many different styles and price ranges of greenhouses, that there's little reason to start from scratch designing your own. The exception to this is if you are building a new house, or are concerned about integrating your greenhouse into the architecture of your home. In this case, it may be wise to seek some professional advice.

Greenhouse kits may be as elaborate as a site-built gazebo room with turrets, or as simple as a box of plans with some hardware and a roll of polyethylene. Send for literature on all the greenhouse kits that interest you. Get on the Internet. Ask other gardeners about their experiences. And be sure to find out whether the supplier provides technical support.

Freestanding or Attached?: Having a greenhouse connected right to your home has many advantages—especially if you want to grow year-round. You can wander in and out to see what's happening at any time, day or night, no matter what the weather. With your plants so close at hand, it's easier to remember about watering and other tasks. Access to water and electricity is also easy. On sunny winter days, an attached greenhouse can add a significant amount of free heat to your home.

But attached greenhouses have a few downsides as well. Without proper venting and a way to isolate the greenhouse from the rest of your house, it may make your home too warm in the summer, and can keep your furnace running day and night in the winter.

Freestanding greenhouses are usually less expensive than attached models, and are much easier to set up. They can be placed right on the ground (though if you intend to heat the greenhouse through the winter, you should consider insulating the foundation down to the frost line). If you will only be using your greenhouse seasonally, a freestanding model will be relatively out of sight during the "down-times" of midwinter and midsummer. Putting in access to power and water may be relatively costly, and many greenhouse gardeners get along just fine with an extension cord and a garden hose.

Classic or Modern?: You will probably want to ensure that the shape or style of the greenhouse is compatible with your home. Even the most elegant Victorian-style greenhouse will not make an attractive addition to a New England saltbox. Northern gardeners must also consider snow load when choosing a greenhouse.

If snow doesn't slide off the roof naturally, you'll have to shovel it off to protect the glazing and allow light to enter the greenhouse. The overall shape of the greenhouse also determines the interior space and how it can work. Make certain that the style you choose provides enough headroom, wall area for displaying plants, a work area and enough roof area for venting.

Glass or Plastic?: Glass is still the traditional choice for greenhouse glazing, but there are now many high-quality horticultural plastics to choose from, including polycarbonate, acrylic, polyethylene and tedlar. When selecting a glazing material, you need to consider appearance, lifespan, whether you need single- or double-glazing, how weathertight your greenhouse needs to be and, unfortunately, price.

Traditional multi-pane glass greenhouses are notoriously difficult to seal. Modern attached greenhouses, with large panes of insulated glass, are usually very weathertight.

If you live where the ground freezes, a glass greenhouse needs to sit on a permanent foundation, or frost heaves could break the glass. Glass lasts almost indefinitely, and its light transmission is very high. That said, plastic glazings offer some distinct advantages over glass. They are far more forgiving of temperature fluctuations. They are easier to handle (lighter weight and non-breakable). They diffuse incoming sunlight, which prevents leaf-scorching. Last but not least, they won't be shattered by an errant frisbee or softball.

GARDENING IN A GREENHOUSE

Owning a greenhouse can give you the opportunity to grow plants from all over the world. But before you stock up on potted citrus, orchids, cacti, scented geraniums and bromeliads, you need to stop and think about what sort of growing environment you will actually be able to provide. A common mistake made by beginning greenhouse gardeners is to fill the greenhouse with any plant that piques their interest.

An eclectic assortment of plants such as this may look fine for a few months, but they will soon begin to suffer. Some plants need cold nights, some need warm nights. Some like lots of bright light, some require filtered shade. Some need water twice a day, some only every few days. The challenge is to decide what sort of environment you will be able to provide, to take advantage of the microclimates within the greenhouse, and to choose plants that will thrive in those conditions.

If you plan to run your greenhouse year-round, you first need to determine what temperature range you want to maintain - both in winter and in summer. Wintertime temperatures ranging from 40 to 60 degrees F may be ideal for growing salad greens, herbs, camellias and for overwintering tender exotics. But these temperatures are too cold for producing healthy tomatoes, gardenias and tuberous begonias.

During the summer months, bright sun and daytime temperatures of 85°–90°F may be fine for potted tomatoes, bananas, figs, and geraniums, but alpine plants, African violets, and many types of orchids will not tolerate the heat.

Microclimates: Within any greenhouse, there are certain areas that are hotter or cooler, brighter or shadier. By taking advantage of these natural microclimates, you can provide optimum growing conditions for a wider range of plants. Shade cloth, lathe, small fans, propagation chambers, heat mats, and other devices can also be used to help create and manage these microclimates.

EXPERT ADVICE ON GREENHOUSE GROWING

A greenhouse is one of the most valuable additions you can make to your property. If you want to be more self-reliant by raising more of your own food, a greenhouse — large or small — can help you meet many of your needs and goals.

With a greenhouse, you can plant fall and winter crops to extend the growing season and enjoy fresh food year-round. It also can provide food and shelter for poultry and livestock, and it's a great place to put worm bins. Here's a little about my greenhouse, and the many ways I use it.

THE GREENHOUSE STRUCTURE

Start With Simple Components. Most greenhouses are made from sheets of plastic stretched over a metal frame. You can buy a kit with all the essential components. Mine is a Paul Boers "gothic" style kit (the arches come to a peak at the top, which is better for shedding snow). I paid more up front to get 1 1/2-inch galvanized steel pipe, rather than 1-inch, for added strength. If your area gets any snow or heavy wind, this heavier pipe is a good investment.

I also recommend using 6-mil plastic that has been treated to resist ultraviolet breakdown. It's readily available from any greenhouse supply, and the version I use is guaranteed for four years. I use two layers of plastic with a small, energy-efficient blower to inflate the space in-between. The inflated "bubble" increases the insulating value of the cover, sheds snow more readily, and resists "chatter" in the wind, resulting in better wear.

Protect Your Foundation. When I first put up my greenhouse, I installed a wooden foundation to attach the "channel lock" into which the plastic cover is secured. Because I avoid using chemically treated wood, I used 2-by-8 pine boards with several coats of linseed oil. That was a bad idea — the boards rotted out after five years. My solution was to install a single course of 4-inch hollow concrete block on a small poured footer, then lock a better grade 2-by-4 (sealed against moisture) onto the top of the block foundation using J-bolts pushed into wet concrete in the holes of the blocks. The channel lock is still screwed into wood, but the wood is never in contact with earth or rain. With applications of sealant as needed, it should last as long as I do.

Choose the Right Size. The larger the greenhouse, the better its ability to buffer temperature extremes. That's because a larger greenhouse will have a larger amount of thermal mass — in the form of soil — that is warmed by the sun during the day, resulting in warmer nighttime temperatures. Another reason to choose a larger greenhouse is that you'll find more and more things you want to do with it.

Most greenhouse kits come in stock sizes, so buying a larger *stock* size may make more sense than ordering a smaller *custom* size. My initial plan was to erect a 20-by-32-foot greenhouse, but I found that by purchasing the 20-by-48 stock size, I picked up 50 percent more growing space for a mere $100.

Provide Adequate Ventilation. If you plan to grow vegetable crops in the greenhouse during the summer, your greenhouse will need heavy-duty exhaust fans and roll-up sides. For most winter growing, however, exhaust fans are superfluous. I know growers with 20-by-96-foot greenhouses who report that winter ventilation is adequate just by leaving the doors open as needed.

Brace for Winter. If you don't remember anything else from this chapter, remember this: If you live in an area that gets snow, brace the hell out of your greenhouse! Snow is so light and fluffy, it's hard to imagine the load it puts on a big structure as it accumulates, but the results can be dire. In February 2003, an unexpected snowstorm crushed my beloved greenhouse leaving inch-and-a-half steel pipes on the ground like spaghetti. After that sad experience, I put up 2-by-4 vertical braces to add support to the framing from the earliest possible date for snow in late fall until the latest possible date in early spring.

CARE FOR THE GREENHOUSE SOIL

Each winter, I grow plots of tightly spaced forage crops to cut for my poultry (usually grain grasses and mixed crucifers), which I rotate over the greenhouse beds. As the spent root systems decompose, they increase tilth, fertility and humus. Of course, using compost in the greenhouse is also a good idea — it will help boost the microbial populations in the soil. Mulches have benefits, too. They will moderate the temperature in the soil, conserve moisture and decompose over time to increase fertility.

There are advantages to leaving the greenhouse soil fallow over the summer: The soil "solarizes" in the intense heat, which burns off soil pathogens and will desiccate even the most die-hard slug. Last summer, however, I realized I wasn't doing anything to improve the soil in my greenhouse that was equivalent to my practice of cover cropping in the garden. So I grew a cover crop of cowpeas, which do well in the concentrated heat and the drier soil of the summer greenhouse. The project required a lot of water, but made a big difference in soil quality.

One caution: Avoid overfertilizing with nitrogen. Green leafy crops can accumulate unhealthy levels of nitrates, especially in the low light conditions of a winter greenhouse. I never add nitrogen fertilizers in the greenhouse, and I always use plant-based rather than manure-based (higher in nitrogen) composts. I am even concerned about the nitrogen added to the soil by my summer cowpea cover crop, and plan to follow it with a quick mixed grain cover to "sop up" some of that excess nitrogen before I plant other crops.

BRING THE CHICKENS INTO THE GREENHOUSE

I've been intrigued for years by the idea of keeping chickens in the greenhouse, and I put it into practice in 2005. We installed 4-inch block, two courses deep, to make partitions for two chicken pens, enclosing them with poultry wire over light wood framing.

There are three benefits derived from keeping chickens in the greenhouse in winter. First, the CO_2 from the poultry's exhalations promotes plant growth. (Before you think I've gone off my rocker factoring in chicken breath, consider that in the Netherlands growers pay good money for bottled CO_2 to pump into their greenhouses.)

Another benefit is that the body heat of the flock moderates the overnight chill in the greenhouse. I cannot test this proposition scientifically, but I had 43 chickens, three ducks and two African geese in there at the height of last winter — more than 250 pounds of warm living bird has to make a difference. Finally, I hate confining my flock in the chicken coop during the winter. Now instead of doing that, I heavily mulch the garden area outside the greenhouse, enclose it with electronet fencing and release the birds onto it during the day. This has many benefits: The mulch protects the soil over the winter, the birds eat earthworms and slugs that live under the mulch, and the cold-hardy poultry enjoy the sun, fresh air and exercise instead of being confined to the boredom and stress of a coop.

Worm Bin: Out-of-Sight Earthworms

I experimented with a 3-by-4-foot worm bin for several years. The greenhouse renovation seemed like the perfect time to step up to more serious vermicomposting. We dug in two courses of 4-inch hollow concrete block for the bins, 40 feet right down the center of the greenhouse. Every 8 feet, we put a cross wall of block, to create five 4-by-8-foot bins, 16 inches deep, each with two 4-by-4-foot lids made of three-fourths inch plywood on 2-by-4 framing. When the flock is out of the greenhouse over the summer, their two 8-by-8 pens are used for an additional 128 square feet of vermicomposting bin.

Because I needed access down the center anyway, I didn't lose much growing space to the new worm bins. And those substantial 4-by-4 lids over the bins have been a godsend. I routinely roll a fully loaded wheelbarrow over them. They are a great place to lay out work projects. We've even set up a table on them and had a picnic there; and I addressed a seated class of 16 on them one raw March day.

Of course all the kitchen throw-offs that don't go to the flock get fed to the worms. But my operation is way beyond the "worms eat my garbage" scale. I haul in pony poop by the pickup load from a neighbor who breeds and boards horses. The worms convert the manure into castings (earthworm poop), one of the best of all natural fertilizers. Last winter, the populations were finally high enough to make regular harvests of earthworms to feed the flock, a nutrient-dense, high-protein addition to their diet.

Winter Gardening Strategy

I don't add any artificial heat to my greenhouse, because I don't think using heat from fossil fuels to grow tomatoes in January is a sustainable practice. Instead, I choose naturally frost-resistant plants and count on the structure of the greenhouse itself to protect them from winter's extremes. You could say my greenhouse gardening strategy is to imitate an unusually mild winter, not to teleport my plants to the tropics. The greenhouse protects plants from winter extremes not only by slowing temperature changes but also by keeping wind and cold rains at bay. Plants such as lettuce are not bothered much by freezing air temperatures. They have learned a neat little trick to survive, which is unsettling the first time you see it: As air temperature drops, the plants move water out of their cells into the intercellular spaces, so that freezing doesn't disrupt the cell walls. The leaves go limp (and the frantic gardener assumes the crop is lost) — but then they perk back up as the sunlight warms the greenhouse and the cells rehydrate.

The more critical factor is to prevent freezing deep into the root zone — this is the key to successful winter gardening. You could think of the soil inside the greenhouse as a rechargeable battery. During the day, it charges from the heat energy of the incoming sunlight. At night, it quickly loses that stored energy, but it has a huge amount of heat to lose before the soil starts to freeze. I've gone into my greenhouse after a 10 degree night to find only a quarter-inch of frost on the surface of the growing beds. Before the frost gets deeper into the root zone, the new day begins the cycle again.

GREENHOUSES: THE MIRROR SEASON

Experienced gardeners might have some difficulty adjusting to the paradoxes of winter gardening. We have to relearn many of our assumptions, particularly about scheduling our crops. Unlike in spring, when the season is opening out into greater warmth and longer days, in the fall it is shutting down into increasing darkness and deeper cold. The biggest challenge will likely be the shorter day length, rather than the lower temperatures.

The bad news: During the darkest time of winter, there is insufficient solar energy to support vigorous growth. If you start your plants too late to accomplish most of their growth before the short days, they will survive the cold temperatures, but instead of growing actively, they will sit and sulk, awaiting sunnier days.

The good news: On the other hand, if you get the timing right, you can produce, say, a mature head of lettuce before the darkest days and it will stay fresh much longer than in the summer. That perfect head of lettuce that would spoil within a matter of days in June will stay in prime condition for two or even three months in the middle of winter.

When you start your crops in the late summer or early fall, start far more than you think you will need. As you harvest, you will not be able to start new crops, but if you have plenty "in the bank" at that point, you can continue making generous harvests until longer days make possible some late-winter crops.

GREENHOUSE CROPS

I start almost all my greenhouse crops as seeds under my growlights in the basement, then move them into the greenhouse when they get too big for the growbench. The greenhouse is simply too hot for direct sowing in late summer and early fall, when most winter crops need to be started. These are some of my favorite greenhouse crops.

Salads. Lettuces are quite resistant to frost, though not as cold hardy as some other winter garden plants. I grow a dozen different varieties — I'm easily bored with only one or two textures, colors and tastes. Chicories are my favorite winter salad. If you've been turned off to stringy, bitter endives and escaroles from the supermarket, be assured that — in the chill and reduced light of the winter greenhouse — chicory's bitterness is tinged with sweet, and the stringy toughness is replaced by a delightful juicy crunch. (An unusually good source for chicory seeds is Seeds from Italy.)

Lesser-known salads include mâche and edible chrysanthemum. Some are astoundingly cold hardy, such as claytonia (or miner's lettuce) and minutina (*Herba stella*). And don't forget scallions as an easily grown addition to winter salads. Cooking Greens. Spinach is extremely cold hardy. I make several sowings during the winter growing season. I also plant crucifers — including mustards, raab, Oriental greens such as pak choi and tatsoi — all are tasty and nutritious "potherbs," or cooking greens. Chard (or Swiss chard) is a type of beet bred for its large tender leaves and rapid re-growth, rather than its roots. It is cold hardy and productive.

Green onion and garlic tops also make great cooking greens. When I plant my garlic crop in the garden in the fall, I set aside the smaller cloves for growing "garlic scallions" in the greenhouse. We also sort out the smaller stored onions, or the ones that have begun sprouting, and plant them in the greenhouse for their beautiful and nutritious green tops. Brassicas that head (such as cabbages and broccoli) are more likely to develop large, tight heads if grown in the late-winter greenhouse rather than in the fall. Loose leafed kale, however, is an excellent crop for the fall-winter greenhouse if you start your transplants early enough. Get an Early Start. Root crops such as beets or carrots are not suitable for planting in the fall greenhouse — they will grow, but do not receive sufficient energy in the shortening days to "make root." I have, however, had excellent results growing carrots, beets, potatoes and daikon (as well as the smaller radishes) in late winter, and harvesting these crops up to two months earlier than their siblings in the garden.

MORE GREENHOUSE GARDENING TECHNIQUES

Know When to Water. It's best to water deeply from time to time in lieu of frequent shallow waterings. Water in the morning, as soon as the frost is off the leaves, to give the plants plenty of time to dry before temperatures fall at night. Avoid overwatering, which makes plants "sappy," less able to withstand cold and other stresses, and less flavorful and nutritious as well. Test the soil with your finger: As long as you feel good moisture half an inch deep or so, it's better not to water. Encourage Natural Ventilation. A closed greenhouse gets surprisingly hot on a sunny day, even if the temperature outside is quite cold. Don't stress your plants by leaving the doors to the greenhouse closed when it's sunny. I typically shut my two large doors (one at either end) at night, then open them wide during the day. If the day is unusually cold, blustery and cloudy, I prop the doors partially open, ensuring air movement through the greenhouse during the day. Good ventilation is important for disease prevention as well.

Balance Your Insects. My general approach to leaf-eating insects is not so much about control, as it is about balance. Therefore, I encourage all the flowering plants I can inside the greenhouse. These flowers provide pollen and nectar that attract lacewings, ladybugs and other beneficial insects. For example, the yarrow I planted last year bloomed early in spring, which encouraged the lady beetle population, so I had far less trouble with aphids this spring. Beneficial insects seem to migrate out of the greenhouse into the garden as it starts to bloom, boosting insect diversity there. Enjoy the Heat! Last but not least, a greenhouse is the perfect cure for the wintertime blahs. It may be 20 degrees with a rude wind blowing over packed snow outside — as long as the sun is shining, you can step into the greenhouse and it's Miami!

TOMATOES IN GREENHOUSE OR GROW HOUSE

GREENHOUSE GROWING : TOMATOES

Cooking Tomatoes

While the tomato is most closely associated with the cuisine of Italy, it first arrived in Europe to Spain from Mexico, not long after Cortes took control of Mexico in 1523.

However, it is perhaps fitting that the earliest documentary mention of the tomato is thought to be an Italian reference to a yellow-skinned form in 1544, hence pomodoro, 'golden apple'. Although tomatoes had been widely cultivated in Mexico before the arrival of the Europeans, there was great suspicion about the tomato when it first arrived in Europe. Botanists of the time knew that many members of the Solanum family are poisonous and they recognised its family features, especially of its flowers.

Tomatoes acquired a reputation as an aphrodisiac and were known as 'love apples' and 'pomme d'amour'. This reputation has faded but it was perhaps instrumental in encouraging people to taste the fruit. While mostly used as a 'vegetable', the tomato is, of course, a fruit and a berry at that. This is more obvious with the small-sized cherry tomatoes that with the usual sizes and the large 'beef' tomatoes.

These latter types are grown for their mealy flesh rather than their juicy seed pulp. A wide variety of fruit shapes is grown, and colours mostly red though yellow and striped too. The tomato plant is a short lived perennial and it is not hardy, though some variety are more tolerant of cool conditions than others.

Cooking Tomatoes

Tomatoes are an incredibly versatile food, being used both cooked and fresh in myriad ways. The flavour of tomatoes complements many other foods, balanced as it is between acid and sweet flavours. The colour of the fruit is valued in many dishes and the tomato has good nutritional value, being a good source of Vitamins A and C, with some fibre and smaller amounts of many other vitamins and minerals. It contains the valuable anitoxidant, lycopene, the concentration of which is actually increased by cooking although some Vitamin C is lost.

Growing tomatoes

Site and soil: Tomatoes can be grown in a greenhouse or outdoors. Greenhouse tomatoes can be grown in pots or in the open ground. Outdoor tomatoes are successful in most years.

Sowing: Plants can be raised from seeds or purchased. The earliest seeds can be sown in the first weeks of the year for early greenhouse planting, and later planting in April can be made form sowings in February or early March. Choose greenhouse varieties for indoor use. Outdoor varieties are raised from seeds sown in the first half of March to make plants of good size for planting out.

Varieties

The seed catalogues list a very wide range of varieties to which new kinds are added all the time. Classic varieties include 'Alicante', 'Gardener's Delight', the beef variety 'Marmande' and the cherry tomato 'Tumbler'.

Planting

Transplant the seedling to a small pot, grow on steadily and plant the tomato plant when it is about pencil height into good fertile soil or compost and do not water much until established and growing actively. Outdoors plant in a sheltered sunny spot in early June. Greenhouse plants must be always just moist at the root, never saturated and never dry.

Flowering

In the greenhouse tomatoes can fail to form on the first flower truss if the plant is too well watered, also the first trusses have a better chance if the plants are gently shaken to release pollen, especially early-sown plants. Outdoor plants will be shaken by air movement.

Training

Greenhouse tomatoes are trained to a single stem, supported by wrapping around a string tied to wires in the roof of the greenhouse, and the side shoots removed continually. Outdoor bush types do not have their side-shoots removed but it is beneficial to tie up the plant to a short stake to assist air movement and ripening.

Picking

The tomatoes are picked when they colour and green fruits that are fully formed will ripen off the plant.

Troubles

Tomatoes have a range of pests and diseases though most of these do not arise. Watch for greenflies and whiteflies in the greenhouse and potato blight outdoors. Tomato wilt caused by root rot diseases can affect tomatoes grown in the same greenhouse soil for some years.

PLANTING OUT TOMATOES

Once the young plants are outgrowing their 3½" (OK - 8.89 cm) pots with the roots coming through the base, it is time to plant on the tomatoes.

For the Growbag

The standard growbag contains between 35ltr and 40 ltr of compost, which is not a lot to grow 3 good plants on. I use a tip I saw on Gardeners World and it works brilliantly.

On top of the growbag I place three 9" bottomless pots. You can buy these for ring culture or just cut the base off some old pots. Using them as a template and a sharp knife, I cut rings into the surface of the bag and 'screw' the pot into the compost below. At the same time, I cut some small slits in the side of the bag about ½ above the base to allow for drainage.

Next, I insert two growbag watering pots to facilitate watering the bag. These are really clever little devices that ensure water and feed gets into the bag. They are re-usable year after year and available from Harrod Horticulture

The also have a ring system that you just screw into the growbag with watering and feeding around the side - take a look here

Having prepared the growbag, I then deep plant the tomato into the pot, leaving just under an inch for watering. A bamboo cane goes in to tie the plant to, which is held in place by going through holes in the top of the growhouse.

You can see small whitish nodules or hairs on a tomato shoot just above soil level. These 'pimples' will grow into roots if they contact the soil, enabling the plant to take on more nutrients and moisture

A good watering then beds everything down.

For the Greenhouse

You can grow tomatoes in a bed down the side of a greenhouse but the soil will need to be changed after a couple of years at least or you will get a build up of disease and the the soil's micro-nutrients will be depleted no matter how much fertilizer you add.

This is more work than you might think and I prefer to grow in large pots using the spent compost as a soil conditioner at the end of the season in the home greenhouse but in the border of the allotment greenhouse as it holds water well if I miss a day.

By large, I mean 12" although you can get away with smaller. Pots are measured across the top, by the way. The different depths and styles mean that the professionals buy according to capacity but I just use my eyes!

Some broken crocks in the bottom to ensure drainage, fill with general purpose compost, plant deep and insert a cane to support the plant. Job Done.

In a full size greenhouse you can use strings from the roof anchored into the pot instead of a cane. I think this was more trouble than using a cane and more of a fiddle to tie the plant to.

Growing On - Cordon Tomatoes

Because of space limitations, I only grow cordon tomatoes under cover rather than the bush varieties, which take up more floor area. The name of the game is growing tomatoes, not foliage, but the tomato is naturally a bushy plant. Left to its own devices, it would spread along the ground, producing many side shoots, which would make more side shoots and so on. It would not make that many tomatoes as its energy would be going into growth.

Fig. Pinching Out Tomato Side Shoot

Tomato Side Shoot Removal

To channel the plant's energy into producing fruit rather than foliage we need to remove the sideshoots These start in the angle between the leaf and stem. The earlier they are removed, the less energy is wasted. A job to be done at least once a week. After the plant is stopped, I have noticed it really goes mad for sideshoots - so watch out.

Be careful not to confuse these shoots with a truss. A truss is the stem that carries the flowers, which turn into tomatoes.

If you let a sideshoot grow to about 6" or more, you can cut it off, pop it into a pot of wet compost and have another plant. Useful if you find yourself short of plants and it is too late to start more from seed.

Stopping Tomatoes

When the plant has set four or five trusses it is time to stop it. You just take the leading (main) shoot at the top and cut it off. This means all the plant's energy can be diverted into fruit, which will hopefully mature before the end of the season.

If you let the plant just carry on you will find yourself with a lot of tiny green tomatoes at the end of the year.

Feeding Your Tomatoes

When the first truss has set, which means the flowers have gone and you can see tomatoes beginning to form, it's time to start feeding. Tomatoes are greedy, we want lots of juicy fruits, so you need a good tomato feed. I use either a bought organic feed, which is based on comfrey, Tomorite or make my own comfrey liquid feed.

Feed weekly at least to keep the plant going.

End of Season

As the season draws to a close, it becomes a race to ripen the crop prior to the frosts. To help this along I remove the lower leaves and expose the fruits to the sun. By this stage the plant does not need as much energy so the leaf removal will not affect it.

At the end of the season before the first frost, I harvest all the green tomatoes of reasonable size and these can either be ripened or used in chutney etc.

You can also hang up the vines with fruit on in a frost-free, cool dark place and they will slowly ripen. If kept in a draw with a ripe banana they will ripen quickly due to the gas given off by the banana

Growhouse Tomatoes

Click on the photo to view larger image

The Tomato Grow House

Here you can see the young plants sitting in the pots, which gives them far more compost to take nutrients up from. As it is early in the season, the top shelves are in place and being utilised for various tender seedlings

Later, these will be removed and the plants will be tied to the crossbars which are part of the grow house structure.

The Tomato Grow House

Here we are in early August and the plants have filled the shelter and been stopped. The pots are hidden under the mass of marigolds which keep whitefly at bay and make for a more attractive item in the garden.

In front our emergency lettuce in a trough (useful when I forget my allotment shopping order) and our cat, Aphy, is watching a butterfly off-shot with great interest.

GREENHOUSE TOMATO PRODUCTION PRACTICES

Tomatoes have been grown in greenhouses for nearly 100 years. For this reason, there are many techniques for growing tomatoes in a greenhouse and there is more written about greenhouse tomatoes than any other greenhouse crop. Additionally, hydroponics was developed for greenhouse tomato production, so there can be many complicated steps to the production of tomato fruit in a greenhouse. There is no single BEST way to grow greenhouse tomatoes, many ways are successful. An individual grower must experience tomato production, in order to determine the best and most economic techniques in his or her greenhouse. This publication is a general summary of greenhouse tomato practices. It is highly recommended that the reader obtain the publications listed below to get a more thorough view of greenhouse tomato production, hydroponics and the production of other vegetables in the greenhouse.

General Aspects of Tomato Production

LIGHT AND TEMPERATURE CONTROL — Tomatoes are a warm season vegetable crop. They grow best under conditions of high light and warm temperatures (summer conditions). Low light in a fall or winter greenhouse, when it is less than 15% of summer light levels, greatly reduces fruit yield when heating costs are highest (Table 1). For this reason, it is difficult to recommend that a greenhouse operator should grow and harvest fruit from December 15 to February 15. Even with the problem of low light and high energy costs, winter greenhouse tomatoes are common in southern Canada and Europe. These greenhouses may use expensive supplementary HID lighting (street lamps) and are able to sell their tomatoes at very high prices because their market is willing to pay a high price for high quality winter tomatoes. Greenhouse tomatoes are not very common in the U.S. or Kentucky, because consumers seem unwilling to pay a high price for winter tomatoes. If you have a market willing to pay for greenhouse tomatoes, then tomatoes may be a successful crop in your winter greenhouse.

Table : Relative percentages of heat costs and percent of light, compared to summer months, for fall, winter and spring months in Kentucky.

	September	October	November	December	January	February	March	April	July
heat	0 %	3	15	26	28	18	8	2	0
light	100%	41	32	14	14	27	50	65	100

Many greenhouses have been built in Kentucky to grow tobacco transplants. Based on many years of experience, tomato production is most successful in the spring. Excellent light, moderate heating costs and good prices annually demonstrate this is the best time for greenhouse tomato production. Yet, tobacco growers have tobacco transplants in their greenhouse in the spring. *Low winter light and high heating costs create a problem for winter production, so trials were completed at the University of Kentucky in 1995 and 1996 to evaluate late summer and fall production for greenhouse tomatoes. Results of these trials are presented throughout this publication.*

Tomato plants grow best when the night temperature is maintained at 60-62 F. Temperatures below 60 will prevent normal pollination and fruit development. This is especially true for standard greenhouse varieties, less so for field varieties, so the grower must be sure that thermostats control heaters properly. In warm or hot outdoor conditions, tomato greenhouses must be ventilated to keep temperatures below 95 F. High temperatures not only effect the leaves and fruit, but increased soil temperatures also reduce root growth.

PLANT SUPPORT — Plants must be tied or clipped with tomato clips to a string or twine suspended from a strong overhead cable. This starts as soon as they are about 10 inches high and continues throughout production. A separate support system must be built inside the greenhouse from pipe, etc. to support the crop. You must remember that each plant may weigh 10 to 15 pounds when it is loaded with fruit so the support system must be quite strong. Typical greenhouse structures are usually NOT strong enough to support a tomato crop, consult the greenhouse manufacturer for details; greenhouses designed to support a tomato crop are available from some manufacturers. Actively growing tomatoes will have to be clipped to the support string or twined around the string every 6-10 days.

WATER, FERTILIZER AND GROWING MEDIA — Tomato production requires that plant nutrition is monitored carefully and regularly. Tomatoes require a well drained growing medium, regular watering and regular applications of fertilizer. The application of water is typically done with a trickle irrigation system composed of distribution lines with drip tubes or spray stakes. Drip tubes or spray stakes are placed at the base of each plant. Tomato plants use a great deal of water, especially in warm weather, so the use of a timeclock to control the irrigation system is highly recommended and relatively inexpensive.

Many types of fertilizer have been used for tomatoes. Generally, the fertilizer is moderate in nitrogen and high in phosphorus, potassium, calcium and magnesium. A grower must be sure that calcium and magnesium are included in the fertilizer program. Normal plant and fruit growth requires these nutrients to be present in the correct amounts. A number of companies - Cropking Inc., Hydro-Gardens, Inc., Totalgro Plant Foods are listed below - have excellent fertilizer mixes for tomatoes. The fertilizer typically comes in two parts, calcium nitrate and a complete fertilizer (without calcium). This is because calcium nitrate is not compatible with other fertilizers in the concentrated form. With two fertilizers, the irrigation system has two injectors, each to inject a specific amount of each type of fertilizer at each watering. *In our 1995 and 1996 tomato trials at UK, we successfully used Scotts (Peters) MiracleGro Excel CalMag, 15-5-15, fertilizer as a single fertilizer from a single injector. This fertilizer combines all nutrients in the same mix; others have reported of the successful use of this fertilizer for greenhouse tomatoes.*

Many growing media can be used successfully for greenhouse tomatoes. Good field soil in the greenhouse floor, packaged commercial growing media composed primarily of composted bark, peat or coir, perlite alone, peat-lite mixes, rock wool slabs, straw bales, uniform river gravel, a thin layer of irrigation water in a plastic tube (NFT - nutrient film technique), controlled water table irrigation system, etc., will work if the grower correctly manages fertilizer and watering. Rock wool slabs seem to be the most economical and are used in most greenhouse tomatoes in Europe and Canada. Perlite is commonly used in the U.S and seems to be the most economical. Commercial growing media are also used because they are quite flexible. The media can be placed into pots or simply left in the bag and the bag is laid on the floor of the greenhouse. Each plant requires ½ to 1 cubic foot of growing medium. *A number of growing media - peat based, bark based, coir based, soil based and muck peat based potting soil - were used in the greenhouse tomato trials at UK in 1995. There were no significant differences in fruit yield between these mixes with the variety 'Solarset.' Tobacco growers involved with the same project used the same medium they used for tobacco transplants with success.*

Table : Tomato fruit yield from the determinate variety 'Solar Set' grown in six different growing media in greenhouse tomato trials in the fall of 1995.

Growing Medium	Average pounds per plant	Average number of fruit per plant	Average ounces per fruit
MetroMix 360 (coir)	7.2	12.8	8.9
MetroMix 360 (peat)	6.4	12.4	8.2
MetroMix 510 (bark)	7.2	13.3	8.6
Progrow (bark)	7.0	12.6	8.8
House Plant Potting Soil (muck peat)	5.9	10.6	8.9
Recycled media (20% soil, 80% peat; sterilized)	6.6	13.0	8.1

Tomato Variety Selection — Tomato variety selection is difficult. Many cultivars have been selected for greenhouse production in Europe, Canada and the U.S. The best varieties in the best greenhouses produce 35 to 45 pounds of fruit per plant in 10-12 months. Most of that production occurs in spring and summer. However, good garden varieties will perform well when grown as a spring or fall crop in greenhouses in Kentucky. Growers should also consider cherry or salad sized tomatoes depending on local market interest. Optimum fruit production will occur from greenhouse tomato cultivars but new growers can learn details of production on good garden cultivars.

The 1995 UK greenhouse tomato trials involved the use of determinate field tomato varieties. We chose these varieties because they produce only 4-6 clusters of fruit. We hoped all fruit would be harvested from October 15 to December 15 in order to reduce the typical high heat costs and low light problems of winter production. Observations in the fall of 1994 demonstrated that the determinate varieties 'Solar Set,' 'Mt. Spring' and 'Sunbeam' might be successful.

Table : Tomato fruit yield from four determinate varieties and one indeterminate variety (Greenhouse 761) from greenhouse trials in the fall of 1995. Seed were sown July 6, 1995 or July 18 (for Solar Set-18) and transplanted August 15. Fruit were harvested from October 20 to December 20, 1995.

Tomato Variety	Average pounds per plant	Average number of fruit per plant	Average ounces per fruit
Florasette	6.3	11.2	9.0
Greenhouse 761	7.8	12.0	10.4
Mountain Spring	6.1	8.7	11.4
Solar Set-6	7.0	12.3	9.1
Solar Set-18	6.8	10.9	10.1
Sunbeam	6.4	10.2	9.9

The average total weight of fruit harvested from each plant ranged from 6.1 to 7.8 pounds (Table 3), but was quite variable between plants ranging from 4 to 13 pounds per plant. Approximately 11 fruit were harvested from each plant, as an overall average, and the average fruit weighed about 10 ounces. There were no statistical differences between the yields of the five varieties in the UK trials in 1995, but we felt 'Solarset' was the best variety for fall performance.

The 1996 UK greenhouse tomato trials compared determinate field tomato varieties with indeterminate garden varieties and indeterminate commercial greenhouse varieties. Two of the garden varieties selected had small fruit size so potential yields of these specialty salad tomatoes could be determined.

The average total weight of fruit harvested from the determinate varieties was quite similar in both years, but fruit size decreased and fruit number per plant increased in 1996 (Table 4). Yields of 'Better Boy' and 'Celebrity' and the commercial indeterminate varieties had significantly higher yields than the determinate varieties. The average total weight of fruit and average fruit number per plant was greater but average fruit weight was variable. However, harvest was delayed 1 to 2 weeks on the greenhouse varieties when compared to the determinate varieties. The small fruited varieties performed reasonably well. The determinate varieties grew to a height of 3 to 4 feet while the indeterminate varieties, topped after the 6th cluster, grew to 6 feet tall. The general yield increase in 1996 could be attributed to better weather in November and December compared to 1995. Ten pounds per plant was the general goal of this demonstration project when it was initiated and this goal was met with standard greenhouse varities. Thus, it is appropriate that greenhouse operators choose commercial greenhouse tomato varieties, e.g. 'Trust,' 'Caruso,' etc. for best yields for fall tomato production.

Flower Pollination — Tomato flowers must be pollinated in order to get fruit set and fruit development. Traditionally, flower clusters are shaken manually with a tomato flower pollinator as soon as the yellow petals open. Pollination must be done every day, seven days a week, usually between 9 a.m. and 1 p.m. Bumblebees are available from insect companies for pollination as well. Simply purchase a box or hive of bees and place them in the greenhouse when tomato flowers open. The bees do a very good job, just be careful to protect the bees from pesticide applications. *In the 1995 and 1996 UK trials, we deliberately did not make a special effort to pollinate the flowers by hand or with purchased bees. We left the greenhouse sidewalls open during the day and feral (native) bees and the wind were responsible for pollination and the fruit yields described above. Additionally, we did not use pesticides while flowers were open. We cannot recommend that all pollination can be done this way, but it was reasonably successful during our trials.*

Table : Tomato fruit yield from five determinate varieties and nine indeterminate varieties (four garden varieties and five commercial greenhouse varieties) from greenhouse trials in the fall of 1996. Seed were sown July 15, 1996 and transplanted August 20. Fruit were harvested from October 20 to January 8, 1997.

Tomato Variety	Average pounds per plant	Average number of fruit per plant	Average ounces per fruit
Common Indeterminate Garden Tomato Varieties from Park Seed Co.			
Better Boy	9.6	18.3	8.5
Celebrity	10.0	21.0	7.7
Enchantment	8.5	40.9	3.4
First Lady	8.2	27.2	4.8
Common Determinate Fresh Market Commercial Tomato Varieties			
Florasette	7.1	15.9	7.0
Mountain Fresh	8.5	15.1	9.1
Mountain Spring	7.4	12.8	9.4
Solar Set	7.3	14.8	7.8
Sunbeam	7.8	14.6	8.6
Commercial Indeterminate Greenhouse Tomato Varieties from DeRuiter Seed Co.			
DRW3579	12.0	23.3	8.3
Furora	9.8	24.3	6.4
Laura	9.1	15.9	9.1
Switch	11.0	23.6	7.5
Twin	10.4	20.4	8.0

Pruning, Suckering — Tomato plants in a greenhouse are pruned to a single stem. All lateral branches or suckers must be removed when they are one to three inches long. This allows for maximum air circulation and simplifies pest control problems. Suckering must be done regularly, plants should be checked at least once per week.

Pest Control — Insects and diseases can be a big problem because so few pesticides are labeled for greenhouse vegetables. Remember, the pesticide label must identify tomatoes and greenhouse applications for it to be legal in the greenhouse (see ENTFACT-36, Controls for Greenhouse Vegetable Insect Pests and PAT-4, Greenhouse Pesticides and Pesticide Safety). The cleared pesticides have low toxicity, so they MUST be applied thoroughly and regularly. Start a regular disease and insect control program after the plants have been set for a week and continue this at 7 to 10 day intervals for the life of the crop. Use sticky yellow cards to monitor the pest population in the greenhouse. Do not wait until your plants are infested to start spraying. All tomato growers should learn about biological control insects and consider using them from the beginning of the crop.

Marketing — The market for fall greenhouse tomatoes is quite good. Tomatoes can be sold directly from the greenhouse at retail prices or sold to wholesale distributors, supermarkets or restaurants at wholesale prices. Be sure to contact tomato buyers early in the season so they will know you will have fruit and so you may learn how they want the tomatoes packaged for their use. We hope that greenhouse tomatoes will always receive at least $1.00 per pound.

Economics — Success in greenhouse tomatoes depends completely on fruit yield. Yields of 4-5 pounds per plant are probably break-even for annual costs. However, you should keep good records through the crop, so you can honestly evaluate your costs and returns. One thousand plants in a greenhouse (4000 square feet) can produce approximately 7,000 to 10,000 pounds of fruit from October 15 to January 1 and thus return approximately $ 7,000. to $10,000. to the greenhouse operator, based on our data from trials in 1995 and 1996.

GREENHOUSE GROWING : CUCUMBERS

Cucumber (*Cucumis sativus*) is a widely cultivated plant in the gourd family, Cucurbitaceae. It is a creeping vine that bears cylindricalfruits that are used as culinary vegetables. There are three main varieties of cucumber: *slicing*, *pickling*, and *burpless*. Within these varieties, several different cultivars have emerged. The cucumber is originally from Southern Asia, but now grows on most continents. Many different varieties are traded on the global market.

DESCRIPTION

The cucumber is a creeping vine that roots in the ground and grows up trellises or other supporting frames, wrapping around supports with thin, spiraling tendrils. The plant has large leaves that form a canopy over the fruit.

The fruit of the cucumber is roughly cylindrical, elongated with tapered ends, and may be as large as 60 centimeters (24 in) long and 10 centimeters (3.9 in) in diameter. Having an enclosed seed and developing from a flower, botanically speaking, cucumbers are classified as pepoes, a type of botanical berry. Much like tomatoes and squash they are often also perceived, prepared and eaten as vegetables. Cucumbers are usually more than 90% water.

Flowering and pollination

A few cultivars of cucumber are parthenocarpic, the blossoms creating seedless fruit without pollination. Pollination for these cultivars degrades the quality. In the United States, these are usually grown in greenhouses, where bees are excluded. In Europe, they are grown outdoors in some regions, and bees are excluded from these areas.

Most cucumber cultivars, however, are seeded and require pollination. Thousands of hives of honey bees are annually carried to cucumber fields just before bloom for this purpose. Cucumbers may also be pollinated by bumblebees and several other bee species. Most cucumbers that require pollination are self-incompatible, so pollen from a different plant is required to form seeds and fruit. Some self-compatible cultivars exist that are related to the 'Lemon' cultivar. Symptoms of inadequate pollination include fruit abortion and misshapen fruit. Partially pollinated flowers may develop fruit that are green and develop normally near the stem end, but are pale yellow and withered at the blossom end. Traditional cultivars produce male blossoms first, then female, in about equivalent numbers. Newer gynoecious hybrid cultivars produce almost all female blossoms. They may have a pollenizer cultivar interplanted, and the number of beehives per unit area is increased, but temperature changes induce male flowers even on these plants, which may be sufficient for pollination to occur.

GENOME

In 2009, an international team of researchers announced they had sequenced the cucumber genome.

Cooking cucumbers

Cucumbers are thought to have originated as a food crop in India over three thousand years ago. A related wild species still grows there, it is a subtropical plant. The ancient Greeks grew cucumbers and the vegetable gradually found its way around Europe. It is a short-lived plant, an annual that in natural conditions would produce seeds and die after a few months. It is related to the pumpkin and the melon. It needs considerable warmth to grow well and did not feature much this far north until glasshouses, or at least glass cloches and frames became available.

There are varieties known as ridge cucumbers which can be grown outdoors after the danger of frost is passed. These are harder than the greenhouse kind, the outer skin is tougher and often has rough bumps and prickles. The flesh is crunchy and they often have seeds since they are open to being pollinated. Greenhouse cucumbers are generally not pollinated as it changes both the shape and the flavour of the cucumber. The shape of a pollinated cucumber often ends up bulbous and the flavour is strong, bitter even. Preventing pollination used to involve screening bees out of the greenhouse but the modern varieties have only female flowers. A fresh cucumber from the greenhouse is crisp and has a lovely mild flavour, easy to grow but a fair challenge to grow well.

Cooking cucumber

Although cucumber is generally considered as a salad ingredient, it can be used in a variety of ways. It makes excellent salad material, either finely sliced or cut in chunks and can be used with a range of other salad ingredients. It is very good, greek style, with yogurt. It is a cooling food and appreciated in hot climates. But it can be lightly cooked, sliced in slender batons for falsh stir-frying and used with delicate flavours. It can b eaten with skin intact, except the tough-skinned ridge types. It is a good source of dietary fibre, Vitamin C, Vitamin K, magnesium, potassium and other vitamins and minerals.

GREENHOUSE GROWING : MELONS

A melon is any of various plants of the family Cucurbitaceae with edible, fleshy fruit. The word "melon" can refer to either the plant or specifically to the fruit. Many different cultivars have been produced, particularly ofmuskmelons. Although the melon is a fruit (specifically, a berry), some varieties may be considered vegetables rather than fruits. The word *melon*derives from Latin melopepo, which is the latinization of the Greek ìçëïðÝðùí (*mçlopepon*), meaning "melon", itself a compound of ìëïí (*mçlon*), "apple" + ðÝðùí (*pepôn*), amongst others "a kind of gourd or melon".

History

Fig. Watermelon and melon in India

Melons originated in Africa and southwest Asia, but they gradually began to appear in Europe toward the end of the Roman Empire. However recent discoveries of melon seeds dated between 1350 and 1120 BC in Nuragic sacred wells have shown that melons were first brought to Europe by the Nuragic civilization of Sardinia during the Bronze age. Melons were among the earliest plants to be domesticated in both the Old and New Worlds. Early European settlers in the New World are recorded as growing honeydew and casaba melons as early as the 1600s. A number of Native American tribes in New Mexico, including Acoma, Cochiti, Isleta, Navajo, Santo Domingo and San Felipe, maintain a tradition of growing their own characteristic melon cultivars, derived from melons originally introduced by the Spanish. Organizations like Native Seeds/SEARCH have made an effort to collect and preserve these and other heritage seeds.

Growing melons | Using melons

The melon, *Cucumis melo*, is a very variable species, native to Africa, and later introduced to Asia, where it developed into a range of subspecies. The Romans knew about melons but did not regard them very highly and this is thought to indicate that the kinds they had were not of great quality. The melon we know really began its current phase with the introduction of some sweet kinds form Turkey to the papal estate at Cantaluppe in Italy in the fifteenth century. This strain or subspecies was sweet and soon found its way around the warmer parts of Europe and took the name 'cantaloupe'.

In later centuries, melons were grown under glass in Northern Europe, often using deep beds of decomposing animal manure, or 'hot beds', to provide additional heat for very early or late crops. Melons became a highly prized fruit and indeed a freshly ripened melon, just picked, is vastly better than shop-bought melon. Being a hot-country plant, melon needs the protection of a greenhouse, low tunnel or cold frame. While they are a bit of a challenge to grow well, they are not very difficult to grow and if only a few fruits are produced, they are delicious!

Growing melons

Greenhouse melons are quite easy to grow and are of excellent flavour. Sow seeds of the varieties 'Ogen' or 'Sweetheart' singly in little pots in late March or April. Plant them into rich greenhouse soil, pots or growing-bags when they are about 15 centimetres high, in May. Pinch out the growing-point.

Side-shoots then develop. Retain the two strongest and train them up strings by twisting them around. These can also be left on the ground to spread, if preferred. Further side-shoots will be produced from the two chosen. These are the fruiting shoots.

When the flowers appear and open, take a male flower, peel away its petals and push it gently into the female flower, which can be recognised by the tiny fruit just behind the petals. Pinch out the side-shoot one or two leaves past the young developing fruit.

Allow only one melon to develop per fruiting side-shoot. Feed and water well once the fruit starts to swell. Melons can also be grown on the ground in a frame or low tunnel. Watch out for red spider mite and spray with Liquid

Derris on a dull day as soon as it is noticed. Repeat spraying will be necessary.

Using Melon

Melon is mostly eaten fresh, ideally just picked from the vine and still warm from the sunshine. Chilled melon loses much of its flavour. Melon can be used in a wide range of fruit desserts, smoothies and drinks. Melon can be used salads, especially fruity salads with cheese. It can also be used in cooked dishes, generally to make a sweet sauce with meat. Low in fat and cholesterol, it is a very good source of Vitamin A, Vitamin C and potassium.

GREENHOUSE GROWING : AUBERGINES

COOKING AUBERGINE

The egg plant or aubergine is a member of the potato family, related to tomato, sweet pepper, chilli pepper and cape gooseberry. It has the typical potato family flowers, purple in colour and flat, star-shaped with a central pointed yellow pistil. Unlike the other potato family crops, the aubergine originated in India, where wild types are still found. Other species occur in various parts of the Far East and are used for food, for instance, in Thailand. It has been used as food for over two thousand years in Asia and several hundred in southern Europe.

It got the name 'egg plant' from the very egg-like fruits on some varieties; these are white or creamy and egg-sized and shaped, unlike the fruits on modern egg plant varieties which are usually purple. However, white varieties still exist and varieties with small fruits and even narrow pointed fruits are still grown in some parts of the world. Aubergine is the french name for egg plant, derived from the Arabic name, the Arabs having introduced it to Spain.

To grow aubergine, it can be treated it much like the tomato, best grown in a greenhouse or tunnel, although it can be grown outdoors reasonably successfully in a warm, sheltered setting. Results will be quite good in a good summer, not so good in a dull, cool year.

Cooking aubergine

Aubergine is a very versatile fruit/vegetable, like the related tomato. It is not a juicy fruit and not as versatile as the tomato but it can be used in many ways - in stews or casseroles, baked and grilled. It is a 'meaty' vegetable that is filling and used for this purpose in vegetarian cookery. It has almost no calories, not much in terms of minerals or vitamins, and its main value is its ability to absorb the flavours of other ingredients. It is an important ingredient of some dishes. It can be a little bitter and some recipes call for salting it before use.

Growing aubergine

Site and soil: Ideally, aubergine is grown in a greenhouse as it benefits from the extra warmth. But it can be grown outdoors in a warm spot. Indoors it is best grown in the open soil rather than in pots or grow bags, and it needs rich, fertile soft soil with lots of well-rotted organic material.

Varieties

'Moneymaker' is a well-known purple skinned variety. 'Balck Enorma' is another. White, egg-sized fruits are carried on 'Mohican' and 'Clara'. Some companies offer mixed varieties.

Sowing

The seeds are sown, much like tomato, in late winter or early spring, starting them in a little warmth and growing them on with protection from frost on cold nights. The plants can be sown several to a pot and thinned to one good seedling.

Growing on

It is important to grow on aubergines without a set-back at any stage, potted on as they grow. If they are checked they often flower early and make poor growth afterwards. About five or six fruits per plant is a reasonable target for the large-fruited varieties, more for the smaller ones.

Planting out

Plant out the young plants from pots, usually thirty centimetres or more tall. Generally they have to wait untill mid-May when other plants are put outside and space is created.

Training

Allow the plants to grow to about fifty centimetres, pinching out the main growing points if they grow too tall. The plants might need the support of a light stake, especially as the fruits begin to swell.

Picking

Pick the fruits when they have made good size.

Troubles

Aubergines are very soft plants and attractive for a range of pests, notably greenflies and white flies. It may be necessary to spray with derris to control these.

GREENHOUSE GROWING : ORNAMENTAL PLANTS

Ornamental plants are plants that are grown for decorative purposes in gardens and landscape design projects, as houseplants, for cut flowers and specimen display. The cultivation of these, called floriculture, forms a major branch of horticulture.

GARDEN PLANTS

Most commonly ornamental garden plants are grown for the display of aesthetic features including: flowers, leaves, scent, overall foliage texture, fruit, stem and bark, and aesthetic form. In some cases, unusual features may be considered to be of interest, such as the prominent and rather vicious thorns of *Rosa sericea* and *cacti*. In all cases, their purpose is for the enjoyment of gardeners, visitors, and/or the public institutions.

SHRUBS AND CLIMBERS

Shrubs and climbers

A wide range of ornamental plants can be grown in a greenhouse or conservatory. Some of these must have the protection of a greenhouse and cannot be grown successfully in the open garden. Other plants, though they can be grown outdoors, grow better with the extra heat provided inside a protective structure.

Flowers

A wide range of herbaceous plants, such as busy lizzie, streptocarpus, pelargonium, cymbidium orchid, canna and peruvian lily, can be grown in the greenhouse. Some of the indoor plants are bulbs, corms or tubers such as gloxinia, tuberous begonia, amaryllis and lily that are potted up in March or April.

Freesia, cyclamen and anemone can be potted up in August or September. Hyacinth, tulip grape hyacinth, crocus and dwarf iris can be potted up in September or October and brought inside in January. Most of these plants come into flower four or five months after potting up.

Many greenhouse flowers can be raised from seed. Cineraria, primula, calceolaria and butterfly flower are sown in June, July or August to flower in March, April or May of the following year. Cyclamen is sown in August to flower 15 months later.

Quite a few bedding plants, both spring and summer, can be used as flowering pot plants. Petunia, everflowering begonia, ageratum, tobacco flower and french marigolds can be sown in March to flower in summer.

Polyanthus and double daisy are sown in early summer, and stock in late summer, to flower in spring. Two very useful greenhouse plants also raised from seed in spring are morning glory and blackeyed susan. These are climbers, but they only last one season.

Many foliage plants, such as spider plant, tradescantia, coleus and ferns can also be grown in a greenhouse. Shading might be necessary to avoid sun scorching and, in winter, some must have frost protection, or be taken indoors.

Alpine plants

Fig. Greenhouse alpine: Primula allionii

Because they need very little space, alpines make excellent greenhouse plants. They enjoy the dry air, but they mostly dislike excessive heat, and are best placed near the door or the ventilator. In winter, it is important to keep air humidity as low as possible.

Special alpine houses with a lot of ventilation are sometimes set up by alpine enthusiasts. Many kinds of alpines, such as primula, raoulia, lewisia, gentiana, rhodohypoxis and many small alpine bulbs, can be grown indoors.

GREENHOUSE GROWING : SWEET PEPPERS

In the U.S. the term sweet pepper covers a wide variety of mild peppers that, like the chile, belong to the capsicum family. The best known sweet peppers are bell peppers, named for their bell-like shape. They have a mild, sweet flavor and crisp juicy flesh. When young most bell peppers are a rich, bright green, but there are also yellow, orange, purple, red and brown bell peppers. Red bell peppers are green bell peppers that have ripened longer and are very sweet. The red heart-shaped pimiento is another popular sweet pepper. Pimientos are the familiar red stuffing found in green olives. Other sweet pepper varieties include cachucha, European sweet, bull horn (thin, curved and green); Cubanelle (long, tapered, yellow to red); and sweet banana pepper (long, yellow, banana-shaped).

The sweet peppers, also called bell peppers and capsicums, are varieties of *Capsicum annuum*, a species to which the hot chilli peppers also belong.

The only differences are the size of the sweet peppers which are many times larger than the chillis and the fac that the sweet peppers have no capsaicin, the agent that causes the hot sensation. The capsicums are native to Mexico and Central America where there are records of cultivation for seven thousand years and perhaps longer. The peppers arrived in Europe about 1500, the hot kinds probably first as a substitute for the true pepper. Their cultivation spread to Asia subsequently.

Although the sweet pepper has been in Europe for over five hundred years, it only found its way on the kitchen table in this country in recent decades, and into greenhouses and gardens even more recently. The capsicum is a warm climate plant and really needs to be grown indoors at this latitude but the newer more vigorous varieties can give good results outdoors in a warm sunny, sheltered place. It is related to tomato and not all that difficult to grow, if the conditions are right. The main colour is red - the green ones are not yet ripe but can be used - and there are yellow, orange and purple varieties too.

Cooking sweet peppers

The sweet pepper is a very versatile fruit. Like the tomato, it can be used in many ways, both cooked and fresh. It can be used as an ingredient in many dishes and it is good at absorbing the flavour of other vegetables and herbs, while imparting its own distinctive taste. It is a very good source of vitamin C and vitamin A, good in fibre with little fat and low in calories.

GREENHOUSE GROWING : LETTUCE

Lettuce (*Lactuca sativa*) is an annual plant of the daisy family Asteraceae. It is most often grown as a leaf vegetable, but sometimes for its stem and seeds. Lettuce was first cultivated by the ancient Egyptians who turned it from a weed, whose seeds were used to produce oil, into a food plant grown for its succulent leaves, in addition to its oil-rich seeds. Lettuce spread to the Greeks and Romans, the latter of whom gave it the name "*lactuca*", from which the English "lettuce" is ultimately derived. By 50 AD, multiple types were described, and lettuce appeared often in medieval writings, including several herbals. The 16th through 18th centuries saw the development of manyvarieties in Europe, and by the mid-18th century cultivars were described that can still be found in gardens. Europe and North America originally dominated the market for lettuce, but by the late 20th century the consumption of lettuce had spread throughout the world.

Generally grown as a hardy annual, lettuce is easily cultivated, although it requires relatively low temperatures to prevent it from flowering quickly. It can be plagued with numerous nutrient deficiencies, as well as insect and mammal pests and fungal and bacterial diseases. *L. sativa* crosses easily within the species and with some other species within the *Lactuca* genus; although this trait can be a problem to home gardeners who attempt to save seeds, biologists have used it to broaden the gene pool of cultivated lettuce varieties. World production of lettuce and chicory for calendar year 2010 stood at 23 620 000/23,620,000 tonnes, half of which came from China.

Lettuce is most often used for salads, although it is also seen in other kinds of food, such as soups, sandwiches and wraps; it can also be grilled. One variety, the Woju () or asparagus lettuce, is grown for its stems, which are eaten either raw or cooked. Lettuce is a rich source of vitamin K and vitamin A, and is a moderate source of folate and iron. Contaminated lettuce is often a source of bacterial, viral and parasitic outbreaks in humans, including *E. coli* and *Salmonella*. In addition to its main use as a leafy green, it has also gathered religious and medicinal significance over centuries of human consumption.

Varieties

Greenhouse-grown lettuce is of better quality than outdoor crops and it is available from November to May when they are not. Sow the variety 'Kwiek' in late August for winter lettuce, and 'Emerald' and 'Kloek' in September/ October for late winter and spring supplies.

These varieties tolerate cold weather, but without frost protection at least, there can be some losses and the plants will not 'heart' up. Watch for greenflies.

Do not splash water about or grey mould will attack some of the plants at soil level. Lettuce can also be grown in frames or in low tunnels.

GREENHOUSE GROWING : PROTECTIVE STRUCTURES

GREENHOUSES

Glass was once the only available glazing material, and it is still the best, letting in light and retaining heat better than any alternative. It is more expensive and not as safe as plastics, but it lasts much longer. Safety glass is available and, though it is more expensive than ordinary glass, it should be considered for a conservatory.

Rigid plastics are not as expensive as glass, and they are safer, but they do not let in as much light; nor do they look as well, except for perspex, but this is expensive, too.

Polythene is cheap and safe, and allows in light well but does not last so well as the other materials. PVC and U-V inhibited films are more expensive than polythene but last longer.

Frames

A garden frame is just a large, low bottomless box with a translucent lid. The sides of the box can be made of wood, concrete, galvanised iron or any other building material – very often salvaged scrap materials will do.

The frame can be any length but should not be wider than 120 centimetres for comfort and safety. It should be 25 centimetres high in front, and about 50 centimetres high at the back. The 'lid' is a number of 'lights', each consisting of a wooden frame with glass or plastic – on it. Each 'light' matches the width of the garden frame in its own length and should be about 75 centimetres wide, and can be made of suitable timber lengths.

Cloches

A 'cloche' originally was a bell-shaped glass jar placed individually over tender plants. The term was extended to include continuous structures of glass sheets supported by iron brackets. These continuous cloches were normally about 45 centimetres high but are now unusual, because low plastic tunnels and cloches have taken over.

Walk-in tunnels

A 'walk-in' tunnel, or polytunnel, can substitute for a glasshouse. Being relatively cheap to put up, it is possible to cover a larger area economically. A polytunnel can be of any length – using a greater number of the tubular steel supporting hoops. Tunnels are generally sold as kits and the standard widths commercially available are 4.2 metres and 5.1 metres. Walk-in tunnels can be difficult to ventilate properly, and the plastic will have to be replaced. It usually lasts two or three years, although there are more durable kinds of plastic film that last for five years.

Low tunnels

A low tunnel is a row of wire hoops – 45 centimetres high, 75 centimetres wide – supporting a 1.8 metre wide polythene film. Length of row is variable. At each end of the low tunnel the film is tied firmly to a short stake. The wire hoops are 1.8 metre lengths of strong wire with an 'eye' twisted into them about 20 centimetres from each end.

Strings tied into each 'eye' and stretched across the polythene hold the tunnel film in place. Although both garden frames and low tunnels are limited in use by their size, they are very successful for low crops such as early and late vegetables, early strawberries, and cuttings.

GREENHOUSE GROWING : HEATING AND VENTILATION

HEAT CONSERVATION

A 'cold' greenhouse means that there is no artificial heat provided. A 'cool' greenhouse has a heating system that will provide some artificial heat – usually just enough to protect against frost. A 'warm' greenhouse has a heating system capable of providing an air temperature of at least 10°Celsius.

Heating systems

If basic frost protection is all that is required, there are two options – paraffin or electricity. A simple paraffin heater is relatively cheap to buy, and to run, but needs to be lit and refuelled, and can give off damaging fumes if not set up correctly.

An electric fan heater is more expensive to buy, but very easy to operate, usually featuring a built-in thermostat. Seek professional advice when installing an electric heater and be sure to set it up so that it does not get wet.

Running costs for a fan-heater are low, if it is used only for frost protection. A two kilowatt fan-heater will keep a 3.6 metres by 2.4 metres greenhouse free of frost on a night when it is minus 8° Celsius outside.

Heating a warm greenhouse to about 10° Celsius is a more difficult proposition. An extra radiator can be taken off the domestic heating system if a conservatory or greenhouse is attached to, or very close, to the house. Most central heating systems are on a time switch that shuts down the system at night – just when the greenhouse needs it most!

However, usually enough heat will have built up earlier to protect plants adequately. A thermostat over-riding the time switch can be installed to prevent very low temperatures.

Electric storage heaters can be used in a conservatory too. These use night-rate electricity. There must be no danger of them getting wet, for safety reasons. They tend to be bulky too. Free-standing greenhouses are difficult to heat economically beyond basic frost protection. A separate hot-water boiler is ideal, but few people would consider this necessary or affordable.

Vents

On a sunny day in summer, greenhouse temperatures could rise above 40° Celsius. Plants dry out quickly and can be scorched or killed at these temperatures. It will be necessary to allow the hot, dry air to escape.

Vents in the roof and sides should be provided. Opening the door helps too. Roof vents are important not only because hot air rises, but also, because it may not be possible to leave side vents or doors open in a conservatory for security reasons.

Polythene tunnels are difficult to ventilate properly, usually relying on leaving the ends open. This is adequate, once the tunnel is not too long.

GREENHOUSE GROWING : SITING A GREENHOUSE

To trap as much heat as possible, a greenhouse should be situated in an open, south-facing position without shading from buildings or trees. The ridge of the roof should point east-west, the broadest part of the glass exposed to the sun. This does have the drawback of heating more on one side, and this can be avoided by running the ridge north south. For warmth, the next best side-on aspect is west because it heats up late in the day, and stays warm longer into the night.

An east-facing side-on site goes cool even before sunset and the morning sun can cause damage to plants by too-quick thawing. A north-facing greenhouse, to be of any use, will need artificial heating – even for the usual range of plants.

Do not site a greenhouse in a hollow where cold air might seep in, nor in a windy position. Do not forget the strong eddies of wind around a house, though the site might seem sheltered.

GREENHOUSE GROWING : GRAPES

A grape is a fruiting berry of the deciduous woody vines of the botanical genus *Vitis*.

- Grapes can be eaten raw or they can be used for making wine, jam, juice, jelly, grape seed extract, raisins, vinegar, and grape seed oil. Grapes are a non-climacteric type of fruit, generally occurring in clusters.

HISTORY

The cultivation of the domesticated grape began 6,000–8,000 years ago in the Near East. Yeast, one of the earliest domesticatedmicroorganisms, occurs naturally on the skins of grapes, leading to the innovation of alcoholic drinks such as wine. The earliest archeological evidence for a dominant position of wine-making in human culture dates from 8,000 years ago in Georgia. The oldest winery was found in Armenia, dating to around 4000 BC. By the 9th century AD the city of Shiraz was known to produce some of the finest wines in the Middle East. Thus it has been proposed that Syrah red wine is named after Shiraz, a city in Persia where the grape was used to make Shirazi wine. Ancient Egyptian hieroglyphics record the cultivation of purple grapes, and history attests to the ancient Greeks, Phoenicians, and Romans growing purple grapes for both eating and wine production. The growing of grapes would later spread to other regions in Europe, as well as North Africa, and eventually in North America.

In North America, native grapes belonging to various species of the *Vitis* genus proliferate in the wild across the continent, and were a part of the diet of many Native Americans, but were considered by European colonists to be unsuitable for wine. *Vitis vinifera*cultivars were imported for that purpose.

DESCRIPTION

Grapes are a type of fruit that grow in clusters of 15 to 300, and can be crimson, black, dark blue, yellow, green, orange, and pink. "White" grapes are actually green in color, and are evolutionarily derived from the purple grape. Mutations in two regulatory genes of white grapes turn off production of anthocyanins, which are responsible for the color of purple grapes. Anthocyanins and otherpigment chemicals of the larger family of polyphenols in purple grapes are responsible for the varying shades of purple in red wines. Grapes are typically an ellipsoid shape resembling a prolate spheroid.

Grapevines

Most grapes come from cultivars of *Vitis vinifera*, the European grapevine native to the Mediterranean and Central Asia. Minor amounts of fruit and wine come from American and Asian species such as:

- *Vitis labrusca*, the North American table and grape juice grapevines (including the Concord cultivar), sometimes used for wine, are native to the Eastern United States and Canada.
- *Vitis riparia*, a wild vine of North America, is sometimes used for winemaking and for jam. It is native to the entire Eastern U.S. and north toQuebec.
- *Vitis rotundifolia*, the muscadines, used for jams and wine, are native to the Southeastern United States from Delaware to the Gulf of Mexico.
- *Vitis amurensis* is the most important Asian species.

PLANTING

Planting

A grapevine can be grown successfully in quite a small greenhouse, but the bigger the better because a grapevine can fill quite a large greenhouse. 'Black Hamburgh' is the best variety for Irish conditions. Planting is usually done when the vine is dormant in December but the plants are pot-grown and can be planted at any time.

Grapevines are often planted with the root outside the greenhouse and the stem taken in through a hole in the wall or wall-base. It is not essential to plant outside, although it reduces the vine's watering needs, but the roots will generally grow out under the wall in any case.

Training

Train the vine to grow up into the roof of the greenhouse. First, train it up to gutter height. Then train a single shoot along the wall at this height. When it reaches the other end, allow side-shoots to grow up the roof on wires, tied into place 30 centimetres apart.

From these side-shoots, which form permanent rods, come the flowering shoots. These arise every 30 centimetres or so. Allow only one shoot to develop at each station and pinch out its tip one or two leaves past the flower bunch. Tap the rods each day, during flowering, to ensure pollination. Pinch out subsequent side-shoots at one leaf.

Grapevines are normally vigorous but if not, mulching the root area in spring will encourage better growth. Use some general fertiliser as well, if growth is weak or after a heavy crop. Watch for red spider mite.

Diseases

Powdery mildew is a serious problem disease. It is important to allow air movement in the greenhouse. Rose and fruit fungicides containing the active ingredient myclobutanil are highly effective, and one or two thorough applications in late spring on the new foliage before flowering will clear the problem.

Grey mould disease can be prevented by ventilation and maintaining a dry atmosphere in late summer. Prune out the fruit-carrying shoots in autumn when the fruit is picked, leaving the framework of permanent rods.

GREENHOUSE GROWING : EARLY STRAWBERRIES

In August, plant strong runners 30 centimetres apart outdoors in good soil. In October, lift the plants and carefully pot then in medium-sized pots. Leave the pots outdoors until the middle of January and then bring them into the greenhouse, or frame.

When the plants begin to grow, check them for greenflies and spray, if necessary. Depending on the level of heat available they will flower in March/ April and fruit in April/ May.

Alternatively, the plants can be covered, where they were planted, by a low tunnel to fruit in May/ June. Plants 'forced' under glass or plastic can be planted out and grown on outdoors, but are not worth forcing again.

GREENHOUSE GROWING : SKILLS OF GREENHOUSE GROWING

WATERING

Plants in a greenhouse need extra care because of the high temperatures generated and the exclusion of natural rainfall.

Cooling

Ventilation on hot days is necessary to keep plants cool. About 25° Celsius is an ideal maximum for most plants. Beyond that, growth slows down and stops. High temperature levels can be reached from late spring onwards.

In summer, ventilation alone might not be enough, so shading can be necessary. Apply Coolglass, or Summer Cloud, in June or early July and remove it at the end of August. A simple way of cooling the house on really hot days is to damp down the floor. Ventilation in winter and spring, on dry, bree days, dries the greenhouse atmosphere, helping disease control.

Feeding

Greenhouse plants must be fed much more often than plants outdoors. The frequent watering that greenhouse plants receive tends to wash the soluble plant nutrients from the restricted reserve of a pot.

Feed little and often – even as often as once a week for large, quick-growing plants early in the growing season. Liquid feeding is simplest to use and most effective. Take care not to feed a dry pot, for fear of scorching the roots.

Hygiene

Pest and disease damage is usually more severe in a greenhouse, where the warm conditions are ideal for insects and fungi, and predators are absent. Remove old and diseased plants, or pest-ridden plants, to break the cycle of infection. Control pests and diseases when they appear.

Wash down the glass, pots, trays and benches in the winter with household disinfectant. There are no products approved for domestic use in disinfection of greenhouse soil. If the soil is 'tired', replace it with fresh soil. If there are root disease problems, grow non-susceptible crops. Flood the greenhouse soil in early spring by watering heavily to leach out excessive salts left over from frequent feeding the previous year.

GREENHOUSE GROWING : PEACHES, NECTARINES AND APRICOTS

Peaches, nectarines and apricots are closely related stone fruits that can be grown in a greenhouse as fan-trained trees on a wall. The trees can take up quite a lot of space, especially the apricot, but they can be hard-pruned too. 'Peregrine' is a common variety of peach and 'Early Rivers' is a nectarine variety.

Peaches can be raised from pips of shop-bought fruit and, unusually among garden fruits which are mostly grafted, will come true to type. Plant a young tree into the open soil and train it to a fan shape by tying in the branches to wires, set 30 centimetres apart, that run the length of the wall to be covered.

Pollinate the peach flowers by hand, using a child's paintbrush, or by tapping the wires each day during flowering. If a lot of fruits set, thin them out to about 15 centimetres apart. When the fruit is picked in August, immediately prune out the shoots that have carried fruit and tie in the new green ones to flower the following year ones.

In the spring, when the buds break, rub away excess young growth, leaving only enough shoots to replace the fruiting shots and maintain the branch framework. These trees always produce too many shoots.

Never let the roots go completely dry. Use a mulch and water as necessary. Watch out for red spider mite and use the predatory mite for biological control, or spray with Sybol, Malathion or Liquid Derris, if necessary.

GREENHOUSE GROWING : OTHER GREENHOUSE VEGETABLES

OTHER GREENHOUSE VEGETABLES

Fig. Early carrots from a cold frame

Early and late season supplies of carrots can be had from the greenhouse, frame or low tunnel. Sow 'Early Nantes' or 'Amsterdam Forcing' in December or January for supplies in late May and June. A late sowing of the same varieties in August gives a December crop.

White turnips, broccoli, radish, scallions and parsley can be grown under protection too. Sowing can start in January in a cold greenhouse or frame, December in a cool greenhouse. Delay sowing until early February under low tunnels but put up the tunnels about three weeks before sowing.

Florence fennel and chinese cabbage are two crops that are difficult to get right outdoors – they both have a tendency to bolt if the weather is not warm and moist. Sow florence fennel in late March and chinese cabbage in May. Keep both well-watered to prevent bolting.

Early and late potatoes can be produced under protection. Planted in December or January they will be ready in May.

ADVANCED ORGANIC GREENHOUSE GROWING

This was a great early season field day consisting of a walk through at Lighthouse Garden's (LG for an abbreviation!) two sites in Lima and Honeoye Falls, NY. Todd had extensive commercial greenhouse experience before starting his own operation in 2005, and it was a great opportunity to learn some tricks of the trade from such an experienced grower. LG is Certified Organic and a NOFA-NY Farmers' Pledge operation, and they both grow retail and wholesale plant starts and produce organic potting soil for gardeners and farmers.

This summary is a quick synopsis of the huge amount of material Todd covered in his tour, including an overview of his greenhouse structures, siting, and operations, using living potting soils, and a look at his propagation house.

GREENHOUSE STRUCTURES AND OPERATIONS

Since we had pretty good winds at the field day, Todd started us off looking at some of LG's greenhouse frames, and focusing on how important it is to work with your prevailing winds, since any greenhouse structure can collapse (for a greenhouse farmer, windy nights are often sleepless nights)! With a ton of wind (largely from the west), LG needs really sturdy houses. They have three 30' by 96' structures from three different manufacturers.

Todd's sturdiest house is from the Canadian manufacturer GGS and has 4' bow spacing. This frame also has extensive wind bracing, including curved purlins that connect to every bow. This adds strength and reduces condensation (the arched shape doesn't trap as much moisture on the purlins to drip onto flats below), but also makes for a longer construction process. This greenhouse looked incredibly sturdy and even survived 80mph winds last year!

With his land, Todd prefers having the end walls face north and south. This puts the sidewall facing the prevailing westerly wind, which allows for better ventilation through the sidewalls. Additionally, greenhouses' arched sidewalls can tolerate significantly more wind stress than their flat end walls. In all three houses, Todd prefers natural ventilation (through sidewall or roof vents) rather than fans, since the fans have significantly higher long term operating costs (such structural venting costs more initially than fans, but generally has a two year payback through reduced electrical costs). The propagation house has a roof vent, but this particular style of roof vent does loosen the plastic (and doesn't work in the rain), so it's not perfect—Todd wants to install one in the future that is either on the peak or further down on the roof to combat these problems. Regardless of vent placement, it's essential to vent away from the wind (so align your houses with the wind rather than the sun direction!).

In the downwind side of the sturdiest house, Todd is using a more economical greenhouse from Sauder's Produce Supply. This house has bows 6 foot on center, which is now more feasible since improved manufacturing allows greenhouse companies to build stronger frame structures with fewer bows. Six foot spacing pushes the limits a bit, but since this house has protection from the wind, does not have to support any hanging baskets, and has a pretty beefy frame, it should be sturdy enough.

For glazing, all three houses have double layer inflated sidewalls, with the inner plastic layer anti-condensate and infrared treated to reduce dripping and boost daytime heat retention. Todd suggested that it's best to inflate the layers using outside air so the air in between plastics stays less humid (and thus blocks less light).

USING LIVING POTTING SOIL

Todd set the stage talking about potting media by explaining how conventional potting soil generally tends to be straight peat moss mixed with wetting agents. In their first year growing organically, Todd used organic peat moss and organic fertilizers, but the fertility didn't seem to be very available to the plants. After being introduced to compost-based potting mixes, Todd immediately saw the difference between media. He likens it to the compost based mixes allowing plants to express more of their fullest potential.

LG began making their own mix right away because they grow so many annuals and ornamentals that shipping costs to buy in mix were prohibitive. (They also began selling potting soil because once you are making a lot for yourself you may as well sell some too!) Right now, Lighthouse Gardens currently uses a paddle mixer to combine their potting soils, but are getting to the point when they need to upgrade from this smaller machine. Todd's mixes strive to have as much compost content as possible, but also include peat moss, vermiculite, and other materials. They are starting to try rice hulls in place of some vermiculite, since they are from the US and fairly sustainable.

LG's goal is to create a rich enough mix to carry the plants through from seed starting to transplanting without any additional fertility inputs. The audience had some questions on foliar feeding and worm castings, however Todd doesn't generally foliar feed because he hasn't found a product that they really like yet. They do apply foliar beneficials and make some custom soil blends with worm castings. Worm castings have been shown to protect plants, however research doesn't yet exactely explain how this process works! Like the other foliar feeds, Todd doesn't use worm castings himself—since their plants are doing fine without the castings, they follow the less-is-more approach of not adding inputs unless they are needed.

In terms of plant pathogen control in the mix, Todd said that his goal is to create a mix where there are so many good microbes active in it, any bad pathogens can't compete. He explained how there are many more beneficial microbes than pathogenic ones, so a good microbial system of a living, non-sterile potting soil should ideally create a natural self-defense against fungal pathogens. In his observation, with a compost-based greenhouse mix, any disease spots that occur spread more slowly than they would in a sterile peat moss greenhouse planting.

Into the Propagation House

LG grows about 500 different varieties of plants—they have a little bit of everything in part because they enjoy the diversity, and in part because their customers really like their ornamentals. They recently purchased a vacuum seeder, but still do the vast amount of seeding by hand. They start most crops in 200 or 288 flats and ideally just pot up one time per crop (since repotting takes a lot of labor and can add 1 to 2 weeks to crop growth). They use a lot of different size containers, depending on the crop, and while they don't like using all the plastic, on their scale, it's not feasible to avoid plugs. They do reuse trays as long as possible, washing and sanitizing them well (with Oxidate) between uses.

In terms of insect management, LG relies strongly on prevention and beneficial insects. Fungus gnats and shore flies pose problems as disease vectors and cosmetic nuisances. Todd focuses on keeping potting media as dry as possible and keeping the greenhouse floors clean (these pests feed off wet organic matter at the soil surface). Aphids can be a pest in any greenhouses—they see them on isolated crops, and monitor populations with yellow sticky cards. Just when the greenhouse gets full each spring, they bring in a batch of lady beetles, which hang out just for a week before flying outside, but do a solid "spring cleaning" of pests in the interim. LG has also used other beneficials successfully, including Athena beetles for fungus gnat larva and parasitic wasps for aphids.

The propagation house has a mix of growing areas, including a germination bed, a set of rolling benches (these are an investment, but are huge space savers and really improve plant airflow), and some ground level growing space. This is their warm house—the goal temperature is 63 degrees. When Todd first stared with just this one open house, it was all one temperature zone, so no crop was entirely happy. Over time, LG added the second (cooler) house, as well as a germination chamber in the propagation house, in order to better control growing conditions by crops' needs.

The germination chamber stays in the 70 to 72 degree range and consists of one bench running the length of the greenhouse. It's a hot water heated radiant tube system running most of the length of the bench top with an automated misting system of five separate misting zones. The germination chamber operates like a conveyor belt, with plants shifting down as they grow from the newly seeded flats on one end, to established crops on the far end. Todd explained how seeds need water vapor to germinate (but not necessarily liquid water), so misting flats every hour on average really helps germination by maintaining the perfect moisture levels.

Outside of the germination chamber, LG's goal is a low humidity environment and they strive to water only on sunny days, so it can evaporate and keep humidity levels down. Most watering outside the germination chamber occurs by hand since that provides the best control. Todd also grows hanging baskets from the purlins, which is a nice way to add a second level of cropping in the same space. The baskets don't cast too much shade if you have good sun alignment with your house. However, one challenge to the baskets is that depending on how you water them, they can really damage flats below them if they drip. To prevent this, LG has automated individual emitter irrigation on the baskets.

Controlling Plant Height Organically

One last area Todd covered was how to grow stockier, hardier plants and control some of their height. You can do this by withholding water, fertility, or temperature, but Todd recommends reducing water, since it is quite compatible a strategy when using compost based mixes. Fan ventilation on plants can be stressful, but you do want some airflow (just not blasting right on the crops). Also, they brush some crops like peppers and tomatoes with cardboard to encourage stockiness.

One fascinating point Todd discussed is the importance of the temperature difference between day and night on plant growth. The greater the difference between these two temperatures, the more the inter-nodal zone grows on plants (so they stretch out and get leggier). Growers often want to take advantage of hot sunny days to speed plant growth, but letting a greenhouse warm up a lot in the day leads to a larger day/night differential and thus creates more potential for leggy plant growth. If you keep your greenhouse warmer at night, it costs more money, but leads to stockier plants. One strategy to try and offset this growth tendency is to recognize that the most inter-nodal growth occurs during the first 2 to 3 hours of daylight. To offset stretch, you can lower the temperature in the house by 5 degrees starting a half an hour before sunrise until 2 to 3 hours after sunrise, which will help lead to stockier plants.

9

Organic Gardening in Horticulture

Organic gardening relies on ecological principles and natural processes to grow and manage garden crops. Although organic gardeners avoid the use of synthetic pesti-cides and fertilizers, organic gardening is not a list of substitutes for synthetic products or a set of home remedies to kill pests. Organic gardening is a holistic approach that involves understanding soil management, integrated pest management, and the life cycles of plants, pests, and the pests' natural enemies. When properly done, organic gardening can produce high quality food and landscapes, enhance the garden environment, protect water quality, and conserve natural resources.

The basic soil management and pest man-agement approaches of organic gardening make sense for all gardeners, whether you avoid all synthetic fertilizers and pesticides or not.

Using these approaches will reduce the amount of fertilizers and pesticides you need, and can improve the quality of your garden.

Other benefits of organic gardening include increasing the number and diversity of beneficial organisms and turning waste mate-rials into valuable composts and fertilizers for the garden. Organic gardening means actively working with nature in your garden. Organic gardeners need to be smart gardeners—knowing the garden environment, observing plants and pests, knowing choices for management, and acting at the appropriate times.

OVERVIEW OF SOIL MANAGEMENT

A good garden soil allows water to enter, and excess water to drain from the root zone. It has the capacity to hold water, air, and nutrients available for plants and microor-ganisms. It has a stable structure that is easy to dig and resists erosion.

Improving and maintaining a garden soil involves:

- Proper use of soil amendments to provide organic matter and plant nutrients
- Tillage at appropriate times
- Prevention of runoff and erosion

ADDING ORGANIC MATTER

Organic matter builds and stabilizes soil structure, improving the porosity, infiltra-tion, and drainage of the soil, and reducing erosion. It holds water and nutrients for plants. Organic matter also is a long-term, slow-release storehouse of nitrogen, phosphorus, and sulfur.

Soil microorganisms continually break down organic matter. Gardeners use composts, plant residues, and mulches to replenish soil organic matter. These materials are relatively low in available nutrients, and can be added to the soil in large amounts.

COMPOSTS

Composts provide an excellent source of organic matter for garden soils. Compost-ing also closes the recycling loop by turning waste materials into a soil amendment. You can make compost at home or buy commercially prepared compost, often made from yard or food waste.

Making Compost

The key to composting is to supply a balance of air, water, energy materials and bulking agent. You don't need to buy additives to stimulate your compost pile. You just need to provide conditions favorable for natural composting organisms.

Home composting can be done in hot or cold piles, in worm bins, or in soil trenches:

- Hot composting produces a high-quality, finished compost in 6 to 8 weeks. To maintain a hot compost pile, balance and mix energy materials and bulking agents, keep the pile moist, and turn the pile frequently to keep it aerated.
- Cold composting requires less work than hot composting. Build the pile, and leave it for months or longer to decompose. Cold composting does not kill weed seeds. Some gardeners have problems with rats and other pests at-tracted to edible wastes in compost piles.
- You can compost fruit and vegetable scraps in a worm bin. This is a good method for urban gardeners who have small amounts of space.
- You also can bury fruit and vegetable scraps and allow them to decompose directly in the soil.

The WSU Extension bulletin, Backyard Composting, EB1784, gives more detailed information on making and using home compost.

Using Compost

You can till or dig composts directly into the garden, or use them as a mulch over the winter or summer before turning them into the soil. One cubic yard of compost covers about 300 square feet of garden one inch deep. Adding

1 to 2 inches of compost each year helps build a productive garden soil. In the first year after application, com-posts that are woody and not fully decom-posed will tie up part of the soil nitrogen, resulting in nitrogen deficiency for the plants. If plants show signs of nitrogen deficiency, add extra nitrogen. In following years, most composts will contribute small amounts of available nitrogen to the soil.

GREEN MANURE

Green manures are cover crops grown spe-cifically to be tilled or dug into the soil. Plant-ing green manure is a way to grow your own organic matter. The value of cover crops goes beyond their contribution of organic matter.

Cover crops also can do the following:

- Capture and recycle nutrients that other-wise would be lost by leaching during the winter
- Protect the soil surface from rainfall im-pact during the winter
- Reduce runoff and erosion
- Help suppress weeds
- Supply nitrogen

No one cover crop provides all of these benefits. Deciding which cover crop or crop combination to grow depends on which ben-efits are most important to you, and which cover crops fit best into your garden plan. You can grow cover crops over the winter or in summer.

Gardeners usually plant cover crops in the fall and till them as green manure in the spring before planting. The earlier cover crops are planted, the more benefits they will provide. Research in western Washington showed that cereal rye planted in September captured three times the amount of nitrogen as an October planting. Legumes, such as vetch and crimson clover, need an early start to cover the soil before cold weather arrives.

Because gardeners often grow crops into November or December, it is not possible to plant early cover crops throughout the gar-den. In this case, plant cover crops in areas that you harvest early, and use mulches on parts of the garden you harvest later. Plant a cover crop in a sweet corn bed immediately following harvest in September. You also can start cover crops around and among late crops where space allows.

Table. Exampls of Cover Crops Grown in Washington.

Cereal Rey	Very hardy, grows quickly;	matures rapidly in spring
Winter wheat	Leafy, covers soil well,	matures slowly
Hairy vetch	Legume, fixes nitrogen, starts,	good companion crop for cereal rey
Crimson clover	Legume, fixes nitrogen, slower	growth than vetch
Buckwheat	Fast growing, frost-sensitive,	summer cover, ready to
till in		30 days

Till or dig cover crops into the soil before they flower. After flowering, the plants become woody and decline in quality. Also, digging the crop into the soil becomes quite difficult if the plants grow too large. If you cannot till a cover crop in time, cut it off and compost it for later addition to the soil. You will still get the short-term benefit of organic matter from the crown and roots when you till your garden.

The fresh organic matter from cover crops stimulates biological activity in the soil and improves soil structure. A good stand of vetch or clover can supply about half of the nitrogen needed by the next garden crop. Because cover crop residues decompose quickly in the soil, these benefits last only about a year. Make cover crops an annual part of your garden rotation to gain their benefits each year. If cover crops do not fit into your gardening plan, use winter mulches as a substitute. WSU Extension Bul-letin EB1824, Cover Crops for Home Gardens in Western Washington and Oregon.

MULCHES

During the summer, mulches control weeds and conserve moisture. Winter mulches also protect the soil from raindrop impact and runoff. Organic mulches mixed into the soil at the end of the season will decompose and add to the soil organic matter.

Mulches are categorized into two groups:

1. Organic mulches include materials such as straw, leaves, compost, grass clippings, and sawdust. Till these materials into the soil at the end of the season or leave them on the surface. Use bark mulches or wood chips around perennial plantings and on paths. Do not till them into the soil.
2. Synthetic mulches include black plastic and weed-blocking geotextiles. Remove and discard these materials when they are no longer useful as mulches. Some people use old newspapers or cardboard as a synthetic mulch that will decompose in the soil. Cover newspapers and card-board with organic mulches to improve the appearance of the garden.

These two types of mulches provide somewhat different benefits, described below. Many organic gardeners avoid plastic mulches because they cannot mix them into the soil or recycle them.

Weed Control

Mulches control weeds by blocking light. Black plastic, geotextile, and cardboard mulches also provide a physical barrier to weed growth. Mulches alone will not control weeds, but they can be a key part of garden weed management. Mulches have limited effectiveness against perennial weeds such as horsetail, quackgrass, and morninglory that can send rhizomes or roots considerable distances.

To control weeds, remove weed seedlings from the area and apply 1 to 2 inches of organic mulches when desirable plants are 2 to 3 inches tall. Be careful not to cover the plants themselves. You may need as much as 6 inches of straw mulch. Although weed seeds can germinate in a mulch, it is easier to pull young weeds from mulch than from soil.

Soil Moisture and Temperature

Organic mulches help maintain soil moisture by improving movement of water into the soil, and by reducing evaporation from the soil surface. Plastic mulches reduce both evaporation and infiltration. We do not recommend plastic mulches in perennial plantings because the mulches make water management more difficult. Soils remain wet later in the spring beneath plastic mulches, creating soil conditions that encourage root rots. In the summer, plastic mulches reduce the effectiveness of overhead irrigation.

Mulches can either increase or decrease soil temperature, depending on the type of mulch. Loose organic mulches insulate the soil. This is a disadvantage in the spring when warm soil temperatures are needed to speed germination and growth. In the heat of summer, organic mulches can be a benefit, keeping soils cooler. Black plastic absorbs heat, and warms the soil in the spring, creat-ing a better environment for warm season crops like melons.

Tilling Mulches into the Soil

You can turn organic mulches into the soil in the fall or spring, depending on your garden plan. Digging or tilling mulches is usually easier than tilling cover crops. Some mulches—sawdust and straw—contain little nitrogen. Once turned into the soil, they will tie up a large amount of nitrogen. To prevent nitrogen deficiency in the next crop, add fertilizer—blood meal, cottonseed meal, or manure.

NUTRIENTS AND FERTILIZERS

Soil is the source of most plant nutrients. Carbon, hydrogen, and oxygen come from air and water. The soil supplies the remaining 13 essential nutrients. We add fertilizers to supplement native soil nutrients. This promotes plant growth and replaces nutrients removed when plants are harvested.

COMPARING ORGANIC AND SYNTHETIC FERTILIZERS

Organic fertilizers are natural materials that have had little or no processing. They in-clude both biological and mineral materials. Organic fertilizers release nutrients through natural processes in the soil, including chemical weathering of mineral materials, and biological breakdown of organic matter. The released nutrients are available to plants in a water-soluble form. These soluble forms of nutrients are the same as those supplied by synthetic fertilizers. When compared with synthetic fertilizers, organic fertilizers usually are less con-centrated in nutrients, and release nutrients more slowly. Larger amounts of organic fertilizers are needed, but their effects last longer. Organic fertilizers contain a variety of nutrients, but the amounts are not always balanced according to plant needs.

Using organic fertilizers recycles mate-rials that otherwise would be discarded as wastes. Production of synthetic fertilizers, on the other hand, can create wastes and use substantial amounts of energy.

SLOW RELEASE OF NUTRIENTS

Organic fertilizers slowly release nutri-ents to plants over the course of the growing season. The rate of release of nutrients from organic materials depends on soil microor-ganism activity, which in turn depends on soil temperature and moisture. Temperature and moisture conditions that favour plant growth also favour the release of nutrients from organic matter.

Nutrients in most synthetic fertilizers are available immediately. They can furnish nutrients to plants in the spring before the soil is warm. However, nitrogen in these fertilizers is vulnerable to leaching loss from heavy rainfall or irrigation. Note: Once nitrogen moves below the root zone, plants can no longer use it, and it may leach into groundwater.

Table. Comparing Organic and Synthetic fertilizer.

	Organic fertilizers	Synthetic fertilizers
Source	Natural materials; little or on processing undergoing extensive	Manufactured or extracted from nature material, often processing
Examples	Manure, cottonseed meal, rock phosphate, fish by-products, ground limestone	Diammonium phosphate, synthetic urea, potassium choloride
Nutrient availability	Usually slow-release; nutrients are released by biological and chemical processes in soil	Nutrients usually are immediately avilable to plants
Nutrient concentration	Usually low concentration	Usually high concentration

Some organic fertilizers contain immediately available and slow-release nutrients, nourishing plants both early in the season and later. Fresh manure, biosolids, and fish emulsions are examples of organic fertilizers containing available nutrients. As manure ages, the most readily available fraction is lost into the air or leached into the soil, leaving slow-release material in the aged manure. Some material in organic fertilizers breaks down so slowly that it does not become available the first season after application. Repeated application of organic fertilizers builds a pool of material that releases nutrients very slowly. In the long run, the pool will decrease the need for supplemental fertilizer.

TYPES OF ORGANIC FERTILIZERS

ANIMAL MANURE

Animal manures vary widely in nutrient content and nutrient availability, depend-ing on the type of animal that produced the manure, and the age and handling of the ma-nure. Mixing with bedding dilutes manure. Exposure to rain leaches nutrients. Composting under cover retains more nutrients, but reduces nutrient availability.

Table compares typical nutrient values of different manures. The nutrient content of manure could differ substantially from the amounts in this table, depending on how the manure was stored and handled.

Applying farmyard manures. It doesn't take much of a nutrientrich manure, such as poultry manure, to fertilize a garden. A 5-gallon bucket of poultry manure contains enough nutrients to fertilize 100 to 150 square feet of garden. If more is applied, you risk over-fertilizing, harming crops, and leaching nitrogen into groundwater.

Dilute manures, such as separated dairy solids and horse manure with bedding, contain far fewer available nutrients and can be applied in larger amounts. You can use as much as an inch of these materials in the garden every year. Use these manures mainly as a source of organic matter.

Experiment with the amount you apply and observe the performanceExperiment with the amount you apply and observe the performance of your crops to fine-tune your application rate. It is better to be conservative and add more manure if the crops appear deficient.

Table. Typical nautrient content of uncomposted animal manures at the time of application.

Type	N	P_2O_5[2]	K_2O
	1b per cu yard as-is[3]		
Broiler with litter	33	29	30
Laying hen	26	40	33
Sheep	13	6	24
Rabbit	11	7	10
Beef	8	4	12
Dry stack dairy	6	3	13
Separated dairy silids			
Horse	6	4	11

1. Divide these number by 40 to estimate the nutrients in a 5-gallon bucket of fresh manure.
2. Phosphorus and potassium in this table are shown in units of izer lables. To convert from P to P_2O_5, multiply P by 2.3. To convert from K to K_2O, multiply K by 1.2.
3. As-is is typical for manure stored under cover.

Commercial manure composts. Composted chicken and steer manures with known nutrient contents are commercially available as bagged products. Table shows typical analyses of these materials. Nutrient levels and availability in steer manure compost are so low that you should use steer compost as a source of organic matter only. Recommended application rates on packages of these products are good guidelines for their use.

Table. Nutrient content of commercial manure composts.

Animal	N	P_2O_5	K_2O
		%	
Chicken	1-3	0.5	1-2
Steer	0.5	1-2	0.5

Using manure safely. Fresh manure sometimes contains pathogens that can cause diseases in humans. These pathogens are not taken up into plant tissue, but they can adhere to soil on plant roots, or on the leaves or fruit of low-growing crops. Cooking destroys pathogens, but raw food carries a risk of pathogen exposure. Washing and peeling raw produce removes most pathogens, but some may remain. The risk from pathogens is greatest for root crops or leaf crops where the edible part touches the soil. The risk is negligible for crops such as sweet corn, which do not come in contact with the soil, or for any crop that is thoroughly cooked.

Consider raw manure to be a potential source of pathogens, and avoid using fresh manure where you grow high-risk crops. Bacterial pathogens die off naturally during composting, extended storage, or after field application. Complete die-off of bacterial pathogens occurs in days to months depending on the pathogen and environmental conditions.

Keep dog, cat, and pig manure out of your home compost and garden. Some of the parasites found in these manures are very persistent, and may survive in both compost and soil. The best time to apply manure is in the spring before planting. You also can apply manure in the fall, but some of the nutrients may be lost over the winter. Environmental risks of leaching and run off also increase. If you do apply manure in the fall, apply it early, and plant a cover crop to help capture nutrients and prevent run off.

Don't over apply fresh manure. Because fresh manure contains available nutrients as well as slow-release nutrients, over application can harm your crops. A safe way to use fresh manure is to mix it into your compost pile and then use the finished compost in your garden. The micro-organisms breaking down the other materi-als in your compost will absorb the available nutrients, reducing the risk of nutrient over-application and leaching.

Because it is hard to maintain the high temperatures needed to kill pathogens quickly in a backyard compost pile, allow your manure compost to age for six months or more before using it in your garden. An alternative is to buy commercially composted manure.

Biosolids

Biosolids are a by-product of municipal wastewater treatment. Federal standards for organic farming do not include biosolids as an organic fertilizer.

However, biosolids do have two important characteristics of organic fertilizers:

1. Their nutrients are released slowly from the organic form by natural processes in the soil, and
2. They are a product of the waste stream that can benefit crop growth.

Most of the biosolids produced in Washington are used to fertilize agricultural and forest crops. The material used on farms is rich in nutrients and acts similarly to poultry manure.

Some communities in Washington produce a special class of biosolids and market them to gardeners. These are called Class A biosolids: they have been treated using heat or composting to reduce pathogens to background levels, making them safe for all garden uses. Three types of Class A biosolids are available in Washington: composts, blends, and heat-dried pellets. Biosolids composts are made from biosolids and yard debris or woody materials, and can be used similarly to other composts.

Biosolids blends are formulated for different uses, including turf topdressing, mulches, and soil amendments. Heat-dried pellets are rich in nutrients and are used similarly to commercial organic fertilizers.

COMMERCIAL ORGANIC FERTILIZERS

Many organic by-products and some unprocessed minerals are sold as commercial organic fertilizers. Table shows approximate nutrient content of some of these materials. Total nutrient contents; because most are slow-release fertilizers, not all of the nutrients will be available the same year they are applied. The table shows that each fertilizer contains one main nutrient. The other nutrients are present in smaller amounts. Several companies produce bal-anced organic fertilizers, blended into a single product that provides all of the primary nutrients.

Commercial organic fertilizers tend to be more expensive per pound of nutrients than either synthetic fertilizers or manures. Sometimes the difference in price can be substantial.

Choosing organic fertilizers involves tradeoffs in cost and convenience. Farmyard manure is usually inexpensive or free, but is less convenient than packaged, commer-cial materials. If you or your neighbours have livestock it makes both environmental and economic sense to recycle the manure pro-duced by the livestock.

Packaged organic fertilizers can be expensive, but gardeners may choose them where convenience or quick availability of nutrients is important, or for small gardens where little fertilizer is needed. The cost per pound of nutrients in organic fertilizers varies widely, depending on the type of material, the concentration of nutrients, and the size of the package. Compare costs and nutrient availabil-ity when shopping for organic fertilizers.

Table. Total nitrogen, phosphate, and potash content typical of some organic fertilizer.

Meterial	N	P_2O_5 %	K_2O
Cottonoseed meal	6-7	2	1
Blood meal[1]	12-15	1	1
Alfalfa	2	0.5	2
Bat guano[1]	10	3	1
Fish meal[1]	10	4	0
Fish emulsions[1]	3-5	1	1
Bone meal	1-4	12-24	0
Rock phosphate[2]	0	25-30 (only 2-3% available)	0
Greensand	0	0	3-7
Kelp meal	1	0.1	2-5

- These materials contain a substantial amount of quickly available nitrogen that plants can use early in the season.
- Very low availability. Useful only in acid soils.

Lime, Gypsum, and Wood Ashes

Lime, gypsum, and wood ashes are all mineral materials used as organic soil amend-ments. Lime and gypsum are commercial products, while wood ashes are produced from home woodstoves and fireplaces.

Lime and pH. Lime is ground limestone, a rock containing calcium carbonate. Lime raises the pH of acid soils, and supplies the essential nutrient, calcium. Dolomitic lime contains magnesium as well as calcium, and is a good choice for organic gardeners in western Washington, where garden soils often are deficient in magnesium.

In strongly acid soils, many nutrients are less available to plants, and some toxic metals are more available to plants. This can be corrected by the proper application of lime. Soils are naturally acidic in humid areas—most of western Washington—and are neutral to alkaline in drier areas—most of eastern Washington. Fertilizers tend to increase soil acidity over time; some eastern Washington topsoils have become acidic from fertilization.

The best way to determine if your soil needs lime is to have your soil tested. In the absence of a soil test, western Washington gardeners can add about 50 pounds of dolomitic lime per 1000 square feet of garden per year. Do not lime areas where you grow acid-loving plants, because they are adapted to acid soils. Lime is a slow-release material. Fall application will benefit a spring crop. Gypsum is not a substi-tute for lime. It provides calcium and sulfur to soils, but has little effect on soil pH. Gypsum has been promoted as a soil amendment to improve soil structure. In the vast majority of cases it will not work. Gypsum improves structure only when the problem results from excess sodium in the soil, a rare condition in Washington. Use organic amendments to improve soil structure, as described earlier. Wood ashes are a readily available source of potassium, calcium, and magnesium. They also act like lime, raising the pH of the soil. High rates of wood ashes may cause short-term salt injury, so keep applications to less than 15-25 pounds per 1000 square feet of garden. We do not recommend using wood ashes in alkaline soils.

ESTIMATING HOW MUCH ORGANIC FERTILIZER TO USE

Estimating how much organic fertilizer to use is a challenge. We have to estimate both the amount of nutrients our crop needs, and the availability of the nutrients in the organic fertilizer. Two standard methods for estimating fertilizer needs are through soil tests and Extension bulletins.

Soil Tests

A soil test will give you the levels of nutrients in your soil and a recommendation for how much fertilizer to add each year based on your soil test results and the crops you are growing. You don't need to test your soil every year—testing every 3 to 5 years is enough.

Washington State University and Or-egon State University no longer test soils, but private labs in both states do tests for garden soils. County Extension offices have lists of testing labs. If you have not worked with a lab before, call them to make sure they are set up to do soil tests and make recommendations for garden soils.

Ask the lab:

- If they routinely test garden soils for plant nutrients and pH
- If they use WSU or OSU test methods and fertilizer guides
- If they give garden recommendations for organic fertilizers
- How much a test costs
- How quickly you will get results

Extension Bulletins

If the cost of a soil test is large compared with your normal gardening costs, you can estimate your fertilizer needs using Extension bulletins instead of soil tests. These bulletins usually give recommendations for synthetic fertilizers. You will need to adapt these for the lower nutrient availability in most or-ganic fertilizers.

TIPS FOR ESTIMATING ORGANIC FERTILIZER RATES

- Organic fertilizers having large proportions of available nutrients can be sub-stituted in direct proportion for synthetic fertilizers.

- For other packaged fertilizers, apply according to their nutrient availability. Composts, rock phosphate, and plant residues generally have lower nutrient availability than more concentrated animal products. Recommendations on the package often are a good guideline for application rates. Check the recommendations against other products to make sure they seem reasonable.
- The nutrient concentration and availability in manures varies widely depending on the type of manure and its handling. Application rates range from 5 gallons per 100 to 150 square feet for high-nitrogen chicken manure to 1 inch deep for steer or horse manure composted with bedding. Estimate application rates based on your manure choice.
- Observe your crops carefully. It is some- times hard to estimate how much organ-ic fertilizer to use. Lush plant growth and delayed fruiting and flowering are signs of high amounts of available nitrogen, and may indicate over-fertilization. You can experiment with different fertilizer rates in different parts of a row and see if you notice differences. Plan your experi-ment carefully, so you are confident that any results come from the fertilizer rates, rather than differences in soil, watering, or other management.
- Soil testing also is valuable in understanding the nutrient status of your soil.

Many established gardens have high levels of soil fertility, and crops will grow just as well using less fertilizer.

AGROECOLOGY

Agroecology is the science of applying ecological concepts and principles to the design, development, and management of sustainable agricultural systems. Agroecology is the science of sustainable agriculture; the methods of agroecology have as their goal achieving sustainability of agricultural systems balanced in all spheres.

This includes the socio-economic and the ecological or environmental. While farming methods vary, traditional manipulated "agroecosystems" generally differ from natural ecosystems in six ways: maintenance at an early successional state, monoculture, crops generally planted in rows, simplification of biodiversity, plough which exposes soil to erosion, use of genetically modified organisms and artificially selected crops meanwhile agroecology tends to minimize the human impact.

The agroecologist views any farming system primarily with an ecologist's eye; that is, it is not firstly economic nor industrial.

FERTILIZER

Fertilizers are soil amendments applied to promote plant growth; the main nutrients present in fertilizer are nitrogen, phosphorus, and potassium and other nutrients are added in smaller amounts. Fertilizers are usually directly applied to soil, and also sprayed on leaves.

Fertilizers are roughly broken up between organic and inorganic fertilizer, with the main difference between the two being sourcing, and not necessarily differences in nutrient content. Organic fertilizers and some mined inorganic fertilizers have been used for many centuries, whereas chemically-synthesized inorganic fertilizers were only widely developed during the industrial revolution. Increased understanding and use of fertilizers were important parts of the pre-industrial British Agricultural Revolution and the industrial green revolution of the 20th century.

Fertilizers typically provide, in varying proportions:

- *The three primary macronutrients*: nitrogen, phosphorus, and potassium.
- *The three secondary macronutrients*: calcium(Ca), sulfur (S), magnesium (Mg).
- *And the micronutrients or trace minerals*: boron (B), chlorine (Cl), manganese (Mn), iron (Fe), zinc (Zn), copper (Cu), molybdenum (Mo) and selenium (Se).

The macronutrients are consumed in larger quantities and are present in plant tissue in quantities from 0.2% to 4.0%. Micronutrients are consumed in smaller quantities and are present in plant tissue in quantities measured in parts per million, ranging from 5 to 200 ppm, or less than 0.02% dry weight.

LABELING OF FERTILIZERS

Macronutrient Fertilizers

Macronutrient fertilizers are labeled with an NPK analysis and also "N-P-K-S" in Australia.

An example of labeling for the fertilizer potash is composed of 1:1 potassium to carbonate or 47% potassium and 53% Carbonate by weight. Traditional analysis of 100g of KCl would yield 60g of K_2O. The percentage yield of K_2O from the original 100g of fertilizer is the number shown on the label. A potash fertilizer would thus be labeled 0-0-60, not 0-0-52.

INORGANIC FERTILIZER (SYNTHETIC FERTILIZER)

Fertilizers are broadly divided into organic fertilizers or inorganic fertilizers.

Inorganic fertilizer is often synthesized using the Haber-Bosch process, which produces ammonia as the end product. This ammonia is used as a feedstock for other nitrogen fertilizers, such as anhydrous ammonium nitrate and urea. These concentrated products may be diluted with water to form a concentrated liquid fertilizer. Ammonia can be combined with rock phosphate and potassium fertilizer in the Odda Process to produce compound fertilizer.

The use of synthetic nitrogen fertilizers has increased steadily in the last 50 years, rising almost 20-fold to the current rate of 1 billion tonnes of nitrogen per year. The use of phosphate fertilizers has also increased from 9 million tonnes per year in 1960 to 40 million tonnes per year in 2000. A maize crop yielding 6-9 tonnes of grain per hectare requires 30–50 kg of phosphate fertilizer to be applied, soybean requires 20–25 kg per hectare. Yara International is the world's largest producer of nitrogen based fertilizers.

Application

Synthetic fertilizers are commonly used to treat fields used for growing maize, followed by barley, sorghum, rapeseed, soy and sunflower. One study has shown that application of nitrogen fertilizer on off-season cover crops can increase the biomass of these crops, while having a beneficial effect on soil nitrogen levels for the main crop planted during the summer season.

Problems of Inorganic Fertilizer

Trace Mineral Depletion

Many inorganic fertilizers do not replace trace mineral elements in the soil which become gradually depleted by crops. This depletion has been linked to studies which have shown a marked fall in the quantities of such minerals present in fruit and vegetables. However, a recent review of 55 scientific studies concluded "there is no evidence of a difference in nutrient quality between organically and conventionally produced foodstuffs" Conversely, a major long-term study funded by the European Union found that organically-produced milk and produce were significantly higher in antioxidants than their conventionally grown counterparts. In Western Australia deficiencies of zinc, copper, manganese, iron and molybdenum were identified as limiting the growth of broad-acre crops and pastures in the 1940s and 1950s. Soils in Western Australia are very old, highly weathered and deficient in many of the major nutrients and trace elements. Since this time these trace elements are routinely added to inorganic fertilizers used in agriculture in this state.

Over-fertilization

Over-fertilization of a vital nutrient can be as detrimental as underfertilization. "Fertilizer burn" can occur when too much fertilizer is applied, resulting in a drying out of the roots and damage or even death of the plant.

High Energy Consumption

The production of synthetic ammonia currently consumes about 5% of global natural gas consumption, which is somewhat under 2% of world energy production. Natural gas is overwhelmingly used for the production of ammonia, but other energy sources, together with a hydrogen source, can be used for the production of nitrogen compounds suitable for fertilizers. The cost of natural gas makes up about 90% of the cost of producing ammonia. The increase in price of natural gases over the past decade, along with other factors such as increasing demand, have contributed to an increase in fertilizer price.

Long-Term Sustainability

Inorganic fertilizers are now produced in ways which cannot be continued indefinitely. Potassium and phosphorus come from mines and such resources are limited. Atmospheric nitrogen is effectively unlimited, but this is not in a form useful to plants. To make nitrogen accessible to plants requires nitrogen fixation. Artificial nitrogen fertilizers are typically synthesized using fossil fuels such as natural gas and coal, which are limited resources. In lieu of converting natural gas to syngas for use in the Haber process, it is also possible to convert renewable biomass to syngas to supply the necessary energy for the process, though the amount of land and resources necessary for such a project may be prohibitive.

ORGANIC FERTILIZER

Organic fertilizers include naturally-occurring organic materials, or naturally occurring mineral deposits.

Benefits of Organic Fertilizer

In addition to increasing yield and fertilizing plants directly, organic fertilizers can improve the biodiversity and long-term productivity of soil, and may prove a large depository for excess carbon dioxide. Organic nutrients increase the abundance of soil organisms by providing organic matter and micronutrients for organisms such as fungal mycorrhiza, and can drastically reduce external inputs of pesticides, energy and fertilizer, at the cost of decreased yield.

Comparison with inorganic fertilizer

Organic fertilizer nutrient content, solubility, and nutrient release rates are typically all lower than inorganic fertilizers.

One study found that over a 140-day period, after 7 leachings:

- Organic fertilizers had released between 25% and 60% of their nitrogen content
- Controlled release fertilizers had a relatively constant rate of release
- Soluble fertilizer released most of its nitrogen content at the first leaching

In general, the nutrients in organic fertilizer are both more dilute and also much less readily available to plants. UC IPM, all organic fertilizers are classified as 'slow-release' fertilizers, and therefore cannot cause nitrogen burn.

Organic Fertilizer Sources

Animal

Animal-sourced Urea, are suitable for application organic agriculture, while pure synthetic forms of urea are not. The common thread that can be seen through these examples is that organic agriculture attempts to define itself through minimal processing as well as being naturally-occurring or via natural biological processes such as composting. Sewage sludge use in organic agricultural operations in the U.S. has been extremely limited and rare due to USDA prohibition of the practice. The USDA now requires 3rd-party certification of high-nitrogen liquid organic fertilizers sold in the U.S.

Plant

Cover crops are also grown to enrich soil as a green manure through nitrogen fixation from the atmosphere; as well as phosphorus content of soils.

Mineral

Naturally mined powdered limestone, mined rock phosphate and sodium nitrate, are inorganic, are energetically-intensive to harvest, yet are approved for usage in organic agriculture in minimal amounts.

ENVIRONMENTAL EFFECTS OF FERTILIZER USE WATER

Eutrophication

The nitrogen-rich compounds found in fertilizer run-off is the primary cause of a serious depletion of oxygen in many parts of the ocean, especially in coastal zones; the resulting lack of dissolved oxygen is greatly reducing the ability of these areas to sustain oceanic fauna.

Visually, water may become cloudy and discoloured. About half of all the lakes in the United States are now eutrophic, while the number of oceanic dead zones near inhabited coastlines are increasing.

As of 2006, the application of nitrogen fertilizer is being increasingly controlled in Britain and the United States. If eutrophication can be reversed, it may take decades before the accumulated nitrates in groundwater can be broken down by natural processes.

High application rates of inorganic nitrogen fertilizers in order to maximize crop yields, combined with the high solubilities of these fertilizers leads to increased runoff into surface water as well as leaching into groundwater. The use of ammonium nitrate in inorganic fertilizers is particularly damaging, as plants absorb ammonium ions preferentially over nitrate ions, while excess nitrate ions which are not absorbed dissolve into runoff or groundwater.

Blue Baby Syndrome

Nitrate levels above 10 mg/L in groundwater can cause 'blue baby syndrome', leading to hypoxia.

Soil

Soil Acidification

Nitrogen-containing inorganic and organic fertilizers can cause soil acidification when added.. This may lead to decreases in nutrient availability which may be offset by liming.

Persistent Organic Pollutants

Toxic persistent organic pollutants ("POPs"), such as Dioxins, polychlorinated dibenzo-p-dioxins (PCDDs), and polychlorinated dibenzofurans (PCDFs) have been detected in agricultural fertilizers and soil amendments

Heavy Metal Accumulation

The concentration of up to 100 mg/kg of cadmium in phosphate minerals increases the contamination of soil with cadmium.

Uranium is another example of a contaminant often found in phosphate fertilizers. Eventually these heavy metals can build up to unacceptable levels and build up in vegetable produce. Average annual intake of uranium by adults is estimated to be about 0.5 mg from ingestion of food and water and 0.6 ìg from breathing air.

Steel industry wastes, recycled into fertilizers for their high levels of zinc, wastes can include the following toxic metals: leadarsenic, cadmium, chromium, and nickel. The most common toxic elements in this type of fertilizer are mercury, lead, and arsenic. Concerns have been raised concerning fish meal mercury content by at least one source in Spain

Also, highly-radioactive Polonium-210 contained in phosphate fertilizers is absorbed by the roots of plants and stored in its tissues; tobacco derived from plants fertilized by rock phosphates contains Polonium-210 which emits alpha radiation estimated to cause about 11,700 lung cancer deaths each year worldwide.

For these reasons, it is recommended that nutrient budgeting, through careful observation and monitoring of crops, take place to mitigate the effects of excess fertilizer application.

Other Problems

Atmospheric Effects

Methane emissions from crop fields are increased by the application of ammonium-based fertilizers; these emissions contribute greatly to global climate change as methane is a potent greenhouse gas. Through the increasing use of nitrogen fertilizer, which is added at a rate of 1 billion tons per year presently to the already existing amount of reactive nitrogen, nitrous oxide has become the third most important greenhouse gas after carbon dioxide and methane. It has a global warming potential 296 times larger than an equal mass of carbon dioxide and it also contributes to stratospheric ozone depletion. Storage and application of some nitrogen fertilizers in some weather or soil conditions can cause emissions of the potent greenhouse gas—nitrous oxide. Ammonia gas may be emitted following application of 'inorganic' fertilizers and/ or manures and slurries.

The use of fertilizers on a global scale emits significant quantities of greenhouse gas into the atmosphere.

Emissions come about through the use of:

- Animal manures and urea, which release methane, nitrous oxide, ammonia, and carbon dioxide in varying quantities depending on their form and management
- Fertilizers that use nitric acid or ammonium bicarbonate, the production and application of which results in emissions of nitrogen oxides, nitrous oxide, ammonia and carbon dioxide into the atmosphere.

By changing processes and procedures, it is possible to mitigate some, but not all, of these effects on anthropogenic climate change.

Increased Pest Health

Excessive nitrogen fertilizer applications can also lead to pest problems by increasing the birth rate, longevity and overall fitness of certain agricultural pests.

ORGANIC HORTICULTURE

Organic horticulture is the science and art of growing fruits, vegetables, flowers, or ornamental plants by following the essential principles of organic agriculture in soil building and conservation, pest management, and heirloom variety preservation.

The Latin words hortus and cultura together form horticulture, classically defined as the culture or growing of garden plants. Horticulture is also sometimes defined simply as "agriculture minus the plough." Instead of the plough, horticulture makes use of human labour and gardener's hand tools, although some small machine tools like rotary tillers are commonly employed now.

GENERAL

Double Digging, Vermicompost, Mulches, cover crops, compost, manures, and mineral supplements are soil-building mainstays that distinguish this type of farming from its commercial counterpart. Through attention to good healthy soil condition, it is expected that insect, fungal, or other problems that sometimes plague plants can be minimized. However, pheromone traps, insecticidal soap sprays, and other pest-control methods available to organic farmers are also sometimes utilized by organic horticulturists.

Horticulture involves five areas of study. These areas are floriculture, landscape horticulture, olericulture and postharvest physiology. All of these can be, and sometimes are, pursued according to the principles of organic cultivation. Organic horticulture is based on knowledge and techniques gathered over thousands of years. In general terms, organic horticulture involves natural processes, often taking place over extended periods of time, and a sustainable, holistic approach - while chemical-based horticulture focuses on immediate, isolated effects and reductionist strategies.

ORGANIC GARDENING SYSTEMS

There are a number of formal organic gardening and farming systems that prescribe specific techniques. They tend to be more specific than, and fit within, general organic standards. Biodynamic farming is an approach based on the esoteric teachings of Rudolf Steiner. The Japanese farmer and writer Masanobu Fukuoka invented a no-till system for small-scale grain production that he called Natural Farming. French intensive and biointensive methods and SPIN Farming are all small scale gardening techniques.

A garden is more than just a means of providing food, it is a model of what is possible in a community - everyone could have a garden of some kind and produce healthy, nutritious organic food, a farmers market, a place to pass on gardening experience, and a sharing of bounty, promoting a more sustainable way of living that would encourage their local economy. A simple 4' x 8' raised bed garden based on the principles of bio-intensive planting and square foot gardening uses fewer nutrients and less water, and could keep a family, or community, supplied with an abundance of healthy, nutritious organic greens, while promoting a more sustainable way of living.

Other methods can also be used to supplement an existing garden. Methods such as composting, or vermicomposting. These practices are ways of recycling organic matter into some of the best organic fertilizers and soil conditioner. Vermicompost is especially easy. The byproduct is also an excellent source of nutrients for an organic garden.

SOIL

Managing the soil is very important. If your garden is healthy then insects will not attack the plants. Insects only attack plants that are unhealthy. As an example illustrating the relative health of plants, insects will not feed on plants which have been genetically modified so as to reduce foliar damage; thus, genetically modified plants are healthier than unmodified ones. To keep your garden healthy give it organic matter and humus to survive. The most important thing is to give your garden lots of attention and your energy.

PEST CONTROL APPROACHES

Differing approaches to pest control are equally notable. In chemical horticulture, a specific insecticide may be applied to quickly kill off a particular insect pest. Chemical controls can dramatically reduce pest populations in the short term, yet by unavoidably killing natural control insects and animals, cause an increase in the pest population in the long term, thereby creating an ever increasing problem. Repeated use of insecticides and herbicides also encourages rapid natural selection of resistant insects, plants and other organisms, necessitating increased use, or requiring new, more powerful controls.In contrast, organic horticulture tends to tolerate some pest populations while taking the long view.

Organic pest control requires a thorough understanding of pest life cycles and interactions, and involves the cumulative effect of many techniques, including:

- Allowing for an acceptable level of pest damage
- Encouraging predatory beneficial insects to flourish and eat pests
- Encouraging beneficial microorganisms
- Careful plant selection, choosing disease-resistant varieties
- Planting companion crops that discourage or divert pests
- Using row covers to protect crop plants during pest migration periods
- Rotating crops to different locations from year to year to interrupt pest reproduction cycles
- Using insect traps to monitor and control insect populations

Each of these techniques also provides other benefits, such as soil protection and improvement, fertilization, pollination, water conservation and season extension. These benefits are both complementary and cumulative in overall effect on site health. Organic pest control and biological pest control can be used as part of integrated pest management. However, IPM can include the use of chemical pesticides that are not part of organic or biological techniques.

ORGANIC HORTICULTURE AND FRUITS GROWING

Organic horticulture is the science and art of growing fruits, vegetables, flowers, or ornamental plants by following the essential principles of organic agriculture in soil building and conservation, pest management, and heirloom variety preservation.

The Latin words hortus and cultura together form horticulture, classically defined as the culture or growing of garden plants. Horticulture is also sometimes defined simply as "agriculture minus the plough." Instead of the plough, horticulture makes use of human labour and gardener's hand tools, although some small machine tools like rotary tillers are commonly employed now.

GENERAL

Double Digging, Vermicompost, Mulches, cover crops, compost, manures, and mineral supplements are soil-building mainstays that distinguish this type of farming from its commercial counterpart. Through attention to good healthy soil condition, it is expected that insect, fungal, or other problems that sometimes plague plants can be minimized. However, pheromone traps, insecticidal soap sprays, and other pest-control methods available to organic farmers are also sometimes utilized by organic horticulturists.

Horticulture involves five areas of study. These areas are floriculture, landscape horticulture, olericulture and postharvest physiology. All of these can be, and sometimes are, pursued according to the principles of organic cultivation.

Organic horticulture is based on knowledge and techniques gathered over thousands of years. In general terms, organic horticulture involves natural processes, often taking place over extended periods of time, and a sustainable, holistic approach - while chemical-based horticulture focuses on immediate, isolated effects and reductionist strategies.

ORGANIC GARDENING SYSTEMS

There are a number of formal organic gardening and farming systems that prescribe specific techniques. They tend to be more specific than, and fit within, general organic standards. Biodynamic farming is an approach based on the esoteric teachings of Rudolf Steiner. The Japanese farmer and writer Masanobu Fukuoka invented a no-till system for small-scale grain production that he called Natural Farming. French intensive and biointensive methods and SPIN Farming are all small scale gardening techniques.

A garden is more than just a means of providing food, it is a model of what is possible in a community - everyone could have a garden of some kind and produce healthy, nutritious organic food, a farmers market, a place to pass on gardening experience, and a sharing of bounty, promoting a more sustainable way of living that would encourage their local economy. A simple 4' x 8' raised bed garden based on the principles of bio-intensive planting and square foot gardening uses fewer nutrients and less water, and could keep a family, or community, supplied with an abundance of healthy, nutritious organic greens, while promoting a more sustainable way of living.

Other methods can also be used to supplement an existing garden. Methods such as composting, or vermicomposting. These practices are ways of recycling organic matter into some of the best organic fertilizers and soil conditioner. Vermicompost is especially easy. The byproduct is also an excellent source of nutrients for an organic garden.

SOIL

Managing the soil is very important. If your garden is healthy then insects will not attack the plants. Insects only attack plants that are unhealthy. As an example illustrating the relative health of plants, insects will not feed on plants which have been genetically modified so as to reduce foliar damage; thus, genetically modified plants are healthier than unmodified ones. To keep your garden healthy give it organic matter and humus to survive. The most important thing is to give your garden lots of attention and your energy.

PEST CONTROL APPROACHES

Differing approaches to pest control are equally notable. In chemical horticulture, a specific insecticide may be applied to quickly kill off a particular insect pest. Chemical controls can dramatically reduce pest populations in the short term, yet by unavoidably killing natural control insects and animals, cause an increase in the pest population in the long term, thereby creating an ever increasing problem. Repeated use of insecticides and herbicides also encourages rapid natural selection of resistant insects, plants and other organisms, necessitating increased use, or requiring new, more powerful controls.In contrast, organic horticulture tends to tolerate some pest populations while taking the long view.

Organic pest control requires a thorough understanding of pest life cycles and interactions, and involves the cumulative effect of many techniques, including:

- Allowing for an acceptable level of pest damage
- Encouraging predatory beneficial insects to flourish and eat pests
- Encouraging beneficial microorganisms
- Careful plant selection, choosing disease-resistant varieties
- Planting companion crops that discourage or divert pests
- Using row covers to protect crop plants during pest migration periods
- Rotating crops to different locations from year to year to interrupt pest reproduction cycles
- Using insect traps to monitor and control insect populations

Each of these techniques also provides other benefits, such as soil protection and improvement, fertilization, pollination, water conservation and season extension. These benefits are both complementary and cumulative in overall effect on site health. Organic pest control and biological pest control can be used as part of integrated pest management. However, IPM can include the use of chemical pesticides that are not part of organic or biological techniques.

VEGAN ORGANIC GARDENING

Vegan organic gardening and farming is the organic cultivation and production of food crops and other crops with a minimal amount of exploitation or harm to any animal. Vegan and vegan-organic farmers use no animal products or by-products, such as bloodmeal, fish products, bone meal, feces, or other animal-origin matter, because they view the production of these materials as either harming animals directly, or as being associated with the exploitation and consequent suffering of animals.

Some of these materials are by-products of animal husbandry, created during the process of cultivating animals for the production of meat, milk, skins, furs, entertainment, labour, or companionship; the sale of by-products decreases expenses and increases profit for those engaged in animal husbandry, and therefore helps support the animal husbandry industry, an outcome most vegans find unacceptable.

Soil fertility is maintained by the use of green manures and composted vegetable matter and minerals. Some vegan gardeners supplement this with human urine and 'humanure' produced from compost toilets; others avoid the potential health risks of using human waste. Such wastes may technically be considered 'animal products', however many vegan organic growers do not consider their usage unacceptable as there is unlikely to have been exploitation associated with their production.

VEGAN ORGANIC GARDENING

Many vegan organic gardeners prepare soil for cultivation using the same time-honoured method used by conventional and organic gardeners of breaking up the soil with hand tools and power tools and allowing the weeds to decompose. Shallow cultivation is also becoming popular among such gardeners: shallowly turning the soil's surface using one of numerous surface cultivating tools that are now available in the market place, including the popular Coleman surface-hoes developed by Eliot Coleman. Shallow tilling disturbs the soil less than deep turning and, combined with avoidance of soil compaction as described by O'Brien helps the soil maintain ecological balance. This minimizes the opportunities for soil diseases, plant diseases, and insect pests to become abundant.

O'BRIEN VEGANIC GARDENING METHOD

The Kenneth Dalziel O'Brien Veganic Gardening Method is a distinct system that was developed by Rosa Dalziell O'Brien, Kenneth Dalziel O'Brien, and May E Bruce, although the term was originally coined by Geoffrey Rudd as a contraction of 'vegetable organic' in order to "denote a clear distinction between conventional chemical based systems and organic ones based on animal manures". The O'Brien system's principal argument is that animal manures are harmful to soil health rather than that their use involves exploitation of and cruelty to animals.

The Kenneth Dalziel O'Brien system employs very specific techniques including the addition of straw and other vegetable wastes to the soil in order to maintain soil fertility. Gardeners following the Dalziel O'Brien system use soil-covering mulches, and employ non-compacting surface cultivation techniques using any short-handled, wide-bladed, hand hoe. They kneel when surface cultivating, placing a board under their knees to spread out the pressure, and prevent soil compaction. Kenneth Dalziel O'Brien published a description of his system in Veganic Gardening, the Alternative System for Healthier Crops.

From Veganic Gardening by Kenneth Dalziel O'Brien: "the veganic method of clearing heavily infested land is to take advantage of a plant's tendencies to move its roots nearer to the soil's surface when it is deprived of light. To make use of this principle, aided by a decaying process of the top growth of weeds, etc., it is necessary to subject such growth to heat and moisture in order to speed up the decay, and this is done by applying lime, then a heavy straw cover, and then the herbal compost activator.... The following are required: Sufficient new straw to cover an area to be leared to a depth of 3 to 4 inches..."

Also part of the O'Brien method is minimal disturbance of the soil by tilling, use of compost, mulch, cover crops, and green manures, use of permanent raised beds and permanent hard-packed paths between them, laying out beds from north to south, putting plants in double rows or more so that not every row has a path on both sides.

ORGANIC AGRICULTURE AND YIELD

Yields relative to comparable conventional systems are directly related to the intensity of farming of the prevailing conventional systems. This is not only the case for comparison between regions, but also between crops within a region, and for individual crops over time8.

An over-simplification of the impact of conversion to organic agriculture on yield indicates that:

- In intensive farming systems, organic agriculture decreases yield; the range depends on the intensity of external input use before conversion9.
- In the so-called green revolution areas, conversion to organic agriculture usually leads to almost identical yields.
- In traditional rain-fed agriculture, organic agriculture has shown the potential to increase yields.

A number of studies have shown that under drought conditions, crops in organic agriculture systems produce significantly higher yields than comparable conventional agricultural crops, often out-yielding conventional crops10 by 7–90 per cent. Others have shown that organic systems have less long-term yield variability. A survey of 208 projects in developing tropical countries in which contemporary organic practices were introduced, showed average yield increases of 5–10 per cent in irrigated crops and 50–100 per cent in rainfed crops.

The so-called organic transition effect, in which a yield decline in the first 1–4 years of transition to organic agriculture, followed by a yield increase when soils have developed adequate biological activity has not been borne out in some reviews of yield comparison studies. Trials conducted on organic cotton at Nagpur indicated that after the third year, the organic plot, which did not receive fertilizers and insecticides, produced as much cotton as that cultivated with them. Similarly, studies conducted in Punjab clearly indicated that organic farming gave higher or equal yields of different cropping systems compared to chemical farming after an initial period of three years.

PROGRESS OF ORGANIC FARMING

The most important constraint felt in the progress of organic farming is the inability of the government policy making level to take a firm decision to promote organic agriculture. Unless such a clear and unambiguous direction is available in terms of both financial and technical supports, from the Centre to the Panchayath levels, mere regulation making will amount to nothing. The following are found to be the major problem areas for the growth of organic farming in the country:

It is a fact that many farmers in the country have only vague ideas about organic farming and its advantages as against the conventional farming methods. Use of bio-fertilizers and bio pesticides requires awareness and willingness on the part of the farming community. Knowledge about the availability and usefulness of supplementary nutrients to enrich the soil is also vital to increase productivity.

Farmers lack knowledge of compost making using the modern techniques and also its application. The maximum they do is making a pit and fill it with small quantities of wastes. Often the pit is flooded with rainwater and result is the top of the compost remains under composted the bottom becomes like a hard cake. Proper training to the farmers will be necessary to make vermi-compost on the modern lines.

Attention on the application of composts/organic manure is also lacking. The organic matter is spread during the months when the right moisture level is absent on the soil. The whole manure turns into wastes in the process. The required operation is of course labour intensive and costly, but it is necessary to obtain the desired results.

It is found that before the beginning of the cultivation of organic crops, their marketability and that too at a premium over the conventional produce has to be assured. Inability to obtain a premium price, at least during the period required to achieve the productivity levels of the conventional crop will be a setback. It was found that the farmers of organic wheat in Rajasthan got lower prices than those of the conventional wheat. The cost of marketing of both types of products was also same and the buyers of wheat were not prepared to pay higher prices to the organic variety. Many experts and well informed farmers are not sure whether all the nutrients with the required quantities can be made available by the organic materials. Even if this problem can be surmounted, they are of the view that the available organic matter is not simply enough to meet the requirements.

The crop residues useful to prepare vermi-compost are removed after harvest from the farms.and they are used as fodder and fuel. Even if some are left out on the farms termites, etc destroy them. Experiments have shown that the crop residues ploughed back into soil will increase productivity and a better alternative is conversion into compost. The small and marginal cultivators have difficulties in getting the organic manures compared to the chemical fertilizers, which can be bought easily, of course if they have the financial ability. But they have to either produce the organic manures by utilizing the bio-mass they have or they have to be collected from the locality with a minimum effort and cost. Increasing pressure of population and the disappearance of the common lands including the wastes and government lands make the task difficult.

In spite of the adoption of the NPOP during 2000, the state governments are yet to formulate policies and a credible mechanism to implement them. There are only four agencies for accreditation and their expertise is limited to fruits and vegetables, tea, coffee and spices. The certiiying agencies are inadequate, the recognized green markets are non-existent, the trade channels are yet to be formed and the infrastructure facilities for verification leading to certification of the farms are inadequate. The small and marginal farmers in India have been practicing a sort of organic farming in the form of the traditional farming system. They use local or own farm renewable resources and carry on the agricultural practices in an ecologically friendly environment. However, now the costs of the organic inputs are higher than those of industrially produced chemical fertilizers and pesticides including other inputs used in the conventional farming system.

The groundnut cake, neem seed and cake, vermi-compost, silt, cow dung, other manures, etc. applied as organic manure are increasingly becoming costly making them unaffordable to the small cultivators.

Marketing Problems of Organic Inputs

Bio-fertilizers and bio-pesticides are yet to become popular in the country. There is a lack of marketing and distribution network for them because the retailers are not interested to deal in these products, as the demand is low. The erratic supplies and the low level of awareness of the cultivators also add to the problem. Higher margins of profit for chemical fertilizers and pesticides for retailing, heavy advertisement campaigns by the manufacturers and dealers are other major problems affecting the markets for organic inputs in India. Promotion of organic agriculture both for export and domestic consumption, the requirements of food security for millions of the poor, national self-sufficiency in food production, product and input supplies, etc. are vital issues which will have to be dealt with in an appropriate agriculture policy of India. These are serious issues the solution for which hard and consistent efforts along with a national consensus will be essential to go forward. Formulation of an appropriate agriculture policy taking care of these complexities is essential to promote organic agriculture in a big way.

The developing countries like India have to design a plethora of national and regional standards in attune with those of the developed countries. The adoption and maintenance of such a regulatory framework and its implementation will be costly. The cost of certification, a major component of which is the periodical inspections carried out by the certifying agencies, which have freedom to fix the timings, type and number of such inspections appears to be burdensome for the small and marginal farmers. Of course, the fees charged by the international agencies working in India before the NPOP were prohibitive and that was a reason for the weak response to organic agriculture even among the large farms in the country. No financial support as being provided in advanced countries like Germany is available in India. Supports for the marketing of the organic products are also not forthcoming neither from the State nor from the Union governments. Even the financial assistance extended to the conventional farming methods are absent for the promotion of organic farming.

In many cases the farmers experience some loss in yields on discarding synthetic inputs on conversion of their farming method from conventional to organic. Restoration of full biological activity in terms of growth of beneficial insect populations, nitrogen fixation from legumes, pest suppression and fertility problems will take some time and the reduction in the yield rates is the result in the interregnum. It may also be possible that it will take years to make organic production possible on the farm. Small and marginal farmers cannot take the risk of low jaelds for the initial 2-3 years on the conversion to organic farming. There are no plans to compensate them during the gestation period. The price premiums on the organic products will not be much of help, as they will disappear once significant quantities of organic farm products are made available. The demand for organic products is high in the advanced countries of the west like USA, European Union and Japan. It is reported that the US consumers are ready to pay a premium price of 60 to 100 per cent for the organic products. The upper classes in India are also following this trend as elsewhere. The market survey done by the International Trade Centre during 2000 indicates that the demand for organic products is growing rapidly in many of the world markets while the supply is unable to match it.

India is known in the world organic market as a tea supplier and there is a good potential to export coffee, vegetables, sugar, herbs, spices and vanilla. In spite of the several initiatives to produce and export organic produces from the country, the aggregate production for export came to only about 14000 tonnes. This also includes the production of organic spices in about 1000 ha under certification. Some export houses like Good Value Marketing Ltd and Burmah Trading Corporation are also engaged in exporting of organic fruits, vegetables and coffee from India. The country could export almost 85 per cent of the production indicating that demand is not a constraint in the international markets for organic products.

Hybrid seeds are designed to respond to fertilizers and chemicals. The seed, fertilizer and pesticide industry as also the importers of these inputs to the country have a stake in the conventional farming. Their opposition to organic farming stems from these interests. The need for fixing standards and quality parameters for bio-fertilizers and biomanures has arisen with the increasing popularity of organic farming in the country. There are a very large number of brands of organic manures, claiming the high levels of natural nutrients and essential elements. But most farmers are not aware of the pitfalls of using the commercially available biomanure products. While the concept of organic farming itself lays great stress on the manures produced on the farm and the farmers' household, many of the branded products available in the market may not be really organic. lements of chemicals slipping into the manures through faulty production methods could make the product not certifiable as organic. The process of composting which is a major activity to be carefully done is achieved usually by one of the two methods, vermi-composting or microbe composting.

While the former is ideal for segregated waste material without foreign matter, microbe composting is suitable for large scale management of solid wastes, especially in cities and metres. Even though the farmers are using manure produced by different methods, proper parameters for biomanure are yet to be finalized. Most farmers are still unaware of the difference between biomanure and bio-fertilizer, it is point out. While biomanure contains organic matter, which improves the soil quality, bio-fertilizers are nutritional additives separated from the organic material, which could be added to the soil, much like taking vitamin pills. Bio-fertilizers do nothing to enhance soil quality while the loss of soil quality has been the major problem faced by farmers these days.

An understanding of the real costs of erosion of soil and human health, the loss of welfare of both humans and other living things and the computation of these costs are necessary to evaluate the benefits of organic farming. These costs will have to be integrated to a plan for the implementation of organic agriculture. A recent study shows the inappropriateness of the cost and return accounting methods adopted to find out the economics of the organic farming. An economic evaluation of the bad effects of inorganic agriculture and their internalization through environmental taxes is proposed for a market based approach to promote organic farming in India.

Political Interventions

Agriculture in India is subject to political interventions with the objectives of dispensing favours for electoral benefits. Subsidies and other supports from both the Central and state governments, government controlled prices of inputs like chemical fertilizers, the public sector units' dominant role in the production of fertilizers, government support/floor prices for many agricultural products, supply of inputs like power and water either free of cost or at a subsidized rate, etc. are the tools often used to achieve political objectives. Any movement for the promotion of organic farming in India will have to counter opposition from the sections who benefit from such policies in the conventional farming system. The political system in a democracy like India is likely to evade the formulation of policies, which affect the interests of the voting blocks unless there are more powerful counter forces demanding changes.

In the absence of alternative employment opportunities and other considerations, the organized workforce particularly in the public sector fertilizer, pesticide and seed industries is also likely to oppose moves on the part of the government to promote organic farming on a large scale.

AGRICULTURAL BENEFITS OF ORGANIC FARMING

Organic agricultural practices are based on a maximum harmonious relationship with nature aiming at the non-destruction of the environment. The developed nations of the world are concerned about the spreading contamination of poisonous chemicals in food, feed, fodder and fibre. Naturally, organic farming system is looked upon as one of the means to remedy these maladies there. However, the major problem in India is the poor productivity of our soils because of the low level content of the organic matter.

The efficiency of the organic inputs in the promotion of productivity depends on the organic contents of the soil. There were many resemblances of organic farming principles in the traditional agriculture of India. But the former gives a more open and verifiable scientific foundation than the latter.

A study conducted in USA on the nutritional values of both organic and conventional foods found that consumption of the former is healthier. Apples, pears, potatoes, corn, wheat and baby foods were analyzed to find out 'bad' elements such as aluminum, cadimum, lead and mercury and also 'good' elements like boron, calcium, iron, magnesium sellenium and zinc. The organic food, in general, had more than 20 per cent less of the bad elements and about 100 per cent more of the good elements.

Increased Crop Productivity and Income

Field trials of organic cotton at Nagpur revealed that during the conversion period, cotton yield was low compared to the conventional and integrated crop management. However, the yields of organic cotton started rising from third year. Cotton yields under organic, conventional and the mixed systems were 898, 623 and 710 kg/ha respectively at the end of the fourth year of the cultivation. The yield of soyabean under organic farming was also the highest compared to the other two systems.

The Central Institute for Cotton Research, Nagpur conducted a study of economics of cotton cultivation in Yavatmal district of Maharashta. The cost of cultivation of cotton was lower in the organic farming than in the modern system. The low costs were due to the non-use of fertilizers and chemical insecticides. As a result of the low yields during the conversion period, the net income from the organic farm was lesser than the conventional farm. But the yield under organic method increased progressively equalling it to that of the conventional system by the sixth year. The input costs were low under organic farming and with a 20 per cent of premium prices of output, the net income increased progressively from fourth year under organic fanning. The appreciation of net income from organic cotton cultivation by the sixth year was 80 per cent over the conventional crop. Results reported from 1050 field demonstration cum trials under the National Project on Development and Use of Biofertilizers in different parts of the country show* an increase of 4 per cent in yield in plantation crops, 7 per cent in fruit crops, 9 per cent in wheat and sugarcane, 10 per cent in millet and vegetable, 11 per cent in fibre, condiments and spice crops, 14 per cent in oilseeds and flowers and 15 per cent in tobacco.

A study of 100 farmers in Himachal Pradesh during a period of 3 years found that the total cost of production of maize and wheat was lower under organic farming and the net income was 2 to 3 times higher. Both productivity and premium prices contributed to the increased profitability. Another study of 100 farmers of organic and conventional methods in five districts of Karnataka indicated that the cost of organic farming was lower by 80 per cent than that of the conventional one.

Low Incidence of Pests

The study of the effectiveness of organic cotton cultivation on pests at the farm of Central Institute for Cotton Research, Nagpur revealed that the mean monthly counts of eggs, larva and adults of American BoUworm were far lesser under organic farming than under the conventional method. Bio-control methods like the neem based pesticides to Ti-ichoderma are available in the country. Indigenous technological products such as Panchagavya which was experimented at the University of Agricultural Sciences, Bangalore found to control effectively wilt disease in tomato.

Employment Opportunities

Organic farming requires more labour input than the conventional farming system. Thus, India which has a very large amount of labour unemployment and under employment will find organic farming an attraction. Moreover, the problem of periodical unemployment will also get mitigated because of the diversification of the crops with their different planting and harvesting schedules resulting in the requirement of a relatively high labour input.

Indirect Benefits

Several indirect benefits from organic farming are available to both the farmers and consumers. While the consumers get healthy foods with better palatability and taste and nutritive values, the farmers are indirectly benefited from healthy soils and farm production environment. Eco-tourism is increasingly becoming popular and organic farms have turned into such favourite spots in countries like Italy. Protection of the ecosystem, flora, fauna and increased biodiversity and the resulting benefits to all human and living things are great advantages of organic farming which are yet to be properly accounted for.

PROGRESS OF ORGANIC FARMING IN INDIA

The first conference of NGOs on organic farming in India was organized by the Association for Propagation of Indigenous Genetic Resources in October 1984 at Wardha. Several other meetings on organic farming were held at different places in the country towards the end of 1980s. Here, mention must be made of the Bordi Conference in Maharashtra, the state which was the focal point for the organic farming movement in India. The Rajasthan College of Agriculture with the support of the state government organized a meeting on organic agriculture in 1992. The United Planters' Association of South India organised two national level conferences on organic farming in 1993 and 1995. ARISE is a major organization in the country engaged in the promotion of organic farming. ARISE was founded in 1995 at a national conference of organic farming held at Auroville. ARISE comprises of a supporting network of regional groups aiming at sustainable environment by protecting bio-diversity and promoting organic agricultural practices. The selection of Auroville for the conference was apt as it housed the Arabindo Ashram and the pioneering work under its auspices on building technology, alternative energy research, wasteland development, afforestation and organic agriculture.

By 1980, three groups of Indians had taken to organic farming. The first one consisted of urban educated technocrats for peripheral interest, which did not last long. Educated farmers consisted of the second group whose farming practices were based on scientific knowledge. The third group practiced organic farming through trial and error. The successful organic farmers in India are those who have access to sufficient natural resources like, water and other organic inputs mostly on their own farms. These farms produce crops like sugarcane, areca, cocoa, coconut, pepper and spices. Many of them have shown that switch over to organic farming do not affect yields and income and more importantly, knowledge/ expertise is available for successful adoption of organic farming in the country.

The International Federation of Organic Agriculture Movements estimates that an area of about 41,000 hectares in India is under organic farming representing about 0.17 per cent of the world organic acreage. It also reveals that the percentage of organic area to the total cultivated area comes to only about 0.03 per cent and the total number of farms comes to about 5,661. But, a comparison of our 41,000 ha to Australia, Argentina, Italy and USA clearly indicates that organic farming in India has to go very far even to catch up with that of the leading nations of the world.

Non Governmental Organizations are spearheading organic farming in India. A report in 2002 indicates that about 14,000 tonnes of organic products have been raised in India. They include tea, coffee, rice, wheat, pulses, fruits, spices and vegetables. India exports organic agricultural produces to European Union, USA, Canada, Saudi Arabia, UAE, Japan, Singapore and Australia, among others.

The International Conference on "Indian Organic Products-Global Markets" at the end of 2002 was the first to be held in India. IFOAM predicts that India and China have great potential to be organic farm produce exporters in the future. An important event in the history of the modern nascent organic farming in India was the unveiling of the National Programme for Organic Production on 8"^ May, 2000 and the subsequent Accreditation and Certification Programme on P' October, 2001. The logo "India Organic" was released on 26'*' July 2002 to support the NPOP.

An important progress towards organic agriculture made by India is the increasing awareness of the ill effects of the modern farming system, which the country adopted about 35 years ago. The threat poised by the conventional food products to the human health and the damage done to the ecology are being viewed seriously. Efforts are made to produce healthy foods and the demand. for them is increasing. The importance of the marketing of the organic products is highlighted for the promotion of organic agriculture. Several individuals and associations have taken to organic farming and organic products are available in the large cities to a very limited extent.

Important Step Towards in Organic Farming

The most important step towards organic farming taken by the government was to draw a regulatory framework. It is true that the initiatives by the government to introduce organic farming by laying down regulations came belatedly as many countries have already done this kind of basic work decades ago. The implementation of NPOP is ensured by the formulation of the National Accreditation Policy and Programme. The regulations make it mandatory that all organic certification bodies should be accredited by an Accreditation Agency. The international certification agencies operating in India even prior to these regulations will also have to get accreditation under the new dispensation.

The regulations lay down the institutional arrangements for implementing the national programme for organic production. The NPOP is administered, monitored and implemented for the benefit of farmers, processors, traders and consumers. It envisages a three tiered organisation under the overall guidance of the Union Government with the Department of Commerce, Ministry of Commerce and Industry as the nodal agency. Policy making and declaration of the standards for organic products, recognition of organic standards of other nations, efforts to get our standards recognized by others and coordination with other arms of the government for the successful management of the organic agriculture are the major functions entrusted to the ministry.

The agencies accredited are the Agricultural and Processed Food Products Export Development Authority, Coffee Board, Tea Board and the Spices Board. The regulations cover exports, imports and the domestic trade of the organic products. But the government regulations are applicable to only the exports. So, an organic farm product can be exported only if it is certified by a certification body accredited for the purpose. The categories of products covered under accreditation are organic crop production, organic animal production, organic processing operations, wild products and forestry.

A national level steering committee is functioning as the apex advisory body for assisting the government to promote organic farming in the country. This body consists of representative's form the Ministries of Agriculture, Food Processing Industries, Forests and Environment, Science and Technology, Rural Development and Commerce.

Organic production requires certification after periodic inspections in order to ensure that all prescribed practices are followed. The inspection and certification are done by the agencies accredited to the Accrediting Agencies dealing with the commodity. Inspection and certification agencies can be government departments, NGOs, trade or consumer or producer organisations. Such agencies should be registered bodies, with managements in position, declaring the persons who shall be held responsible for any miscarriage of certification and having proof of adequate field staff to undertake periodic inspections. The continued accreditation of such bodies is dependent upon their record of fidelity to the principles of organic production. They are authorised to award certificates after due satisfaction that practices conformed to those enunciated by the Accrediting Agency in relation to the item concerned. The charges levied by the certifying agencies are fixed by the Accrediting Agencies.

SEVERAL PROJECTS AND INITIATIVES TO PROMOTE ORGANIC FARMING

Several projects and initiatives to promote organic farming in the country have begun at the behest of individuals and institutions. A project aided by the World Bank to empower the rural communities in the country to grow organic products for exports had come up in 2002. The programme aims at the improvement and promotion of organic production of spices, certification and export of black pepper, white pepper, ginger, turmeric, cardamom, clove, nutmeg and herbals like rosemary, thyme, oregano and parsley. The implementation of the progamme is done by the NGOs, and Idukki and Waynad districts of Kerala, Nilgiri district of Tamil Nadu and Kandhamal district of Orissa are the areas selected for the purpose. Imparting training to both the JNTGOs and the farmers on organic production methods, basic standards required, documentation, inspection and certification is a major objective of the programme. The assistance to NGOs includes among others computer hardware and software especially for market promotion of their produces.

An initiative for the spread of organic farming by various stakeholders in the Indian organic agriculture sector is their coming together to constitute an apex body for providing centralized services and expertise for the increasing number of organic farmers in the country. Initial steps for setting up the Indian Competence Centre for Organic Agriculture has been taken at a meeting held at the National Academy for Agricultural Sciences in New Delhi in 2003 under the joint auspices of INDOCERT, a Kerala based organic certification agency and the Swiss based FiBL. The decision was the outcome of an Indian team's visit to Switzerland in 2003 to study the structure of Swiss organic farming.

The meeting elected a nine member promoter board of directors to facilitate the setting up of ICCOA, which would be registered as a charitable society. The Centre would strive to strengthen and supplement the efforts of the state governments in promoting the development of organic agriculture in the country.

In Haryana, an enterprising farmer who began farming on his 16 acre land in the Sonepat district in 1971 could establish an organic farm on 108 acres, raising vegetables and other crops. It appears that his success is mainly attributable to the efforts made by him to market the products. NGOs functioning in the neighbourhood of Delhi buy the produces like rice, wheat, pulses and vegetables from his farm at a premium price of 30 to 50 per cent. An exporting firm at a premium of 20 to 30 per cent buys his basmathi rice. Almost 70 per cent of his farm production is sold through advance agreements/ contracts. Presently he and his friends are working with the resident associations in Delhi to market their organic products at a premium of about 25 per cent. In Rajasthan, the Morarka Foundation, established in 1995, promotes sustainable agriculture. It has about 10,000 partners producing vermi-compost and the Foundation is said to be the single largest producer of this organic input in Asia. It encourages the production of bio-pesticides and supports procurement of certified organic products. It has set up a joint venture to promote agri-biotechnology parks and a model park of such a nature has come up in Jaipur on 20 acres of land.

The campaign launched by the Foundation in the Sheldiawati region of the state in favour of organic farming has resulted in reduction of cultivation costs and improvement in the quality of the produces. Small and marginal farmers in the districts of Sikar and Jhunjhunu, who had been complaining of degradation of their agricultural land and declining productivity, were benefited. The efforts of the Foundation to popularize the use of vermi-compost in place of the chemical fertilizer by creating awareness and imparting training to the farmers have been successful. The Foundation too has a large facility to produce vermi-compost. Application of vermi-compost reduces irrigation, increases the flavour of the products and results in a decline in the damage to the crops by insects. The Foundation is presently engaged in developing techniques to enrich vermi-compost through micro-organisms to make it suitable for location and crop specific application. The promotion of organic farming is encouraged through natural resource management based on ecology protection and sustainable agricultural methods.

In Kerala, the POABS Organic Estate at Nelliyampathy is engaged in the organic cultivation of several agricultural produces. Research on organic farming methods including manures and pesticides is also undertaken there. Liquid manures, mixtures of slurry, cow urine and some herbal preparations are also made for use in the estate.

Several people have taken to organic farming in the state fully convinced of its beneficial effects on man and nature. A farmer who took organic farming as a mission in the district of Kottayam was an example. His estate grew only green crops, from vegetables to rubber. When the rubber plantation was raised on organic methods, the yields were low during the initial years. On the application of the organic inputs, they increased and after three years the yields were on par with the conventional rubber trees.

An initiative to make the state of Kerala fully organic has begun with the formulation of a draft policy in 2003. A workshop on Organic Sustainability of Kerala - A Global Model was organised jointly by the state agriculture department and the Confederation of Indian Industry to deliberate on the organic farming in Kerala. The government policy will focus on conversion of land, produces and budgetary support. Assistance will also be available for certification and inputs, promoting the local certifying bodies, development of agronomic practices, extension support and training to farmers. Creation of consumer awareness, quality considerations, and emphasis on income rather than on yield will also be part of the policy. A campaign to promote organic farming on the lines of the programme on Literate Kerala is proposed to be launched. Organic farming, it is suggested, can be promoted among the educated youth who are presently averse to conventional agriculture.

The Peerumedu Development Society is a cooperative society in the Idukki district, which promotes organic farming for the last 12 years. Pepper, cardamom, coffee, tea, nutmeg, clove, etc. are the crops raised by about 20000 farmers of the PDS who are encouraged to adopt organic farming. PDS collects the products from its member farmers and exports too. It has also started an organic tea processing factory in district.

A view currently gaining ground in the state is that organic farming has almost become necessary for the Kerala farmer, reeling under the onslaught of the highly sensitive international markets for agriculture products. The close linking of solid waste management with bio-manure production is opening up new avenues in city planning in Kerala. The State has short listed three organizations for conducting solid waste management programmmes. The possibilities of making fuel pellets out of the rejected wastes are also being explored. 'Jaivam' or organic is the catchword now gaining popularity in Kerala. The tide seems to be turning in favour of bio-manure, bio-pest control and bio-disease control in all forms of agriculture. The state controlled Vegetable and Fruits Promotion Council, Keralam is also taking slow steps in promoting the 'bio' trend as against the overriding importance given to the chemical methods of farming.

An Association of Agriculturists Functioning in the State

'Infam' is an association of agriculturists functioning in the state. As a part of its efforts to promote organic farming, it is planning to launch a producers' company for marketing of organic produces with a view to assist the growing trend of organic farming in the state. In the initial stage, the functioning of the company will be confined to the Wayanad district. The company will have about 3200 farmers of the district as members who have decided to switch over to organic mode of cultivation. Steps are also being taken to forge collaboration with the Indian Institute of Rural Management, Anand. The proposed tie up with IRMA will be for technical help and also for marketing of the products. The Infam has conducted about 300 training programmes in Wayanad district, which had motivated the farmers to adopt organic farming methods of cultivation.

The MS Swaminathan Research Foundation, Chennai that has been operating in the area, assists the movement. Wayanad district is on the verge of an environmental calamity due to the excessive use of chemical fertilizers and pesticides that depleted the soil beyond redemption. The top soil is fast losing its fertility and is becoming barren in many areas. About 2100 banana farmers used tonnes of Furidan, an insecticide annually in the district alone.

The increased use of chemicals was also posing a health hazard. A survey conducted by the Infam among the school children in Thavingal Panchayath recently revealed that 250 of them were cancer patients. The cancer disease in the region is alarmingly on the rise. Karnataka has finalized the policy on organic farming and thus has become the first state in the country to adopt it. It encourages the farmers to adopt organic farming and gradually give up the use of chemical fertilizers and pesticides. The government has earmarked Rs 20 crores in the state budget of 2004-05 for the purpose.

The organic farming movement in the state has reached a stage in which the creation of markets for the products has become essential. Association for Promotion of Organic Farming at Bangalore consists of 150 voluntary members. It has been promoting organic farming by creating awareness, inspecting and giving organic certification to the farms. Organic farm production in the state is not very significant. However, some NGOs and individuals are buying organic produces although the movement to convert the land to organic farming has not been successful. There is no organised market for organic produces and if not sold out in the right time, they are left with the conventional produce at the same prices. At the same time, while the farmers are interested in the organic cultivation the consumers are willing to pay for such products. But the link between the two simply does not exist. Consumers demand consistent supplies of good quality organic products and the farmers want an assured market for such produces.

APOP is making the farmers aware of the organic farming methods, particularly about the preparation of the soil for the purpose. The principles behind the healthy soil through the use of the on-farm inputs and compost making are explained to them. Purushotthom Rao who owned 10 acres of land in the Shimoga district took up organic farming in 1989. He raised coconut and paddy along with several other crops in place of arecanut which was destroyed due to strong winds. The yield of coconut he obtained was 80 per cent more than that of his conventional farming friends. The cost of paddy cultivation incurred was 80 per cent lesser than his said friends.

An enterprising farmer practicing organic farming could export several products to the European market. His firm sent 5000 kg of black pepper, 1000 kg of nutmeg, 500 kg of mace, 4000 kg of white pepper, 1000 kg of clove, 300 kg of vanilla, 2000 kg of turmeric, 2000 kg of ginger, 5000 kg of white hibiscus, 80000 kg of henna and 500 kg of cardamom. His firm is certified by a European agency as organic since 1994.

The state of Manipur in the north-east> of India has decided to encourage organic agriculture. The north-east region with its unique characteristics and agricultural practices can be a potential area for the introduction of organic farming. Manipur is aiming at the encouragement of the eco-friendly farm practices and pollution free industry in the state. Dependence of the agrochemicals will be avoided and factories and industries causing harm to plants and humans will be discouraged. The emphasis on protection of environment is in perfect harmony with the identification of the entire north-east as the mega diversity spot containing rich reserves of flora and fauna. Given the geographical location and agro-climatic zones, the state gives importance to horticulture and agro-industries. The National Horticulture Board has identified 2.77 lakh hectares for the exclusive development of horticulture in the state. It has been decided to encourage organic farming in this development area. The state has proposed to the setting up of an exclusive export zone for organic products in collaboration with the Agriculture Processed Food Export Development Authority. Tamil Nadu plans to encourage organic farming in horticulture and plantation crops to increase the income of the farmers of the state. The state government also wants to promote organic cultivation of fruits, vegetables and tea. The Tamil Nadu Agricultural University has established a model organic farm on a 2.5 hectare area in the campus.

The National Bank for Agriculture and Rural Development has decided to promote organic cultivation of horticultural crops in the mango producing areas of southern Tamil Nadu districts. Theni and Dindigul are major mango growing areas and the fact that the state government has decided to promote an agri export zone for mangoes in these districts will quicken the efforts for organic farming. The aim is to take the benefits of the premium prices for organic products in the developed countries through exports of mangoes. NABARD has funded a farmer in Theni district to the tune of Rs 3.5 crores for organic mango cultivation on a 252 acre area. Identification of land for organic cultivation was a difficult process and it took one year for the farmer to do so and another three years to convince the banks. Search for the ideal planting materials took several months and he incurred an annual cost of Rs 46000 for certification.

A seminar organised at Shri Murugappa Chettiar Research Centre at Chennai focused on the need for natural cultivation of food products. Application of farm manure, biological pest control, companion planting, inter cropping, introduction of beneficial microbes and fungies were advocated for natural food farming. The importance of earthworms and the harm caused to them by chemical farming were highlighted at the discussions. In the history of organic farming in Tamil Nadu, the efforts made in 1970s to revive the traditional methods of agriculture at Chennai were praiseworthy. A study held by MCRC in the city revealed that 58 per cent of the people were aware of the benefits of organic farming and 82 per cent were ready to buy organic foods if the prices were competitive.

A few farmers in Puliangudi village in Tirunelveli district have successfully adopted a package of eco-friendly technologies in the paddy cultivation. It is found that these practices show good results on the indigenous rice varieties. The cost of cultivation has substantially been reduced and the farmers receive a premium for the organic rice. The cost of cultivation worked out comes to about Rs 8,750 per hectare. The price of rice obtained was Rs 30 per kg. The cultivation turned out to be rewarding economically besides being environmentally acceptable. Several farmers are coming forward to practice the method of organic farming after witnessing the results. Another farmer of the same village revealed that he got about 9,250 kg of paddy per ha and no plant protection was done after adoption of the new method. His cost of cultivation worked out was about Rs 12,500 per ha.

In Goa, a co-operative institution, the Adarsha Krishi Sahakari Kharedi Vikri Prakriya Sanstha, pioneered organic farming of cashew and coconut crops. The organisation has 1000 members and is led by its Chairman under whose leadership the organic cultivation is launched. The Cooperative Society has been receiving export orders from traders from abroad for supply of organic cashew nuts. The Society has helped more than 450 cashew growers to convert to organic farming by imparting training and other supports. It also has a processing facility for about 100 tonnes of cashew nuts during the season. The price paid for a kg of organic raw nuts is Rs 35.50. The processed nuts are taken to Mumbai and Delhi by the Society for sale.

The state of Madhya Pradesh has gone for organic soya cultivation. Plans are also ready to convert maize, wheat and pulse cultivation to organic on the principle of crop rotation. Organic soyabean is cultivated in the Malwa region of the state in the districts of Khargone and Dhar on an area of 8,700 hectares under contract farming. Farmers who have not used chemical fertilizers and pesticides during the last two years on the land offered for organic farming are selected. This condition was necessary to restore the soil health to make the land suitable for organic cultivation. Certification of the farm has been done by SKAL, an international agency accredited to APEDA. On getting the certificate, the farm can use the logo 'India Organic' on soyabean and its products like soya oil and deoiled cake.

The production is meant for both the national and international markets. It is said that the conventional yellow soyabean fetches Rs 12,000 per tonne in the local market, while the organic soyabean rules at Rs 34,000 per tonne in Delhi. However, a price premium of 50 per cent is the least expected for the organic soya. This will be financially beneficial to the farmers, even though the productivity of conventional soyabean is put at 800-900 kg, which is higher than 500-600 kg of the organic soya. The genetically modified soya crops dominate the international market for soyabean and its products. However, the demand for organic soya is high ensuring a good premium for exports from the country.

IMPORTANT OF ORGANIC FARMING

This is important because organic farming embodies the elements of a sound agriculture — traditional practices that have been proven over time. In fact, a good, convenient, working definition for organic agriculture is *good farming practice without using synthetic chemicals*. This working definition distinguishes organic practice from the general milieu of agriculture that existed in the pre-chemical era, much of which was exploitative and unsustainable. Organic farming was never intended to be a "throwback" or regressive form of agriculture.

A truly significant event in the history of organics took place in 1962, with the publication of Rachel Carson's *Silent Spring*. *Silent Spring* is a strong and dramatic statement about the impact of pesticides on the environment. It was one of the key documents that gave birth to environmental consciousness in the 1960s and 1970s.

When environmentalists and others began looking around for an alternative to pesticides and industrial agriculture, organic farming was there. Not only was it an approach that did not use synthetic pesticides, it also had an attractive counter-culture name that grew to signify a philosophy of living as well as a method of farming.

While *Silent Spring* and the environmental movement were not about organic farming *per se*, they brought it to public consciousness on a vast scale. It is not uncommon, in fact, for some writers to suggest that organic agriculture began with Rachel Carson's book. Though this assertion is untrue, the book clearly played a major role in stimulating industry growth and in altering public perceptions. From the mid-1960s onward, organics was increasingly identified with pesticide issues. It became the idealized alternative for providing clean, healthy food and environmental protection.

NOTIONS OF ORGANIC

As organic farming and marketing entered the 1970s, it began to develop as an industry. As a result, a clearer definition was needed to distinguish it and its products from conventional agriculture. This was no straightforward task. Environmental issues and other alternative agriculture philosophies had created diverse notions about what organic agriculture was and what it should be. A particularly problematic image grew unexpectedly from the anti-pesticide movement of the 1960s.

This was the romantic notion that organic simply meant "doing next-to-nothing." In this exploitative approach, not only were pesticides avoided, sound farming practices that built the soil were also largely ignored. The results achieved on such farms were predictable, as yields were low and the quality poor. These approaches became collectively known as organic by neglect and are a far cry from the responsible farming models proposed by Albert Howard and J.I. Rodale.

It is unclear how many farmers actually chose to farm "by neglect" and advertise themselves as organic over the years. However, this extreme representation of organic agriculture was quickly taken up by critics who tried to characterize all of organic agriculture as soil depleting and unproductive. To counter this, current standards for certified organic production require an "organic plan" outlining the use of soil building activities and natural pest management.

There is a further notion that organic farming also describes farm systems based on soil building, but that continue to use some prohibited fertilizers and pesticides in a limited or selective manner. A USDA study of U.S., organic farms made note of many such individuals who readily and sincerely referred to themselves as organic farmers. While these growers were largely conscientious and would, in most instances, fall under the modern umbrella of "sustainable farmers," industry standards evolved to preclude all synthetic pesticides or commercial fertilizers. The approach to farming by this loose-knit group of growers and their supporters has come to be called "eco-farming" or "eco-agriculture" — terms coined by Acres USA editor Charles Walters, Jr.

Bibliography

A.K. Tiwari: *Fundamentals of Ornamental Horticulture and Landscape Gardening*, New India Publishing Agency, 2012.

Arun K. Zingare: *A Manual of Gardening*, Satyam Publishers, Delhi, 2013.

Aruna Ludra: *Four Seasons Gardening in India*, Originals, Publication, Delhi, 2000.

B. L. Jana:*Hydroponics: Soilless Gardening*, Aavishkar Publishers, Delhi, 2015.

Buckland, Toby: *Gardeners' World Practical Gardening Handbook*, Random House India, 2004.

G Marshall Woodrow: *Gardening in India*, Daya, Publication, Delhi, 2001.

J. Coutts, A. Osborn and A. Edwards: *The Complete Book of Gardening*, Srishti Book, Delhi, 2004.

Kaushal Kumar Misra: *Ornamental Gardening in India*, Biotech Books, Delhi, 2011.

L.C. De: *Handbook of Gardening*, Aavishkar, Publication, Delhi, 2012.

L.H. Bailey and Ethel Zoe Bailey *Dictionary of Gardening and General Horticulture:* , Biotech, 2003.

L.L. Somani: *Dictionary of Gardening*, Agrotech, Publication, Delhi, 2009.

Laeeq Futehally: *A Sahib's Manual for the Mali : Everyday Gardening in India*, Permanent Black, 2004.

Leendertz, Lia: *Gardening SOS*, Random House India, 2008.

R.K. Chauhan: *Encyclopaedia of General Gardening for Common People*, Dominant, Publication, 2011.

R.L. Misra and Sanyat Misra: *Landscape Gardening : Design Elements Garden Planning and Pollution Monitoring*, Westville Publishing House, 2012.

Roy Edwin Biles: *The Complete Book of Gardening*, Biotech, 2003.

S.C. Dey: *Complete Home Gardening*, Agrobios, Publication, Delhi, 2012.

S.C. Dey: *Indoor Gardening*, Agrobios, Publication, Delhi, 2003.

Sudeep Guha: *Organic Methods for Ornamental Gardening and Floriculture*, Dominant, Publication, Delhi, 2011.

Supriya Kumar Bhattacharjee: *Landscape Gardening and Design With Plants*, Aavishkar, Publication, Delhi, 2012.

Syed Mahboob Ashraf: *A Handbook of Landscape Gardening and Environment*, Agrobios, Publication, Delhi, 2010.

Titchmarsh, Alan: *Alan Titchmarsh How To Garden: Greenhouse Gardening*, Random House India, 2004.

Titchmarsh, Alan: *lan Titchmarsh How To Garden: Greenhouse Gardening*, Random House India, 2004.

V.L. Chopra and Markandey Singh: *Ornamental Plants for Gardening*, Scientific, Publication, Delhi, 2013.

W.E. Shewell-Cooper: *Vegetable Gardening*, Biotech Books, 2005.

W.F. Gericke: *Soilless Gardening : A Complete Guide*, Biotech Books, Delhi, 2007.

Walter P Wright: *Encyclopaedia of Horticulture and Gardening*, Biotech, Publication, Delhi, 2002.

Index